THE EXERCISE OF SOVEREIGNTY

THE EXERCISE

OF

SOVEREIGNTY:

Papers on Foreign Policy

by

CHARLES BURTON MARSHALL

The Johns Hopkins Press, Baltimore, Maryland

© 1965 by The Johns Hopkins Press, Baltimore, Maryland 21218
Printed in the United States of America
Library of Congress Catalogue Card No. 65-11665

FOREWORD

Mr. Marshall begins one of the essays in this volume, "In a conversation a while back a lady of high civic zeal referred to her experiences in diplomacy as constituting the pleasantest way to spend a summer within her recollection." An even better way would be on a steamer chair in the shade, a long, cool drink near one hand and this book in the other, sipping alternate refreshment from both. For with a seductively easy style, Mr. Marshall provides refreshing instruction and wisdom about the world around us, both the physical world and the world of ideas.

He has learned and thought in many roles and from many vantage points—the halls of academe, committee chambers on Capitol Hill, secret councils in the State Department, active practice in foreign missions. Finally and importantly, he demonstrates Mr. Justice Holmes's aphorism that to be weighty one need not be heavy.

In the field of foreign affairs, it is not really understood—though it surely ought to be, since it is plain enough—that there is and should be division of labor. A friend has observed that most New York lawyers over fifty spend their days imagining that they are the Secretary of State and dispensing foreign policy decisions at their luncheon clubs. In the division of labor first come the hired practitioners. They work for the government. These unfortunates are so close to the harsh necessity of daily action decisions that they have no opportunity to "generalize it all and write it in continuous, logical, philosophical exposition . . . with its roots in history and its justifications of expedience, real or supposed."

Second in the division of labor come the expounders of foreign policy, divided into two groups. Their members work for those of us who are trying to understand what is going on. In one group are tri-weekly pundits and less continuous Congressional critics who issue spot criticism of yesterday's action. Their work is, of necessity, likely to be topical, ephemeral, and shallow. The other group, their luckier brethren, are the essayists or lecturers who take a longer look, think more deeply, and do have a chance to relate the roots in history to the justifications of expedience.

One is tempted to go on and suggest another group in this division: the historians, scanning broader and farther horizons, and taking deeper soundings. But today history is written so contemporaneously that one finds historians merging into the ranks of the essayists, and vice versa. Mr. Marshall's writing, and this volume in particular, springs right from the point of merger.

Maynard Keynes entitled a small volume of his, *Essays in Persuasion*. This one might be entitled, *Essays in Education*. For it helps us to find our way through that lush, tangled, and dangerous jungle which is our times—through the clichés, the moralism, the emotionalism, the bad history, faulty analysis, and just plain ignorance which suffocate most discussion of foreign affairs. Mr. Marshall cuts through this fetid growth, with both wit, to lighten the way, and ruthless analysis, to clear it. To a lofty commentator who dazzled the disciples by such show of learning as "Mr. Khrushchev thinks more like Richelieu and Metternich than like Woodrow Wilson," he once observed, "Yet one should beware of likening him to Metternich or Richelieu—in the sense that saying a tiger is more like a horse than an octopus should not be stretched into a conclusion about saddling a tiger." Mr. Marshall's own comment states far more keenly what was possibly meant: Mr. Khrushchev's "peasant rotundity gives an essentially subtle operator an advantage of not appearing subtle at all."

Each of the essays in this book brings the stimulation of new light and new thought. If I had to choose the one which brings most help with perplexities and confusion of councils, it would be, "Détente: Effects on the Alliance." Here clarity of analysis, wealth of historical knowledge, perceptive insight, and wisdom are brought together with a method of exposition in itself of great help to understanding. The result is exposition of a Euclidian type, which marches forward to its conclusions.

His main points are these:

The hopes raised during World War II and its immediate sequel for a reliable order in world affairs, resting on a scheme for collective security premised on continuity of the prevailing coalition and objectified in the Charter of the United Nations, foundered on an array of divisive issues of dominion preeminently involving the disposition of Germany.

The North Atlantic Treaty, growing out of frustration of that hope, substituted regional defense for universal collective security.

Though not free of problems and issues in this respect, it has worked as a framework for military security of the area, developing in response to unfolding demands of the situation. A highly significant event in this course has been the inclusion of the German Federal Republic in the scheme of military—and, as a corollary, political—collaboration.

Beyond the defensive purpose, the Alliance was intended to create conditions to render the adversary amenable to an acceptable settlement in Europe. In this respect, the undertaking of the Alliance implicitly represented, at least in the American view, not abandonment but deferment of hope for world concord as a basis for peace. The Alliance was, and remains, ambiguous regarding modes and conditions for such a settlement.

The urge for détente, reflecting lingering fascination with that hope, accentuates relevant ambiguities in the Alliance. The crux of the problem of settlement remains the disposition of Germany.

The effect is disintegrative. The danger is that of impairing the Alliance, even dismantling it, by premature and ill-considered gestures toward détente. The outcome is all too likely to be loss of the Alliance without gaining a settlement.

From beginning to end this piece is solid reasoning from solid fact.

Not all the essays are so rigorously analytical. "The Golden Age in Perspective" is one for that summer afternoon in the steamer chair, mentioned at the outset. And "On Understanding the Unaligned" eases a feeling of guilt at not understanding persons of diverse cultural backgrounds. Neutralism, Mr. Marshall explains, "is a way not of withdrawing, but of playing a role in global politics, of getting into the game, but staying out of the scrimmages." It should not be equated, he warns, to the tenor of Washington's Farewell Address, as was attempted by a returning American good will traveler.

In short, one finds here the equivalent of several evenings' good talk, as Mr. Marshall, speaking in varying moods and modes, enlightens and entertains.

DEAN ACHESON

AUTHOR'S NOTE

By far the larger portion of what I have written about foreign affairs either never emerged from the recesses of bureaucracy or was issued in the form of anonymous documents or as speeches delivered by someone else. My files, however, contain notes and texts of about 200 lectures and some 95 essays done in my own name over the last dozen years or so. It was my wife's idea to winnow through them and to make selections and combinations for a book.

It has been her method to put aside discussions of issues and problems of only passing moment and to focus on ideas of more enduring relevance. The result is a book on ways of thinking about foreign policy, more than on events. She has trimmed away much duplication. What duplication remains is probably irreducible, unless one should undertake to rewrite all the way through. The pieces selected fall—with fair precision and with scant regard for chronology—into three broad topics: the conditions of foreign policy, alliance and confrontation, and relations with new states. For each section I have written a brief introduction.

The pervading attitude may seem to some pessimistic, though it does not seem so to me. The emphasis is on the world of nations as it is, more than as one might like it to be. Real situations interest me more than dreams and aspirations, which get sufficient attention from others anyway.

I can claim no novelty of content. This circumstance does not trouble me. In Bertrand de Jouvenel's words,

> Man is no great inventor of ideas. The good ones are far from new, and the bad ones are no less antiquated. The

band-waggon of heresy, though done up in new colors, runs back into the thousand-year-old ruts. Our intelligence, it might be said, holds certain models, which serve as the skeletons to the flesh of all its theories. The doctrines of today are but a silhouette of yesterday's, in a new dress.[1]

In a poet's safe prediction,

> Far away beyond her myriad coming changes
> earth will be
> Something other than the wildest modern guess
> of you and me.[2]

One change I am not inclined to count on heavily is a sweeping improvement of the human personality. According to a notion often heard, the natural sciences have been dynamically producing wonders, while the social sciences unhappily have remained static, so that what is needed now is for the social sciences to hurry ahead to close the gap between man's mastery of his environment and his lack of mastery over himself, and to point mankind to a happy, tranquil future. The fallacy is a simple one. As Sir David Kelly once pointed out, the social sciences have burst upon the world as recently, as actively, as expansively, and as pervasively as the natural sciences.[3] We know ever so much more about human affairs than our predecessors knew, just as men today know more about the physical and natural environment than did previous generations. People may know more, but they have not thereby transcended or transformed themselves any more than they have altered the inherent character of natural phenomena. I should not count on their being able to do so.

I do not regard this attitude as pessimistic. In falling short of Utopia, mankind would not be missing much, in my view. I once attempted to express this thought in metrics:

---

[1] Bertrand de Jouvenel, *Sovereignty* (Chicago: University of Chicago Press, 1957), p. 199.

[2] Alfred Lord Tennyson, *Complete Works* (Cambridge, Mass.: Houghton Mifflin, 1898), p. 523.

[3] Sir David Kelly, *The Hungry Sheep* (London: Hollis & Carter, 1955), p. 119.

A fecund woman living in a shoe
Improvidently multiplied her kind
For lack of knowing other things to do.
A full house showed an emptiness of mind.
No such excuse for earth's redundant brood!
Best brains were put to work promoting life.
In rational and scientific mood,
They ended havoc, pestilence, and strife,
Enrolled all ages in a world police,
Prescribed unending protocols and pills
To keep the world perpetually at peace
And immunize the human race to ills.
In this secure and regulated trance
Men found the teeming happiness of ants.

Besides being deeply grateful to Betty L. Marshall for the idea of this collection and for all her effort, I am indebted to the following for permission to use copyrighted items: the American Academy of Political and Social Science; the Commonweal Publishing Company; Farrar, Straus, & Company; *The Johns Hopkins Magazine;* The Johns Hopkins Press; the *Journal of International Affairs; The New Republic,* and the Public Affairs Conference Center of the University of Chicago. For affording me time to contemplate foreign affairs in a congenial atmosphere I am grateful to The Washington Center of Foreign Policy Research, an affiliate of the School of Advanced International Studies of The Johns Hopkins University. My colleagues there may find some of their own ideas reflected herein but unacknowledged.

CHARLES BURTON MARSHALL

Arlington, Virginia
May, 1964

CONTENTS

III. RELATIONS WITH NEW STATES

I.

THE CONDITIONS OF
FOREIGN POLICY

INTRODUCTION:

THE MEANING OF

BEING SOVEREIGN

A heading—"Sovereignty Outmoded, Says Rusk"—on a
newspaper at hand as I write is interesting.[1] The account below
it details a speech given as part of a labored dialogue between
this government and that of Charles de Gaulle's France. The
speech is more restrained than the heading. What it consigns to
obsoletencss is expressed as "absolute national sovereignty."

As the context makes evident, the key phrase is invoked to
describe President de Gaulle's notions about structuring authority in the North Atlantic Alliance. Implicitly what worries the
United States Secretary of State is not really the obsoleteness of
opposed ideas but a possibility of their having a future. The
debating device employed is a familiar one. In foreign affairs, as
in other aspects of political life, it is a regular part of interchange for proponents to claim present vitality for their own
preferences and to label opponents' designs as archaisms. A
variant of the technique currently in high vogue is to call one's
own interpretations and wishes realities and to dismiss all contrary assumptions as myths. A sophisticated observer learns to
bracket such expressions in his mind—just part of the game.

The particular setting and application of the Secretary's remarks are of less concern to me here than the abstractions
called up. The key ideas—absoluteness and sovereignty—are
tricky ones. Anyone undertaking to explore their meanings is
likely to find himself deep in. I have no intention of following
the tracings of Bodin, Hobbes, Austin, and all the rest of that

[1] *Washington Post and Times-Herald*, May 10, 1964.

3

distinguished company into a logical and conceptual swamp. Nevertheless, with respect to sovereignty, the idea of the obsoleteness of its absoluteness prompts me to question the absoluteness of its obsoleteness.

For simplicity and clarity, the absolute modifier *absolute* applied to sovereignty can well be disposed of at once. Whatever its relevance in the realm of pure ideas, the term usually serves only to clutter up discussion of actual human affairs. I wonder whether the idea of *absolute,* otherwise than in connection with absolute zero, has utility. I can scarcely imagine any faculty or endeavor wholly untrammeled, infinite, or wholly beyond contingency. On the other hand—and to recognize this point is to avoid a common fallacy—entities and their purposes and characteristics do not have to be absolute in order to exist at all, to operate, and to be valid, and one does not disprove them merely by denying their absoluteness.

So we come to the focus of discussion—sovereignty. At root, the term merely denotes superiority. That concept, however, requires a referent. One must ask: superior with respect to what? Applied to a finite government, sovereignty merely is a term implicit of ascendancy established with respect to matters bearing on the government's capacity to function as a going concern. Sovereignty denotes capacity to make and to give effect to public decisions. Sovereignty is the situation of being in charge of a domain.

Speaking to audiences on foreign policy, I often encounter the notion pronounced by the Secretary of State—the obsoleteness of sovereignty. The proponent customarily employs a tone of discovery and solution—as if uttering a formula to end vicissitude and to achieve concord. Usually I reply by naming over some of the constituent characteristics summed up as sovereignty and then asking the proponent to specify which of the characteristics he would mark for elimination. In the general case, it turns out that my questioner finds national responsibility awesome, risky, and expensive. Sovereignty to him epitomizes the risks and burdens, and by getting rid of the concept or the word he hopes to alleviate them. He is merely wishing to pass the buck, though he would prefer a more dignifying term for his aim.

It is worth a moment to consider some of the practical components of sovereignty. Sovereignty entails having a scheme of authority—a ruling group—capable of maintaining dependable social order pervasively over a demarcated area. Sovereignty entails command of the allegiance of a determining portion of persons and groups encompassed in that area. Sovereignty entails having a common set of recollections from the past and expectations for the future forming a pattern of identity among such persons and groups. Sovereignty entails a conscious general purpose to amount to something significant in the world's annals. Sovereignty entails a capacity and a will to command means and to devote them to give effect to common preferences. Sovereignty involves capacity to enter into and to effectuate obligations. Sovereignty involves capacity to affect environing conditions as well as to be affected by them. Sovereignty requires having some system of agency capable of representing the realm in external dealings—able to communicate authentically and conclusively on its behalf to others beyond the span of jurisdiction.

These faculties and qualities listed are not easy to come by. Even under most favorable circumstances, they require continuous cultivation. No society can afford to assume them to be an inherent endowment, a fixed reality. I should wish my own society to prize, to hold on to, and to go on cultivating every one of those faculties and attributes. It would forfeit any one of them at its peril. The notion of solving great problems through planned obsolescence of sovereignty is simply one of the airy generalizations abundant in discussions of international relations—something handy to say before an assemblage but not of much account in engaging with actualities. The perils and perplexities in the world about us rise not so much from an excess of the constituent qualities of sovereignty in the entities passing as nation states, as from an entirely opposite circumstance. A great many of them have not achieved those qualities. Realizing them may be beyond the ultimate capabilities of some.

For the time being at least, we of the United States can look upon ourselves as belonging to one of the more fortunate of the entities participating in world affairs as nation states—fortunate not only in regard to scope and advantage of geographic position and material endowments but also in respect of the level of reality of the faculties and attributes expressed in sovereign status. That is to say, the United States is a great power: an organized society with considerable capacity to achieve intended results. Its relative importance puts it, willing or not, in position to affect conditions in the world at large. As such, the United States and its people need to be concerned—in particular, but not to the exclusion of other aspects—with the last two of the constituents of sovereignty listed, which pertain to linkage between sovereignty conceived as the sum of a nation's attributes as a going concern and sovereignty expressing a nation's role and significance among other entities on the same formal footing.

With respect to this facet of the matter, community has become a watchword of our time. My purpose is not to inveigh misanthropically against community but rather to put a proportion upon a widely affirmed disposition to regard the government's and the nation's highest and indeed engrossing function in world affairs as that of reflecting whatever values and preferences may be found to prevail in areas beyond the span of national jurisdiction. To note utterances of this idea by columnists, psychiatrists, physicists, and politicians is not astonishing. What has astonished me is having thrice in recent months heard the notion voiced by theologians, even distinguished ones, for theologians should know better than to interpret life and duty in terms of being an echo chamber.

My point may be clarified by a personal reference. As a young man my father got his first job in the South as foreman in a brick plant in South Carolina. His new employers briefed him on conditions and requirements and detailed the methods in vogue for handling the local labor force, mainly Negro. My father said he would not follow the methods described. His employers retorted that they were only explaining the situation.

My father said that the situation had changed. His employers asked: how? The change, my father said, consisted in the circumstance that he was now on the scene.

The difference made by the fact of one's presence is a way of explaining what one amounts to in the world—for a nation as well as for a person. The measure, moreover, is not what one reflects but what one projects. To the degree of filling that measure, a nation may be said to be creative and may be accounted sovereign. Filling that measure, the United States is bound to find some degree of tension between itself and other wills and forces in the world—and the prevalent talk about relaxing tensions is therefore mostly vain and misguided.

To be sovereign, in the sense that those who look upon the world from the standpoint of a great power must think of being sovereign, is to be able to have an effective foreign policy. Having an effective foreign policy requires continuous rigor about methods and meanings and purposes. Upon these considerations the essays selected for this first section are focused.

RENDER UNTO CAESAR

In the State Department back in 1952, acting for the Secretary, I received a group of ladies seeking official endorsement of a plan to solve world political issues and establish peace once and for all. The kernel of the idea was to transcend the state system in the making of great decisions. The trouble with the state system, as their spokeswoman explained, was its divisiveness. It partitioned humankind off into some dozens of societies, whereas in the interest of peace mankind must be grouped as one. The common denominator must be motherhood.

The proponents of the scheme were mothers—not necessarily all in a literal sense, it was explained, but at least in viewpoint. All humanity was linked by motherhood. Half of the race had a capability for maternity, if not indeed the experience of it, and everyone was linked to motherhood at least in the sense of having had a mother. Mothers, moreover, were mothers wherever found. No mother could ever wish anything but good for her own offspring or anyone else's. Thus through motherhood all the world could be harmonized and redeemed. The solution of the obdurate political problems confronting governments and threatening the peace lay in translating them into the discourse of mothers, who understood each other around the globe.

The ladies were planning to make their way by charter flight around the world, going first to the Far East, then through South Asia to the Middle East, to Africa, and thence to Europe. In each country, they would get into touch with mothers and

From *The Johns Hopkins Magazine*, May–June, 1962; *The Foreign Service Journal*, September, 1962; *The National Observer*, October 1, 1962.

recruit increments for their pilgrimage. They appreciated the fact of want in many other lands. They would take along clothes from last year's wardrobe lest their affluence prove a barrier. They supposed that mothers joining the movement from poorer lands might well have to proceed by tourist class. Multiplying into thousands as they progressed, the mothers would congregate for a climactic meeting in a city behind the Iron Curtain, where, after singing the choral parts of Beethoven's *Ninth Symphony* simultaneously in the diverse tongues represented, they would resolve the views of mothers on world issues. Statesmen, all having learned obedience in the cradle, would scarcely dare defy the consolidated will of the world's mothers. Moral force would supersede political power. The authority of mothers over the courses of nations would be established to stay.

I regret my success in dissuading the ladies from their venture if only for curiosity over the technical problems of translating Schiller's ode for simultaneous rendition in such a variety of idioms and of accommodating Beethoven's counterpoint to the limits of the five-tone scale prevailing in most other cultures.

My notes on the session with the ladies are filed along with a number of items of like sort: for example, a clipping concerning a resolution by a nudists' convention urging the practice of their particular persuasion on those in high authority in world affairs as a way of opening their eyes to what mankind has in common and thereby resolving world tensions, or another reporting an action by a convention of luncheon club executives calling for special voice for their vocation at highly sensitive international conferences in view of their peculiar understanding of the arts of smoothing things over. I cite these not for facetious extremity but for their representativeness of many formulas for elevating the conduct of international relations above the prevailing unsatisfactory level.

The unsatisfactoriness of the basic condition of politics was touched upon by a child in one of Rudyard Kipling's verses:

> All the people like us are We,
>   And everyone else is They.

> And They live over the sea,
>   While We live over the way,
> But—would you believe it?—They look upon We
>   As only a sort of They!

Carrying on relationships between a "we" and a "they" disposed to look upon us as "they" is an onerous and often baffling business. The factors keep shifting. The fringes of the groups tend to be unsteady. Sometimes groups change sides. No sooner is some accommodation worked out than it becomes obsolete and a new issue rises to attention. Assumptions tend to be repeatedly confounded by events. Even the best plans go amiss in some respect. Successes are never perfect and seldom final. Most of the tasks are Sisyphean.

It is not difficult, and it is indeed appealing, to imagine better alternatives. The factor of purported improvement is almost invariably a greater community of attributes among the entities counting in world affairs. The standard concepts of heaven tend to be of this sort—a place where tensions are absent and harmony abounds because all inhabitants have been brought along to a glorious sameness of outlook and intention. Those liking to think up heavens on earth usually hit upon a similar formula. More often than not, the characteristics projected as desirable universals in a plan for rising above the vicissitudes of a political world are those of the person or group doing the projecting. The first chapter of Genesis provides an explanation for this in relating God's creation of man in God's image—that is, I take it, to be creative in his own modest way and, alas, to project his own image in applying the aptitude.

The idea of improving international relations by having them managed by persons like oneself thus comes naturally—and the same applies within states, though this is an aspect beyond the topic. It is neither necessary nor typical to go so far as to imagine the acceptance of the proponent's outlook and preferences by everyone. The people who count—the ones in authority—are enough. Then great decisions would be made as if the choice were left to the author of the wish. The environment would be wholly reassuring and problems susceptible of rational solution. There would only be a "we" formed according to the wisher's views and unencumbered by having to deal with a differentiated "they." Our discourse would become the sovereign discourse. Our perspectives about truth would be the prevailing ones.

Plato called the state "man written large." Preferably what kind of man? Plato—a philosopher, mind you—gave his answer in a hope "that there might be a reform of the State if only one change were made, which is not a slight or easy though still a possible one," namely, to have philosophers to be kings and kings be philosophers, thereby substituting the universal terms of his own discipline for the particulars of politics.

A distinguished evangelist, heard recently on the subject of bettering world politics, had a parallel version—to wit, that potentates should be seized by a selfless and evangelical zeal like his own.

A United Nations bureaucrat whose company I experienced a few months ago pressed unremittingly upon his audience the urgency of raising the great decisions above all considerations of national advantage by placing them in the hands of a disinterested international bureaucracy. Imagine, if you can, a disinterested bureaucracy!

I have had an exchange of letters with an industrial engineer intent on promoting a scheme for setting up in each country a panel of industrial engineers to handle foreign policy—"the only group that basically understands," according to one of his letters. "They think in common terms," it adds. "Their problems are alike everywhere."

Boris Pasternak, a man of artistic bent, on being asked to what class he would entrust a world government, replied, "Perhaps to artists," seeing the artist as having "a unique vocation to be a human creature with all the love and all the freedom which this state implies."

I might go on and on with instances from my files and notes of self-projection—of seeing the state as oneself written large— in formulas for saving the world. I wish I could. I should like to dwell at length on the implications of an idea treasured among anthropologists looking to the achievement of concord in world affairs through general acceptance of their professional attitude of avoiding judgments of good or bad in regard to the practices of other societies; on the literature of psychiatrists who pursue solutions by imagining nations in the role of patients under their care; on books by fanciers of the diplomatic tradition calling for a return to the usages of a dreamed-up time when foreign policy was left to the charge of unaccountable diplomatic technicians; and on a grand enterprise of lawyers for abating dangers in the world by translating its issues into terms of their litigious speciality. A lawyer serving as counsel with one of the delegations at the United Nations reproved my skepticism regarding that last named project. "It really is true," he insisted. "As lawyers we all get along together wonderfully. Much of the world's trouble would vanish if left to lawyers to work out."

Much as in the thirteenth century with the theologian, in our age the man written large is pre-eminently the scientist, and so I reserve special comment for a relevant outlook of the breed— an attitude given its clearest expression, in my judgment, in an address given by Werner Heisenberg to students at Göttingen in 1946 and included in his *Philosophic Problems of Nuclear Science*. He described political life in terms of "a constant change of values, a struggle of one set of illusions and misleading ideas against another set of illusions and equally misleading ideas," whereas there would "always be a 'right or wrong' in science," where "a higher power, not influenced by our wishes . . . finally decides and judges." The core, he went on, consisted of "the pure sciences . . . not concerned with practical applications." He waved aside any objection based upon the inaccessibility of this power to the great masses of people; ". . . it may be that people today will be satisfied to know that though the gate is not open to everyone there can be no deceit beyond the gate. We have no power there—the decisions are taken by a higher power. . . ." Moreover, "any world order must be based" on this center and "guided by men who have not lost sight of it."

In more recent times, Heisenberg has become less assured about the title to a sovereign role for his discipline, as evidenced by a warning in his *Physics and Philosophy*: "Of course, the influence of science should not be overstated." The spirit of his earlier pronouncement, however, marches with show and confidence through an array of current literature, enough of it to snow us under. That spirit is maintained as dedicatedly by scientists who do not write as by those who do, and, in my tentative conclusion, no dogmatism exceeds that of a scientist expounding outside the field of his particular competence. The claim of special insights and determinative prerogatives for the profession typically parallels those made on behalf of such groups—a view already assumed to be above interests, a bond of community with foreign counterparts, and a universal frame of discourse. World problems would all become negotiable if left to scientists, one of the calling told me. There were no barriers as in ideology and politics, he explained, and an equation in physics meant the same in Moscow as here—tantamount to what has been said of mothers, artists, legalists, and philosophers.

Putting aside the obviously absurd ones of the approaches cited, I wish to discuss relevant motivations, as I understand them, more seriously than I have done so far. All of them reflect pride in vocation or other basis of identity—quite a human characteristic. Excesses of enthusiasm in looking to the precepts of one's groups for canons for wider application—an easy and common error—may appropriately be discounted with skepticism rather than dismissed with scorn. Each of the group identities involved in the dignified examples obviously has a bearing, even if not the central bearing, on solving the world's great problems. That goes even for the function of maternity, especially if its rate can be slowed in regions of critical disparity between numbers and supplies.

One motivating consideration common to the approaches is clearly anxiety over the potential for force inherent in international relations. It lurks in all business of states, whose authority, as Philip Melancthon pointed out, rests essentially on power to take life. It is especially critical in relations between states—

where force is least clearly and systematically bridled—and the inherent danger grows steadily greater with untrammeled progress in technology of weapons. However impracticable, the urge to substitute, in place of the usages of state conduct, group attitudes and codes free of the sanction of force is obviously not hard to account for.

Closely related is a desire to be more solidly assured concerning the moral basis of choices in foreign policy. The plurality of values and interests involved in all great international issues, accentuated by their remoteness from personal experience, is perplexing. The complexity of values and interests is what gives rise to so much temporizing in this field of endeavor—a factor making way for a suspicion of expediency, in a pejorative sense, about foreign policy. It comes naturally, if uncritically, to imagine great virtue and benefit in providing a set of values less complicated, closer to one's ken, and supposedly bearing more elements of community among nations. How to do this? Well, it would be easier if kindred spirits had charge everywhere—and, as I used to hear in the Army, you can't be court-martialed for dreaming.

My observations have a bearing on traditional arguments over expediency versus morality and interests versus principles in foreign policy—hardy topics invariably good for an editorial, a classroom lecture, or a Sunday afternoon at a civic forum. In my experience, those wont to speak up for morality in this connection, as if settling issues by invoking the term, use it generally to denote the way they imagine their kind would run affairs if in charge. Expediency, in contrast, is an invidious term employed to describe the temporizing occasioned by the diversity of interests and attitudes counting in the world as it is. Principles mean the interests one thinks his group would look after if in authority, and interests mean any concept of principles deviant from them.

I see small usefulness or importance in arguing about foreign policy in these terms. They are rarely, if ever, pertinent to resolution of a real issue in the line of responsibility; that is to say, I cannot imagine a President or a Secretary of State posing a question whether to be expedient or inexpedient in a particular line of action, to uphold or to abandon morality on an issue, to serve or to disserve our interest, or to honor or to flout principles.

I can imagine doubters asking what about morality and principle in relation to painful episodes of springtime in 1960 and then a year later. As for the U-2 scrape—few would question the necessity of espionage; governments continually intrude upon one another with unacknowledged prying. The fault in that embarrassment lay not in our failure to be history's first big exception but in a default of preparing to handle consequences of mischance—inadequate forethought, bad timing, and inept performance, all adding up to something hugely inexpedient. As to the fiasco at the Bay of Pigs, the Under Secretary of State reported to have voiced advance doubts and the Senator who interposed objections did invoke principles. They were vindicated—no doubt of it. My only question is whether the lesson was one of principle or an expediential one. As a hypothesis, suppose our intelligence to have been correct and the plans and execution tolerably adequate. Suppose masses of Cubans had risen to dispel the five o'clock shadow. Suppose, after a tactical success with minimal slaughter, the Cubans had managed to rally to a reasonable political arrangement. How different, how bold and noble, the undertaking would have seemed then! In actuality, it was a botch. It proved untimely. Factors of feasibility were misappraised or mismanaged. Means chosen were inapposite to the purposes—in sum, an exercise in inexpediency. Hands were wrung over the wickedness of intervention. Yet no cries of offended principle were raised when in unequivocal intervention, our warships stood in to ensure and to quicken the departure of certain ambitious scoundrels from the Dominican Republic a short time later—just as no great display of rue had been occasioned by a provident venture in Guatemala a half dozen years earlier.

Though reconciled to being misunderstood and misquoted on the point, I really do not suggest renouncing morality and principles or embracing a characterless sort of relativism in foreign policy. I mean only that the possibilities relevant to real questions coming up for settlement can rarely be sorted with such litmus-paper conclusiveness.

As an illustrative example, I recall from some years back an issue over repatriation of prisoners in Korea. The argument within the government over whether to make our reluctance forcibly to repatriate prisoners a sticking point in the armistice negotiations was strenuous. The doubters referred to the novelty of the proposed position, the difficulties of making it understood abroad, the likelihood of splitting our coalition, and the danger of prolonging hostilities, widening the theater of conflict, and incurring large avoidable casualties. The affirmers saw danger of branding the United States with faithlessness, alienating allies, and weakening our place among nations in any other course. They were confident of generating support for a position involving not mere abstractions but the lives and liberty of actual, ascertainable people in significant numbers. They rated higher than the doubters the probability of the adversary's giving in on the issue in face of manifest firmness. While discounting it somewhat, they accepted the chance of prolonging and widening hostilities. They contended that the United States still had great resources to draw on, was not deprived of options, and should not regard the issue as if in extremity. These arguments prevailed and proved correct. The United States was saved from taking a wholly wrong way out.

I retrospected on that issue once with a friend much interested in moral aspects of foreign policy. He described the decision as epitomizing moral judgment in this field. In fact it was not that simple. Those on either side of the issue within this government had wished to do the right thing. Both sides also tried to take full account of prudential factors. Both wanted their government to act morally and expediently at the same time. Each sought a course both workable and right. Such is generally the case.

The instance illustrates yet another basic characteristic. To have yielded on forcible repatriation would have required bringing terrible compulsion to bear on men in our care as prisoners.

To reject this way out involved additional casualties and some degree of risk of incurring many more. Either course was charged with peril and pain hugely beyond any choice ever put up to us as private individuals. In our lives and vocations as private men we are relieved from having to make choices involving death and destruction—thanks to the existence of institutions of state and government vested with a monopoly of rightful coercion over the span of their jurisdiction.

We may regret rationally the finiteness and multiplicity of states and wish, however remote the prospect, for one great monopoly of coercion to subsume them all. We are not entitled to assume a fastidious pose about the state's problems in this respect, looking with condescension or aversion on the institution and its authorities because they have to deal with onerous and painful problems from which we are exempted in our personal existences. We are not entitled to think to ourselves how much better and cleaner the state's business might be if given over to be operated in accord with the standards of our personal and professional relationships; at least we are not entitled to assume any usefulness in that line of thought.

Moral judgment does have to be brought to bear on the problems of states—especially so with respect to the perilous problems central to the control of the coercive apparatus—but not vain judgment based on a fallacy of ignoring the limits of the state's situation, not the sort of moral judgment we imagine ourselves giving when we fancy being philosopher kings.

A colleague of mine in the State Department was wont to assume that mantle in the face of a new and difficult issue. His customary first step was to observe that such a problem could not even arise in a properly ordered world. His second was to balance causes and effects concerning the problem and, having thus explained it, to assume a tone of having explained it away. His third—following a device of philosophers—was to analyze the entities in contention according to essential and accidental characteristics. The first were the ones supposed to be important. The accidental were relegated to secondary status—and thereafter ignored in his discourse. All problems were thus elevated to a philosophic level of consideration, their troublesome aspects sloughed off. At that rare level, ourselves and our adversaries were pared down to central essences as states and shown to be quite alike, with all differences eliminated by definition.

The rejoinder to this intriguing Platonic exercise was obvious. For analogy, suppose a man on the street sticks a gun in my ribs and makes demands. I might say to myself that such a thing should not happen. I might assure myself that the effects confronting me could all be balanced out against causes. I might then make note of the bandit's status as a man like myself, enumerating the essential attributes shared with me, reminding myself of his parity with me in God's sight, of the equality of concern which a priest might feel for the state of our souls, and of the equality of interest which an anthropologist might take as between the customs of the gunman's culture and mine or which a psychologist might take in the workings of our respective minds. The problem of the exigent man with a gun in my ribs would still be there, and the aspect of him most important for me at the moment would be his accidental characteristics as a bandit.

The state operates in a realm of imperfection, attending to an array of problems at the level of accidental and particular characteristics of the human situation—a level different from the essential and universal qualities of fascination to philosophers. This one should keep in mind in considering the problems of foreign policy—honoring the injunction to give unto Caesar the things that are Caesar's.

STRATEGY AND PURPOSE

IN UNITED STATES

FOREIGN POLICY

THE MEANING OF STRATEGY.

A little more than five decades ago a writer named Homer Lea was widely derided as heretical, deluded, irrelevant, and mischievous for attempting to deal with the United States' relations to its environment in such martial terms as radiuses of attack, comparative resources for levying war, states of military proficiency, and looming conflicts of dominion. Such ideas—so the critics' argument went—had no bearing on the American future. A short time later, after the outbreak of World War I, an American president, Woodrow Wilson, was enraged on learning of the War Department General Staff's having quietly considered plans against a hypothetical involvement in the hostilities. He issued reprimands and ordered immediate discontinuance of activities so obviously irrelevant to the country's course. Even after the advent of World War II, John Nicholas Spykman's *America's Strategy in World Affairs* incurred wide skepticism for its disposition to view concern with the geography and technology of security as a thenceforth abiding aspect of national life rather than a passing abnormal necessity due to be alleviated upon defeat of the moment's adversaries.

From a volume of essays on foreign and military policy, edited by Robert A. Goldwin (Chicago: Rand McNally, forthcoming 1965). Copyright © 1963 by the Public Affairs Conference Center, The University of Chicago. All Rights Reserved.
Also from *The Key Reporter*, Spring, 1964.

Attitudes so recently regarded as exceptional have come to be taken generally for granted. The circumstance undoubtedly has much to do with a now quite common practice of using the term *strategy* to denote enduring and engrossing considerations relevant to foreign policy. The key word is by origin a military expression cognate with the Greek *strategos,* signifying a general or one in supreme command and relevant to generalship at its most recondite level and, by strict standards of meaning authorized by the dictionary, remains exclusively such.

The practice of applying it virtually as a synonym of higher policy is of fairly recent origin. I first became aware of the usage in an official context fourteen years ago in connection with production of a basic paper regarding national security— NSC 68—whose contents were then closely guarded but have since become widely known. That same year, as I recall, the Secretary of State of the time used the phrase "Strategy of Peace" as a title for a major speech on foreign policy. A decade later an aspiring senator applied the same phrase to a book consisting of his collected addresses on world affairs. Subsequently, during his tragically shortened tenure as President, the key word used to turn up often in his discourses at press conferences and on more formal occasions. Others widely echo the use. Various institutions focusing on foreign policy purport to be strategic in intent and adopt the word in their names.

Maybe the usage is here to stay, notwithstanding the restrictiveness of the dictionary definition. In part the vogue may be a matter of style. The term sounds big. Individuals sometimes invoke it to vest their ideas with thoughtfulness, dimension, and authority without attention to its meaning. In part, however, the vogue has a measure of validity due not only to steady concern with security considerations in foreign policy under present conditions but also to ideas implicit in the term but not so clearly derivable from the companion word *policy. Strategy* suggests the idea of discriminating choices. More dimensions are implicit in it than in the other word. Any response or purpose might qualify to be called a policy, but a strategy seems to suggest deliberateness, scope, and complex calculation. So probably the prevalence of the term reflects a sense of our having gone beyond the simplicities characteristic of earlier times in world affairs.

Testing the appropriateness of the term in application to national undertakings in the broad calls for taking into account some characteristics of warfare. Its nature is obscured by a current tendency to refer to a type of conflict as limited war—implicitly as if some contrasting sort of war were infinite. All wars are limited. No war, whether experienced or merely notional, presents infinite possibilities. Wars vary not between being finite and measureless but in the manner of their finiteness.

The phenomenon of war occurs when adversary political societies or groups of such, disposing armed forces, seek to resolve conflicting purposes by acting upon each other's wills through effecting a determinative shift of relative capabilities for bringing force to bear—each side to its own advantage and to the disadvantage of the antagonist—and to that end, as an essential part of the process, use their armed forces to expend energy destructively upon the respective adversary establishments. The numbers of political entities drawn in on either side, the purposes put at issue in combat, the levels of force capabilities generated, the areas chosen for destructive expenditure of energy, the range of devices used, the intensity of the destructive expenditure, the amounts of matériel and of manpower committed to the effort, and the time entailed—such are the interdependent variables, directly or inversely related according to circumstances, involved in the measurement and therefore in the management of warfare.

Strategy concerns calculation of interrelations among such factors. How, in broadest terms, to interweave potential and purposes is its focus. Strategy relates to the establishment and application of a pattern of ends and a framework of means, whereby to assess tactical opportunities, to choose which areas to yield, to contest, or to overrun, and to appraise what initiatives in coercing others or for winning their support may help or hinder the broad cause. The occasion for strategy is a situation of choice—to wit, a situation of having means enough to afford some exercise of preferences but lacking such abundance as to be able to effectuate every desire. Strategy involves renunciation and deferment as well as pursuit and achievement of ends. It entails choice among purposes brought into conflict because of limitation of means.

The strategic content of thinking involved in planning and levying war varies from one instance to another. In uncomplicated cases, as for example between antagonists so inherently incommensurate in capabilities as to spare one side appreciable need to calculate the interrelated magnitudes and to afford the other side little opportunity to do so, the management of war may be mostly a matter for tacticians. The closer the two sides are to being even in potential, the greater becomes the requirement of systematic calculation of the interacting factors of magnitude: the greater, in other words, the role of strategy.

The prominence of the term owes something also to an awareness of being in a phase of pervasive and unremitting contest in world affairs. The main elements of changed circumstance accounting for this intensification of concern about external affairs can only be named here, for each is so complex as to deserve book-length explanation. They are:

The establishment of positions of great scope and importance—namely the Soviet Union and the Chinese People's Republic and appurtenant areas—for revolutionary purposes in world affairs.

The emergence of weapon systems characterized by prodigious destructive capabilities and instant readiness for delivery over spans of thousands of miles.

The sharing of pre-eminence in such weapons by two societies—one the United States, the other the Soviet Union—based beyond the confines of what used to be the central theater of military significance and political importance in world affairs, namely Central and Western Europe.

The progressive disappearance—a major phenomenon of our times—of the Europe-based, inequalitarian imperial order once serving as a framework of relationship between economically and politically advanced societies and the less-developed and tradition-bound lands and peoples.

As a corollary, the proliferation of juridically independent new states, entering into the public life of the world often without having as yet established adequate bases of public life within themselves and participating in the making of history without, in many instances, canons of relevant historic experience of their own.

As a further corollary, the approach to universalization of the equalitarian usages of diplomacy in succession to the inequalitarian arrangements of empire.

The existence and continuous activity of an institution—to wit, the United Nations—now also approaching universality and designed for and devoted to what is called parliamentary diplomacy.

Some of these developments were never willed by the United States and have been thrust upon its consciousness by forces and events beyond its ordaining. Others, though encouraged by the United States, differ widely in actuality from the hopes which prompted sponsorship. In sum, they illustrate the inherent adventitiousness of foreign affairs and the limitations on power of even a first-rank government for affecting its environment. In consequence of them, attending to the external concerns of the United States has become a hugely more involuted and rigorous business than it was in previous epochs. The inherent necessity of choice and renunciation in exterior relations is borne in upon general and official consciousness constantly rather than being a point of intermittent concern, as in earlier and less exacting stages of national experience. The margin for error has shrunk. Interactiveness among the globe's quadrants has become increasingly manifest. A need for seeing the world steadily and whole has become patent. Foreign policy itself has no traditional terms for distinguishing readily between pervasive and lasting considerations and immediate and local problems. The borrowing of a discriminating analogy from military discourse is natural and convenient.

TWO BASIC VIEWS OF NATIONAL PURPOSE.

However novel some features of the situation in which the United States now defines the purposes of policy, the basic premises from which it conceives those purposes are part of a memory reaching back to the national origins and far beyond. In some degree, the premises tend to come into contradiction. Policy must strive to maintain a workable compatibility between them. In this sense, policy is a matter of making ends meet. Contrasting premises about the character and role of the American nation in relation to other peoples are most fundamental in this regard. These premises reflect divergent perspectives about societies and their origins and courses.

The more sanguine outlook may be described as rooted in Genesis, in Isaiah, in the Book of Daniel, in the account in the Book of Acts of Paul's sermon at Mars Hill, and in Revelation. It has been—in a phrase from Abraham Lincoln—"dished up in as many varieties as a French cook can produce soup from potatoes." Medieval theocratic thought was preoccupied with it. It was reflected in the beliefs of Anabaptists in the Rhine Valley in the 1500's and of Levelers and the Fifth Monarchy sect in England a century later. Bossuet and Fenlon exhorted cognate ideas in Louis XIV's time. Marxist and Darwinian thinkers have produced their counterpart notions. Another version of the concepts appear in the late Pope John's encyclical, *Pacem in Terris.*

By the line of thought common to such diverse exemplars, humankind had a common origin: "God . . . hath made of one blood all nations of men for to dwell on all the face of the earth," according to Paul's version of the matter. Variations of culture are a product of man's wanderings away from the original base or reflect some divisive catastrophe like that of the Tower of Babel. Institutional structures called states and governments are a product of, and epitomize, such aberrant developments. Behind, beneath, or despite them, mankind remains inherently a unity. In this vein, as a contemporary example, George F. Kennan, in *The Realities of American Foreign Policy,* speaks of "these unsatisfactory but indispensable arrangements we call governments" and describes peoples as "separated from one another" by them.

According to this outlook, moreover, mankind has a potential—has indeed a destiny—of becoming reunified in some climax lying ahead. Politics, arising from accidents of diversity within human society, will then fade out. A new Jerusalem, marking an end to conflict and a final heightening of enlightenment and prosperity, is to emerge. Particularism will fall away. The nations, transcended, will pay homage. Thus goes the vision portrayed in the twenty-first chapter of Revelation. For men involved in the vicissitudes and uncertainties of temporal experience, no idea has had a more compelling and pervasive appeal than that of a new Jerusalem. "Earth at last a warless world, a single race, a single tongue," in Tennyson's summation.

By a contrasting perspective, diversity has been characteristic of the human situation back as far as the evidence is adducible. Societies took shape at diverse points, in diverse times, and under divergent circumstances. As the matter is put in Bertrand de Jouvenel's *On Power:*

. . . It is no longer treated as proved that there was only one primitive society; now, on the contrary, it is readily admitted that different groups of men have from the beginning presented different characteristics, which, as the case might be, either caused them to develop differently or prevented them from developing at all. . . .

According to this concept—put before us in a popular and titillating version in Robert Ardrey's *African Genesis*—such order, security, and continuity of authority as men have achieved have been realized by the combined efforts of particular groups in particular localities by dint of getting and maintaining control of territory. The limited monopolies of force called governments, however imperfect and contingent, form the basis of whatever experience men have had in living together in peace. Governments, by this view, are not divisive of mankind but afford such opportunity as there is, limited as it may be, for men to live peaceably together. A group living an established existence under one span of government identified with some marked-off area of the earth's surface has interests of its own and a legitimate right as well as an inherent necessity to uphold them; and if such a group is unable or indisposed to fend for its own interests, then surely no one else will.

Diversity is what makes political relationships necessary. Community makes them possible. Any version of policy which seeks to renounce and to transcend the differences represents a flight into Utopia. Any version which undertakes to make an absolute of diversity amounts to a declaration of war against or an instrument of secession from mankind in the large. Community and diversity are thus complementary characteristics, each varying in degree from one relationship to another. It is not my purpose here to choose between these two concepts. Here we are concerned with the roles of these two contrasting ideas in the American consciousness regarding the world at large. They are crystallized for us by two documents forming parts of the national foundation—namely, the Declaration of Independence and the Constitution. I do not imply them to be the only channels of these ideas to us, but surely they have served to articulate them for us in an important way.

WORLD MISSION AND NATIONAL INTEREST.

The Declaration is to be understood as essentially a document in foreign relations. It presents a bid for entry into the nexus of diplomacy—for assuming "among the powers of the earth . . . separate and equal station"—instead of continuing to acquiesce in the management of American relationships to the outside world by the vicarious, inequalitarian usages of empire. It solicits sympathy and support abroad. It asserts norms for relationships among diverse peoples and areas. It does this last on the basis of an assumption of a universal sort of rationality—holding truths to be self-evident to the world at large. As an unexceptionably valid idea, it argues the abhorrence of absentee rulership, of government from afar, to basic laws of nature and God.

Such are the proclaimed notions basic to American nationhood. Such a line of argument was not logically inevitable. The founders might have seized upon practical and particular arguments: the impracticability of control of the colonies from a base so far away, the miscomprehension of American desires and needs in London, the tendency of the new lands to outstrip the mother country, and so on. In the style of the times, however, they predicated universal principles. So ideas of the Enlightenment are echoed to us in the Declaration—universal rationality, harmony of interest, and the like.

One better understands all this by taking account of linkage between the Declaration and Thomas Paine's ideas in his *Common Sense*, as elucidated for us in Felix Gilbert's brilliant small book, *To the Farewell Address*. Paine exhorted not only for separation from the Crown but for renunciation of all alliances. Force would be necessary only for sundering the ties to the Crown and thereafter was to be dispensed with as an instrument of policy or a basis for security. In Paine's view, ties to the motherland only made the colonies heirs to the motherland's enmities. Freed from those ties, the colonies, as states, would enjoy the universal friendship assumed as latent in all relationships among nations. As unencumbered markets, they would serve the interests of all, and all would thereby be constrained to honor and to protect American independence. Thus security was to reside in detachment. America would be attuned to a harmony of interest inherent among nations but concealed by obsolete practices of empire. General interest would be made to flourish simply by eschewing particular interests.

American independence, in Paine's world view, was not merely to serve American interests but to discharge a duty to all mankind. The withdrawal into autonomy would be true only in a juridic sense. Emerging America was to set a republican example destined for general emulation. Power was not to be sought or husbanded. It was to come paradoxically in consequence of being avoided—power arising from rational purpose and good example. Such was the source of a persistent set of clichés—a hardy tradition—against power politics. The new nation was conceived then as an exemplar to all mankind, a guide to a new Jerusalem, achieving power by rising above considerations of power, forwarding its interests by forgetting about them, making its way in security without having to take provident thought about its security.

How different is the cast of thought in the Constitution! I do not mean to go so far as to suggest mutual exclusiveness between the ideas of the respective documents. Many men subscribed to both. Some of the bright expectations of the Declaration lingered on and do so even yet. Even so, the national leadership echoed in the Constitution has become less hortatory. The content reflects recognition of needing more than declaratory purposes and abstract good ideas in order to maintain a going concern. A bitter lesson has been learned: independence hinges on capacity and willingness to meet obligations. It is not enough simply to keep attuned to a supposed harmony of interest. The nation must put itself in position the better to attend to its own concerns. No universals are proclaimed, and no language of world mission. The document is intent on perfecting the union of states. It is concerned with justice within—justice not as a spontaneous abstraction, but justice as linked to, and a function of, authority. The tranquility asserted as an aim is domestic. The common defense must be striven for as security for a national base. The welfare postulated is that of the generality of Americans. The blessings of liberty are coveted for ourselves and our posterity. Domestic concerns they all are. Quite a contrast! On the one hand is the concept of a nation founded upon and exemplifying universally applicable principles—taking the lead in a new order of the ages, portraying for others what their future is to be like, setting an example for all to follow; on the other hand, a nation—in Alexander Hamilton's phrase—"likely to experience a common portion of the vicissitudes and calamities which have fallen to the lot of other nations" and constrained therefore to do what it can to fend off trouble and to look out for itself.

POWER AND RESPONSIBILITY.

At the moment of the American challenge for independence the world situation represented order in an appreciable degree. The governments—mainly, indeed almost exlusively, European—participating in the world's public life had learned long since to desist from interference in each other's domestic arrangements, accepting each other's autonomy and confining their quarrels to marginal issues. In the main, each participant could look ahead with solid assurance against destructive violence and change. The tenor was interrupted by two decades of turmoil prompted by the French Revolution. A century of order, apparently more engrossing and solid than ever before, succeeded.

Perhaps history has never provided an equivalent of the pleasant and successful time enjoyed by the United States in its relationships with the world during that century. The world was still only loosely drawn together during most of that period, though progressively less so as time advanced. The power situation presented opportunity rather than danger to the new nation. The country could even afford in the 1860's the luxury of a massively violent internal division without incurring lasting and serious disadvantages in the environment. The Americans' field of real concern lay close to hand. Issues emerging afar were remote in import as well as in distance. The nation itself represented almost—not quite, but almost—the sum of its preoccupations. In this it enjoyed reciprocity: even as late as 1914 the foreign offices and war offices of the European powers going through the fateful steps preliminary to the first of the two world wars gave not a moment's attention, as revealed in their archives, to the question of the United States' possible relation to the emerging hostilities—something never to happen again except in a sequel to some now unforeseeable obliterative catastrophe to the nation.

With respect to the world at large, Paine's prophecies of the universal efficacy of the American example were far from vindicated. The sweeping propositions of the Declaration retained vitality, however, in the national consciousness. A dialogue between the two contrasting ideas of universal mission and national interest persisted through the nineteenth century. It would oversimplify and overclarify matters to represent the dialogue as having been developed with studied logic and by consistent proponents. The nation was portrayed at once as standing apart from the world and yet as affecting it pervasively. The nation was destined to be puissant, but it was to eschew power—an echo of ideas underlying the Declaration. "I hope our wisdom will grow with our power, and teach us that the less we use our power, the greater it will be" ran Thomas Jefferson's formula in answer to a nice question as to how to be both self-denying and self-aggrandizing.

Yet it was mostly a rhetorical dialogue rather than a debate about actual policy choices. In the circumstances of the time, relating America to the nations of the transoceanic continents required of the American people attitudes rather than actions and commitments. Jefferson, giving counsel for dealing with what he called the enmities of Europe, might foretell a time "at no distant future" when "we may shake a rod over the heads of all, which may make the stoutest tremble" and assert that "even should the cloud of barbarism and despotism again obscure the science and liberties of Europe, this country remains to preserve and restore light and liberty to them." Walt Whitman, moreover, might turn recurringly to a theme of America ascendant in the world and bearing the destinies of all nations. For all practical intents the United States was following the counsel of George Washington's Farewell Address, abiding by more restricted and less lofty policy concepts of the Constitution as distinguished from the Declaration.

America was then concerned mainly with acquiring room to

grow, establishing grounds for fending off encroachments from abroad, and gaining positions and privileges conducive to American commerical success in the world. The Jay Treaty, the southwestward expansion in the 1840's bringing on hostilities with Mexico, and the accessions of Hawaii and the Philippines caused transient qualms, but in general in relations with external entities the Americans got ahead by doing what came naturally. They usually found their own resources for action sufficient for success, which was demonstrably grand in broad outlines and usually prompt and complete in particulars.

To be sure, in the Jefferson and Madison presidencies, performance fell short of the aim to compel British acknowledgment of the nation's asserted neutral rights in oceanic commerce, but the absence of important maritime wars in the succeeding century made this failure more an affront to pride than an impediment to destiny. The nation had to reconcile itself to a delay of a couple of decades, but no more, between the onset and the consummation of desire to acquire Texas. For roughly a half-century, moreover, it had to put up with some frustration of its desire for exclusive control of a projected trans-isthmian canal. These instances aside, the Americans generally not only knew but also got—and right away—what they wanted, whether in getting the British off the Northwest frontier, the Mediterranean pirates off the necks of American mariners, the French out of the trans-Mississippi West, the Spanish out of Florida, the Mexicans out of the present Southwest, the British out of the Far Northwest, the Russians out of Alaska, or the Spanish out of Cuba.

The abiding concern related to filling out and consolidating the continental position. It is not enough merely to call that position unique. All national positions are so. It is necessary to understand its particular combination of characteristics—a generally healthful land of great range and endowment generally accessible in all its parts, located in both the northern and the western hemispheres, and facing both upon the Atlantic and the Pacific. In earlier but still recent times it was possible still to speak cogently of that position as a basis for a policy of standing apart. Thus Samuel Flagg Bemis wrote in 1936, closing his distinguished *Diplomatic History of the United States:*

> The continental position has always been the strength of the United States in the world. American successes in diplomacy have been based on a continental policy. The interests of the United States today rest on the same support. It is a safe ground on which to watch and wait for a better world. A *continental* policy was instinctive with the Fathers. Its pursuit has been most consonant with the genius and the welfare of the American people. Where they have left it, to "become of age" or "to take their place"—on other continents—among the great powers of the world, they have made their mistakes. Where they have followed it, they have **not gone astray.**

The words seem to belong to another age rather than to a time less than three decades ago. There is no question now of watchfully waiting aside for the emergence of a better world—no question, moreover, of whether or not to stand among the great powers, for pre-eminence in that respect has been thrust upon the United States by events. The nation is involved in an endless discourse with itself growing out of consciousness of this pre-eminence and a contrasting awareness of its having been first among the once colonial peoples beyond Europe to challenge successfully to a place in the nexus of diplomacy and to the prerogatives of a history-maker. While engrossed in the affairs of the northern hemisphere, its people and its officials still retain habits of thinking of the United States as being located in the western hemisphere in a way more intimate and basic than its place in the northern. Thus the President and the Secretary of State are wont to say "this hemisphere" in referring to the Americas. The dialogue between the concept of a world mission—that is, the view of the nation as the bearer of universal values destined to prevail at large in the future—and the concept of the nation as a finite entity constrained to look to its own interests is no longer one merely of academic or literary interest separate from the practical issues of policy. Rather, it involves issues of continuous exigent concern.

THE SHORT RUN AND THE LONG.

Undertaking war against Spain in hope of clearing up a nuisance near the national periphery, the Congress re-enunciated the grand propositions of the Declaration of Independence. Pondering whether to make avail of opportunity to take over the Philippines, President McKinley implored divine guidance and then explained the action in terms of universal altruism. In a series of actions relevant to the traditional policy known as the Monroe Doctrine, the United States government adopted a posture described as follows by Dexter Perkins in *The United States and Latin America:*

> . . . it is remarkable how little emphasis was placed
> . . . on . . . national safety. No doubt the foreign offices
> of all countries indulge in high sounding generalities. . . .
> But this fact is conspicuously true in . . . American di-
> plomacy. Again and again . . . the emphasis is on ideol-
> ogy, rather than on security. . . .

Invoking war against Germany in 1917, the United States was not content to rest its cause upon the security issues involved but was constrained—borrowing a phrase from a British publicist, H. G. Wells—to "make the world safe for democracy." Interposing American resources against the Axis a generation later, Franklin D. Roosevelt propounded an Atlantic Charter with its four freedoms, all universal.

Reviewing the many such instances, a skeptic might well agree with Perkins:

> . . . American statesmen have believed, and acted on
> the belief, that the best way to rally American opinion be-
> hind their purposes is to assert a moral principle. In doing
> so, they have often gone far beyond the boundaries of ex-

pediency. And perhaps it is fair to say that in underempha-
sizing security, they have helped to form a national habit
which unduly subordinates the necessities of national defense
to the assertion of lofty moral principles.

The record reflects more than merely the rhetoric of policy propaganda, however. The universalistic assumptions of the Declaration are fixed in conscience as well as consciousness. The
Enlightenment is echoed to us in our great normative document
—and with it an age-old assumption about the original and
inherent unity of mankind. Under a deep national predisposition,
actions in world affairs undertaken in pursuance of the more
finite purposes of the Constitution are not *ipso facto* justified
but require vindication consonant with a universal scheme of
good. Like Thomas Paine, this part of the national psyche—of
which I personally do not completely partake—feels better in
identifying national purposes with service to all mankind.

This attitude dwells upon ultimate goals and conceives them
as including resolution of all differences and harmonization of
all interests—in sum, the transcending by policy of politics
among nations. This view tends to assume the omnipotence of
mankind for solving all problems. It subscribes to the feasibility
of new starts. It puts great store by the power of example alone.
It places great confidence in the power of documents to transform
situations and to enter into the general conscience—an understandable assumption in view of the efficacy of the Declaration
in affecting our own national approach.

The repeated invocations of this frame of thought in regard
to external affairs are not a mere matter of presidential guesswork as to what will go over with the public. The makers of
policy—that is, successive Presidents and their spokesmen and
principal counselors—do not simply humor these preconceptions but, in the usual case, share them in some significant
portion. The relevant notions are essential to a framework for
justifying policy undertakings to those themselves in charge and
are not a mere device for persuasion.

As a world power, the United States states its case and vests its ultimate hopes in propositions which guided it at the beginning of its national history, back when this country was the ugly duckling among states. Centrally involved in trying to create the conditions of a new order in world affairs, the nation abides by the discourse of times when it stood afar from the centers of the world's political concerns and enjoyed the benefits of an order largely maintained by others.

True to the frame of thought of the Declaration, national policy is steadfast in devotion to universalizing of independence. It abides by Paine's postulate of the inherent incapacity for justice in all rulerships exercised from afar. It has been, and continues, assiduous in establishing self-determination as a political absolute of our time. The inherent capacity of any people in whatever area to find within itself the canons of nationhood and to make its way as a going concern is taken for granted. The faith has shifted somewhat from Wilsonian premises of the efficacy of democratic forms and institutions in ensuring success. Emphasis, for the time being, is on economic factors as the key to the venture. A span of time and a proper level of investment will bring everything around.

The community of nations—along with an inherent community of interests among nations—is premised. The universalizing of independence—the introduction of increasing diversities into the nexus of diplomacy—is seen as helping community along to full realization. The ease, the virtual automaticity, of the process of bringing community into play is not assumed as it was in Paine's discourse. More time and more organizing effort are seen as required, but the reconciling end is sure, and will enfold even our adversaries. Fending off a cliché about having a no-win policy, the Secretary of State has countered with a cliché about having a set of purposes by which everybody will win. Thus also the Assistant Secretary of State in charge of policy planning postulates hopes in encouraging Communist governments "to perceive that the world we . . . are trying to create . . . has a place of dignity for all nations which pursue their national interests with integrity, which respect the hard imperatives of interdependence and the rights of other nations and peoples." It is as if conciliation were awaiting the reassertion of irreproachable abstractions, as if divisive issues were rooted in miscomprehension, and as if indeed an inherent unity of purpose needed right modes of expression to become revealed and made operative.

A danger of sorts inheres in uncritical acceptance of the optimistic postulates of the eighteenth century reflected in the Declaration. The case for universal independence, for example, poses diversity as right, proper, good—along with the assumptions of inherent harmony of interest and community among nations. Opposed qualities are thus placed in apposition. The case for freedom, stated by its most committed proponents, is linked to a concept of historical momentum amounting to an ineluctable force. Free will is seen as borne along toward triumph by deterministic currents. The danger is one of logical contradiction, but this troubles the discourse of policy no more than it did the Enlightenment. Community and diversity come on the same package, like gold dust twins.

We are out to promote them both—along with a theory combining the best parts of two other opposed ideas, freedom and determinism. "No one who examines the modern world can doubt that the great currents of history are carrying the world . . . toward the pluralistic idea . . . ," in the late President's words. "No one can doubt that the wave of the future is . . . the liberation of the diverse energies of free nations and free men." An Under Secretary of State has added a gloss. "Free will, not historical determinism, is the credo of free men," he has said. Free will, in his version, however, is a sure thing— "This is the only acceptable working hypothesis for free men today: We are on the side of history, and the trends are running our way."

Old happy assumptions from our early past are reflected in the government's proffered solution for the armament dilemma embodied in an official document called *Blueprint for the Peace Race.* All disputes about particulars are to be engrossed in a general agreement on global conditions of legitimacy. This is to be documented and made contractually binding. The agreement is to become by stages a basis for a world monopoly of force subservient not to any national or regional interest but only to a general good—irresistible power harnessed to an all-embracing benefit. The nations are to become secure, tame, inoffensive—as in Paine's vision of the future or in Revelation—being subsumed into a general order and intimidated by a force made irresistible by definition. Disarmed, the structures of particular governments will no longer be divisive of mankind. On a grand scale, one span of community and authority such as imagined to have obtained by the outset of human experience is to be renewed.

Thus our government spins a dream. For the long run, policy remains faithful to the spirit of the Declaration. At the same time, policy-makers are oath-bound to the Constitution and to the more immediate and limited obligations laid upon them by the world as it is rather than as it should be or might be in one's dreams. Such is the world written of by Leopold Schwartzchild in *World in Trance* a score of years ago:

> Never again can we believe that any new magic can achieve what we ourselves must achieve by hard work. Mankind is not capable of sudden rebirths. . . . There are good reasons for the fact that the millennium has never materialized. . . . Against the eternally lurking jungle, weapons and compulsion are always the only defense and nothing liberates us from the duty of doing the utmost for ourselves. . . . And if the great powers have a common will, everything is well. If not, there is no collectivity, and once again we are alone; with our nearest friends we are thrown back on our resources. We must always be prepared for that eventuality. . . .

With such a world—not the world of our preferences or our dreams—policy has to come to grips every day. In such a world national purposes are tested, and, as Cassandra says in Giraudoux's *Tiger at the Gates*, destiny is "simply the relentless logic of each day we live." In the world as it is, no universal frame of legitimacy prevails. The governments all sincerely avow a preference for peace over war, but the conditions of universal order nevertheless remain obdurately at issue. Governments vie in invoking the concept of community as a matter of habit, while the constituents of community remain unevenly spread—fairly strong between some, indifferent as between others, and almost nonexistent in other instances. Governments feel constrained to deprecate the high level of destructiveness in armaments and yet constrained also to maintain it because of the lack of mutual trust and divergence on the conditions of legitimacy. Governments and men are habituated to invoke the idea of international authority, but such authority in fact, far from being effective and continuous, is only something occasionally and contingently contrived, issue by issue. In the world as it is, deep disparities among peoples are a fact, and the dour prospect is that success as going concerns may simply be beyond the means and capacities of many societies and beyond reach of any precept or example that others may set for them. I do not suggest, in all this, a cause for rejoicing, but, in the immortal words of Jimmy Durante, "dem is da conditions dat prevail."

THE NATURE OF

FOREIGN POLICY

I shall define the foreign policy of the United States as the courses of action undertaken by authority of the United States in pursuit of national objectives beyond the span of jurisdiction of the United States. That is a lot of big words. Let me put the idea another way. Our foreign policy unfolds in the things done by the U.S. government to influence forces and situations abroad. The meaning of the phrase "things done" should not be construed too narrowly. In this field, utterance is a form of action, and pronouncements may be deeds, especially when they convey meaning about intended or possible actions rather than merely expressing abstractions and moralizations.

My definition of foreign policy may sound strange. Let me justify it. Foreign policy may be viewed as something distilled into chapters of a book or as a process involving a lot of daily hard work by many people. I am discussing it in the second sense—in the way that one might talk of a painting as a resultant in a process of putting paint on canvas, rather than as an ultimate effect hanging statically in a museum.

The two elements in my definition to be stressed are these: foreign policy is generated in actions; the things acted upon in foreign policy are things lying beyond the direct control of this country.

Those two things are simple and obvious. Yet they are often overlooked. The overlooking of them leads to a lot of misunderstanding.

A year or so ago I spoke in a midwestern city. In the question

From *The Department of State Bulletin*, March 17, 1952.

period a lady in the audience asked me to lay out briefly the course of policy for the next ten years. I declined, saying I could not foresee events that far ahead. The lady reduced to five years the span of the prophecy she sought. I disavowed clairvoyance even in that more modest degree. She became impatient. She said surely I could tell something about the future—something to be counted on—something to be taken for granted by a policy planner such as I in the laying of plans. I said there was indeed a sure element in the future: it was trouble; it was bound to occur; its timing, its points of arrival, and its guises were unpredictable; but that trouble would come was as safe a proposition as I could imagine.

My lady questioner became more impatient. She asked: If foreign policy was not a design to keep trouble away, then why have one—since one obviously could find trouble without the expense, effort, and time required for attending to foreign policy?

I said that the test for a nation as for an individual was not its success in abolishing trouble but its success in keeping trouble manageable—in generating the moral strength to face it and the capacity for handling it.

She spurned that answer. The lady said that if the Department of State was full of individuals like me, who took trouble for granted, then it was no wonder that the United States found itself in so much of it all the time.

A few weeks ago I had a different—yet in some ways similar—experience. I took part in a round-table. Another participant appeared to hold me personally to blame for the shortcomings of what he described as a foreign policy of expediency. My question as to whether he preferred a foreign policy of inexpediency did nothing to stem the tide of his scorn. He said a foreign policy must consist of principles discovered in natural law and not susceptible of being compromised or tampered with and that the only way to conduct a successful foreign policy was to set these principles up as absolute standards of conduct and then persevere in them without regard to the limitations of circumstance. The limitations of circumstance as a factor in foreign policy, he assured me, were figments of the craven mind that wants to avoid trouble instead of seeing national life as the opportunity of service to the eternal principles of right.

I did not fare very well in either of those arguments. In both cases the other participants were thinking about foreign policy only in terms of objectives. I was thinking of foreign policy as relating to means and ends and to the gap between them.

Ends are concepts. Means are facts. Making foreign policy consists of meshing concepts and facts in the field of action.

Suppose money grew on trees. Suppose power were for the asking. Suppose time could be expanded and contracted by a machine as in the story by H. G. Wells. Suppose Aladdin's lamp, the seven-league boots, and the other fairy tale formulas for complete efficacy were to come true and to be made monopolistically available to Americans. We would have then a situation in which we could do anything we wanted. We could then equate our policy with our goals.

In the world of fact, however, making foreign policy is not like that at all. It is not like cheerleading. It is like quarterbacking. The real work comes not in deciding where you want to go—that is the easiest part of it—but in figuring out how to get there. One could no more describe a nation's foreign policy in terms solely of objectives than one could write a man's biography in terms of his New Year's resolutions. Foreign policy consists of what a nation does in the world—not what it yearns for or aspires to. The sphere of doing, as distinguished from the sphere of desire and aspiration, is governed by limits. Adam Smith pointed out that economic behavior derives from imbalance between means and ends and the circumstance that ends therefore tend to conflict. The same is true in foreign policy.

I shall illustrate that in terms of present problems.

To begin, let me identify the fundamental purpose enlightening our conduct as that of preserving a world situation and enabling our constitutional values to survive.

That we must keep in mind when speaking of national interest as the basis of our foreign policy. To me the phrase "national interest" does not mean a set of aims arrived at without regard to values. I cannot think of our foreign policy except in relation to the character of the nation and its political institutions.

That has a bearing on the choice of means in the conduct of foreign policy. An accountable government cannot lead a double life. It is foreclosed from using such means as would destroy the very values it would save.

The main purpose enlightening our foreign policy holds true in all stages of our national life. It will continue as long as our country continues in the tradition we know. It is objectified in different ways as the world situation changes.

The world situation concerning us in the recent past and the present has been characterized by five main elements. The first is the result of complex historic changes, notably two world wars. A falling away in power among several nations once of primary greatness has occurred. This leaves two states of first magnitude, each with a great geographic span and great resources of power. One of these is our country.

The second relates to the situation of the other main element in this bipolar world of power, the Soviet Union. It is ruled by tyrants, who reached the seat of power through conspiracy and, having achieved power, have not dared to risk their hold on it by resort to a valid procedure of consent. They have remained conspirators after becoming governors, combining the usages of conspiracy with the prerogatives of the state. Both at home and in the world at large, the conspiracy that walks like a state requires tension and conflict to maintain its grip. It uses in the service of this aim a political doctrine emphasizing the patterns of violence—class conflict, subversion, and so on.

As the third element, I cite the climate of intimidation and fear in much of the world resulting from the circumstance that the Soviet Union has great military forces either under direct control or amenable to its purposes and that these forces are deployed along a huge span bearing on Northern and Central Europe, the Mediterranean area, the Middle East, Southeast Asia, and Japan.

Fourth, the dislocation of economic patterns and the exhaustion and demoralization of peoples in consequence of invasion, occupation, and oppression in World War II have created situations affording special opportunities for Soviet communism working within other countries as a conspiratorial force in the service of the Soviet rulers.

Fifth, the weakening of old restraints in Africa, the Middle East, and East Asia and the impulse to wayward use of freedom among peoples unaccustomed to the usages of responsibility and preoccupied with redressing old grievances, real or fancied, have created opportunities for the Soviet Union, alert as it is to the quest of advantage in the troubles of others.

In these circumstances our endeavor has been along four general lines. First, we have sought to develop stronger situations in the areas where the choices made by the peoples and governments in the great confrontation coincide with ours. We have done this so as to relieve the sense of anxiety—and with it the intimidatory power of the Kremlin—among the nations disposed to go along with us. In this category I put our alliances, military and economic assistance to our allies, and our efforts to return our former enemies to full relationships with other nations.

Second, we have sought to insure that the areas where the crisis of politics is sharpest—the areas of contest, such as Southeast Asia, the Middle East, and the Arab areas—shall not be lost.

Third, we have sought to exercise leadership in working toward the ideas of responsibility and peaceful adjustment in contra-distinction to the Soviet pattern of turmoil and conflict. This aim enlightens our attitude of trying to combine responsibility with new found freedom among the Middle Eastern and the Southeast Asian countries. It reflects itself in our support of the United Nations pattern, in our confrontation of aggression in Korea, and in our attempts to bring about a system of arms limitation that will not reward faithless performance.

Fourth, we have sought to steer away from the tragedy of another world war.

I am referring here not to objectives divided into neat categories distinct from each other but to concurrent phases of a process. That sounds very bureaucratic, but I do not know how better to convey the idea that in reality these things do not have such nice separateness as they seem to have when one talks or writes about them. These interrelated aims tend in part to support each other, and in part they also tend to contradict each other.

For example, at a certain point the pace of generating military strength may run counter to the requirements for a sound economic basis among our allies. In another instance, the effort at countering aggression might be carried to lengths that bear against the aim to avoid a general war. In still another, the impulse to deal sympathetically with the aspirations of a people new to freedom and not adjusted to its obligations may run counter to the economic necessities of another country which is allied with us or to the strategic necessities of our allies and ourselves. Again, trying to help with the military needs of one area may require the diversion of arms and supplies from others who also need them. Such are the dilemmas that arise when our power is not sufficient for doing all the things we want to do.

What requires judgment and timing in the highest degree, along with the fortitude that can defer hopes without surrendering them, is the job of threading a course through such contradictions as these and striving as best one can to find choices of action consistent with all of the aims concurrently. That is the job of making the best of situations in the knowledge that such is the only way of making them better. The job consists mainly of the rationing of power among aims. There—not in the formulation of aims but in the rationing of power among aims—is where a foreign policy really takes form.

In my definition at the outset I said that the decisions were made under authority of the United States. That authority exists in the grant of the executive power to the President and in the grant of legislative power to the Congress. I shall wave aside the constitutional question and the political question of the paramountcy of authority in these matters. The agencies and departments of the government concerned in foreign policy serve as staff advisors to the President and, under his direction, to the Congress in the making of the fundamental decisions. A staff function of this character carries duties but no prerogatives. The President and the Congress are entitled to seek counsel where they wish within the government or outside it. The same holds true within the Department of State. In making up his mind as to what advice to give the President, the Secretary is certainly entitled to seek counsel where he wishes.

I am one of several members of a staff which is only one among many elements within the Department of State producing advice for the Secretary of State. I am setting forth here not the conclusive word but only my own views, developed not in theory, but by observations. As I see it, the job of making the decisions which generate foreign policy calls for two ranges of perception. The first of these is the sense of the situation being dealt with. By that I mean knowledge of the background and of the local factors. The second is a sense of perspective. By that I mean a grasp of the relation and proportions between the instant problem and all other problems arising in other places and foreseeable in other ranges of time and competing with the instant problem in the apportionment of power.

These two ranges of perception are not mutually exclusive things. A situation can exist only in an environment. An environment entails a relation to other things. Moreover, a perspective can be taken only from a point in space or a moment in time—and a point in space and moment in time mean a situation. The differences between these two senses are differences in emphasis. As I see it, the planning function in foreign policy relates to a particular sense of responsibility for the perspectives.

The usefulness of planning is as an essential ingredient in the process of bringing problems to decision. The job of keeping clear on proportions and relations is indispensable in this business. Only systematic and continuous forethought can insure that a problem will be viewed in all its implications before a decision is made and action launched. Without it, decision and action would all too likely be quixotically impulsive, and the resources of capability would all too likely be overdrawn and the policy itself rendered insolvent.

I do not suggest that this special attention to perspectives originated only when the Policy Planning Staff was established in 1947. No doubt the Jeffersons, the John Quincy Adamses, and the Sewards had recourse to forethought in making up their minds. In recent years, however, the concerns of the United States have become unprecedentedly various and their scope unprecedentedly vast. That circumstance accounts for the usefulness of having within the Department of State a staff with a frame of reference as wide as that of the Secretary, the Under Secretary, and the Deputy Under Secretary for Political Affairs.

It is exacting business. Our problems reflect upon and from each other like the facets of a crystal. An alteration in any facet shifts the light that shines from and through all the rest. The proportions and interrelation of our problems undergo unceasing change.

I take note of a fallacy that planning contains the remedy for all vexations and points the way around every dilemma. The idea that all our problems can be solved through the employment of total planning is persistently put forth. Since some planning is good, more would be better, and the most possible best of all—thus runs the reasoning. Imagine trying to salt a stew according to that scheme of logic. The limit of utility in planning inheres in this. At any moment it is possible to draw one's perspectives on the future in the light of the data at hand, but it is not possible to draw a perspective on what one's perspective will be at some later stage in time. Wisdom cannot be stockpiled. Brains are not susceptible of being carried around in a brief case. There is no sound way of pre-empting judgment. It is not possible to tell better today how to handle a problem arising six months hence than it will be when the time comes.

It may be—it is—possible and necessary to keep proportions intact and up to date so as to have them ready for the moment of decision, but the judgment of the moment itself cannot be foreclosed.

I take note also of the notion that planning is a self-inductive process and that planners should stay remote from the arena of responsibility and plan and plan and plan in communion with other planners who plan and plan and plan. Quite the contrary, the important thing is for the planner to keep the roots of his thinking in the exigencies of real problems. I recall the story of the shingler who became so fascinated with his work on a foggy day that he shingled five feet beyond the eaves. That is what would happen if planning were carried on as a self-contained activity complete within its own system of logic.

The idea that planning can make everything tidy, answer all problems before they happen, foresee all eventualities, and prepare in advance the pat answer for every exigency is first cousin to the idea that power can be just as great as you want to make it. Power is the capacity to achieve intended results. It is always limited. Not all the elements bearing on a nation's destiny can ever be brought completely within the nation's control. Machiavelli pondered this in *The Prince*. He concluded that a .500 average on the field of destiny was about as much as might be hoped for.

The figure strikes me as too high, but many persons expect much more than the Florentine did. I refer not to their personal expectations. Most people are not dismayed by having to manage their financial problems along month to month. People go on driving cars year after year without ever permanently solving their parking problems. Yet some of my friends, and many persons in this country, some of whom write editorials or sit in seats of authority, persist in believing the desirable and achievable situation for the state to be one of perfect efficacy in its world relations. When perfect efficacy is not obtained, these people feel dismay and sense betrayal.

I recall a story told in Mexico. A man heavy in need and great in faith wrote a letter asking for one hundred pesos. He addressed it to God and mailed it. The postmaster had no idea how to handle the letter. He opened it, seeking a clue. He was touched by the man's story of need. He passed the hat among the postal employees. Thus seventy-five pesos were raised. These were placed in an envelope to await the return of the importuning man. A few days later he was back, inquiring for mail. He was given the envelope, opened it, counted the money, and glowered. Then he went to the counter and scribbled out another letter. It read: "Dear God: I am still twenty-five pesos short. Please make up the difference. But don't send it through the local post office. I think it is full of thieves."

The expectation of perfect efficacy in the conduct of foreign affairs reflects itself in the "whodunit" approach to world problems. I am concerned here, however, not so much with the tendency to ascribe to personal villainies all the difficulties of national existence as with the question of the proper proportions in which to view the problems. This is consequential. As an accountable government, our government must stay within the limits permitted by public opinion. To the degree that unrealistic notions about what is feasible are factors in public opinion, unnecessary limits are imposed on the scope of action in foreign affairs, and rigidities harmful to our true interests result. This is borne constantly upon the mind of anyone having responsibilities in the making of foreign policy.

Several things occur to me as sources of the expectation of complete efficacy. One of them is the consciousness of an extraordinarily successful past. The diplomatic course in the evolution from a colonial beachhead to a power of highest magnitude was one of matchless performance. Just as a man may lose his perspectives in calling up his departed youth, it is all too easy for us to lose a sense of proportion about our national problems by harking back to what we did when horizons were open and distance and the balance of power afforded us a shield.

Another influence I might call faith in engineering. That stems from our natural pride in the physical development of our country. Popular tradition treasures the idea that in the realm of creation all things are possible to those who will them. The margins available to us have made this almost true so far as the development of our own country is concerned. Some of the popular ideas derived from science reflect this same material optimism. I think these are due not so much to the leaders of science themselves as to the popular interpreters of scientific achievement. From them we get the notion that cumulative knowledge can solve anything and that every problem is by definition solvable. Whatever may be the validity of this notion in the material relations which are the field of science, an error comes in trying to apply it as a universal.

Another contributing circumstance is that so much of foreign policy now stems from legislation. Legislation is law, law is to be obeyed, and an objective expressed in law is bound to be achieved. So goes the notion. This idea bears particularly on congressional expectations in relation to foreign aid. The Congress has written into foreign aid legislation as conditions upon recipients many purposes whose consummation is devoutly to be wished. Some of these are such that they could be realized only in considerable spans of time and under governments with great margins of political power derived from energized and purposeful public support. The lack of such conditions in Europe is the heart of the difficulty. I find incredible the idea that phrases enacted by one country's legislature can *ipso facto* solve problems, the solution of which requires redressing the factors of political power in another country.

This topic came up the other day in a conversation with a friend of mine who serves very ably in the House of Representatives. He was perturbed at the lag among European nations in realizing some of the domestic and international reforms prescribed by the Congress in the foreign aid legislation. I commented along the same line as I have spoken here. He agreed with me. Then he added that the Congress would have to write the conditions tighter next time. Thus runs the endless faith in the compulsiveness of law.

Besides faith in making laws, let me mention faith in advertising. Where a perfume is marketed not only for its odor but also as a guarantee of domestic bliss, where automobiles are sold as means to capture the esteem of neighbors as well as means of transport, and where life insurance is offered not only as protection but also as a help for insomnia, it is natural to demand of foreign policy not only that it should handle the problems at hand but also that it should lead to a transfiguration of history. This idea and all its implications are fit to be spurned. I shudder whenever I hear anyone refer to "selling" our foreign policy. Let me say for my Planning Staff colleagues and for myself that we regard foreign policy not as a commodity but as a responsibility, the American public not as our customers but as our masters, and ourselves not as salesmen but as stewards.

I spoke along these lines recently to a very able group of business men visiting the State Department, Sloan Foundation Fellows from the Massachusetts Institute of Technology. One of them commented that by disclosing its foreign policy too much in terms of moral purposes rather than in terms of actual problems to be handled within practical limits of capability, the government itself encouraged the tendency that I was decrying. That was a good point. I was reminded of the story that at the Battle of New Orleans, General Jackson, seeing that the targets were being missed, ordered his artillerymen to elevate the guns a little lower. That counsel applies here.

As one other influence, a very important one, giving rise to the expectation of perfect performance, I shall cite the confusion of force and power. By force I mean first the capacity to transmit energy and so to expend it as to do vital harm to a foe, and second, the deterrent, compulsive effect exerted by the existence of this capacity. The capacity for force is only one of many elements in a nation's power reservoir. The others pertain to its economic strength, the internal integrity of its political position, the degree of confidence and good will which it commands abroad, and many other factors.

A nation's intentions and its power interact on each other. What we seek is in part determined by what we can do. What we can do is determined in part by what we are after. Furthermore, our own aims and power acting as functions of each other are in an interactive relation with adversary intentions and capabilities, which also relate to each other as interdependent variables. Foreign affairs is a complex business. Gross errors result in the attempt to treat them on the basis of the misleading notion that all the problems of power can be reduced to the nice simplicity of calculations of force.

Wars occur when nations seek to impose their wills by effecting drastic changes in the ratios of power through radical action in the factors of force. The force factors are susceptible of precision in military planning. The elements are concrete. The speeds of ships, their capabilities for carrying men and cargo, the distances, the fuel requirements of planes and tanks, and the fire power of divisions, and so on are known factors. The military planning process, in so far as it relates to the ponderables of real or hypothetical campaigns, turns out tidy and complete results. I do not mean that battles and campaigns are fought according to preconceived schedules. I mean only that in so far as advance planning is employed in the military field, the quotients are precise, the columns are even, and the conclusions concrete. Furthermore, within the time and space limits of a campaign, the problem of force can be brought to an absolute solution. It really is possible to achieve the surrender of all of an enemy's forces or to eliminate armed resistance in a particular place for a particular time.

I speak here in no sense of professional disdain for military methods. I have served more of my life as a staff officer in the Army than in the line of foreign policy. I recognize the utility and necessity of military methods of thinking for military purposes. I am aware also of their limitations for other purposes. It is easy for the unwary to jump to a fallacious conclusion that if all human affairs were laid out with the precision of military plans, then all problems could be brought to as complete solution as can the problem of force in the conduct of a victorious military campaign.

This is the sort of thing one gets to when one tries to find the solution of all the nation's problems in the world, instead of taking the historically realistic view that the job is one of managing the problems, not of getting rid of them. It is only a few steps from the notion of solution to the notion of employing force as a solvent. This is an easy fallacy for those souls anxious for history to be tidy and all conclusions certain. The exercise of force, however, is only an incident. The problems of power are endless. Wars only occur. Politics endures.

Some of my colleagues who bore with me as I tried out these comments thought I discounted too heavily the qualitative importance of objectives in foreign policy and reflected too somber an outlook. Let me make the proportions clear. I do not disparage the importance of objectives. Only in the light of ultimate purposes can one know how to proceed problem by problem in this field. Moreover, I do not believe that good is forever beyond reach, but I am sure that the way to it is difficult and long.

The young Gladstone was advised by his mentor that politics was an unsatisfactory business and that he would have to learn to accept imperfect results. That advice has wisdom for the conduct of a foreign policy. The never-ending dilemmas inherent in measuring what we would like to do against what we can do impose great moral burdens. These are beyond the capacity of some individuals to bear. Sometimes they become intolerable for whole societies. The rebellion against that burden sometimes takes the form of an abdication of will, and relief is sought in a passive fatalism about the problems of national existence. Again the rebellion may take the form of resorting to the counsel of violence as the solvent for the difficulties and restraints which life imposes. In either form, the rejection is a rejection of life itself, for life imposes on nations, as on men, the obligation to strive without despair even though the way may be long and the burdens heavy. To recognize this is in itself a source of strength. As Keats tells us,

> . . . To bear all naked truths;
> And to envisage circumstance, all calm;
> That is the top of sovereignty.

NOTES ON CONFERENCEMANSHIP

Despite having sworn off, I let myself be enticed into two recent conferences on foreign policy. In both I kept notes and kept quiet. Here are some of the thoughts which were left unspoken.

ON CONFERENCEMANSHIP AND GOALS.

General propositions abound. Some are too obviously fallacious to be considered or so obviously true as to be of no help. Most are simply ambiguous. According to the late John Nicholas Spykman, most general propositions about foreign policy would stand up equally well with or without a *not* inserted by the verb. A Senator urges utmost central direction and control of policy; he is applauded. A call for creation of a monolith would have raised doubts. The same audience liked another speaker's insistence on wider sharing of responsibility.

Speakers and audience are for exploiting every opportunity, but they are against opportunism; for firmness, but against rigidity; for flexibility, but against pliability; for sticking to our principles, but against being dogmatic; against putting all our eggs in one basket and against scattering our shots; for concentrating our efforts, but also for leaving no stone unturned; for more daring and also for greater prudence.

The audience is for having long-term goals; yet a warning against preoccupation with remote horizons, in disregard of imminent perils, went over equally well. These arguments about

From *The New Republic*, February 16, 1963.

long-term versus short-term goals and plans are misleading. What counts is paying heed to the long-range effects of present decisions.

ON THE AMBIGUITY OF REALITIES.

Someone—Albert Sorel, I think—once referred to "an eternal dispute between those who imagine the world to suit their policy, and those who correct their policy to suit the world." The dispute dominates the session at hand. Those imagining a world to suit their policy project a harmonized globe—no clashes of aims and interests, all regimes drawing upon and guiding by a common store of reason. For them, the vision takes on reality. Those who would correct policy to suit the world speak of responding to reality. In their discourse reality takes on wholeness, continuity, and ascertainability; it is something susceptible of measurement to set a course by, as a ship's master takes bearings by the stars. They portray policy-making as merely taking one's cue from reality. Reality, as they assume it, is visionary.

Reality, as the sum of environing circumstances in which the nation must make its way, is a hodgepodge of interacting phenomena. They tend to conflict. Constructing a policy to mesh with them all would be impossible. Some of the factors are for all practical purposes intractable. Others are changing or changeable. Our actions and intentions form a portion of reality as viewed by counterpart entities taken into account in our own appraisal of reality. The nub of policy is the effects we will and produce to affect their appraisals of reality, thereby producing effects in reality as it affects us. Responding to reality is only half—the less important half at that—of policy-making. The big thing is to act on reality—to make it respond. To speak of reality as something imperious and irreducible is misleading. A speaker just appealed for basing our policy on reality and abandoning myths—a prescription for mutability. The test is how to base reality on policy—so far as one can. How poor a society would be if it abandoned its myths! Myths are what endure and give a nation its bearings. Realities here today may be gone tomorrow.

ON GETTING THE BEST PEOPLE.

The Senator pleads that we find and enlist the best people for top policy posts. One also wants to draft the best people for our overseas undertakings. Apparently they are available in droves. Should we export them wholesale? Spain is said never to have recovered from the loss of talent sent abroad in the sixteenth century.

Anyway, who are the best people? The question sends most of us to the mirror. The Senator's aim is probably overstated. The really and truly best, if identifiable, would wreck the policy machine, and vice versa. John Quincy Adams seems superb in retrospect, but a biographer once described him aptly as a first-rate second-rate man. A platoon of his quality might help. A more apt but less rousing version of the Senator's plea would be to get more truly second-rate people into important posts. The quality gap has persisted since Adam. The late Henry F. Ash-urst once recalled his maiden speech as one of Arizona's first U.S. Senators. In his eulogy of the new state, he described it as needing only adequate water and a good population to be a paradise. A colleague interposed to apply the same observation to hell.

ON CLASH OF INTERESTS.

A man and his wife repulsed and killed a bandit; a newspaper on my lap gives the account. The couple and the bandit had common interests in a roll of legal tender and in survival. The couple had joint interests. The distinction is important. Cats and mice, lions and lambs, and rival bull elks have common but not joint interests. Some people infer too much from interests we have in common with the Communists—such as the interest in survival. Common interests are plentiful, joint interests problematic.

ON BIG MEDICINE.

Three speakers have just resoundingly recommended more effective policies and strategies without much of a clue as to means. This sort of thing is as correct and vapid as an answer once given by a college classmate who, without credentials or authorization, sneaked into a lecture given by a distinguished clinician to medical school seniors. The lecturer described hypothetical symptoms and asked how to proceed with the case, pointing to my friend for a reply. The young man answered, "I would call a doctor."

ON UNSOLUTIONS.

I asked directions of a man in St. Louis thirty years ago. He replied with details about proceeding to a third traffic light, turning left, and going another half mile to a dead end at a white house with a yard full of dogs. He concluded, "That's not the right way," and walked on. I still recall this discourse of his as an unsolution.

I have just heard another one. After urging us to bear witness to our principles throughout the world, the speaker said of the emerging nations: (a) they need efficiency and progress; (b) democracy is not applicable; (c) neither are Western standards.

It helps little to tell how not to solve a problem. The emerging peoples claim the rights of self-government, the benefits of modernity, and importance in world affairs without knowing how to fulfill them. Characteristically, they need to work out a basis of public life, to develop a bond of trust within their societies, to establish canons of procedural decency so that the force of the state is not brought to bear for private revenge. Many of them have yet to develop a pattern of politeness—meaning a code of conduct enabling strangers to deal with each other and enabling men to transcend the strictures of tribe and sect. They need to learn lessons of accountability. These matters may be beyond their power to realize in some cases, but at least we should know what to suggest as agenda—if asked.

A great many persons of scholarly mien think in shallow pseudo-syllogisms like the following: Democracy and dictatorship are opposites; inefficiency and efficiency are opposites; democracy tends to inefficiency and frustration; dictatorship therefore must mean efficacy. Should we rate Ghana's oppression above Nigeria's attempts to hold onto something of a free system? True, not every aspirant to democracy is a Jefferson, but neither is every despot another Ataturk.

While serving as political adviser in a new state, I used to hear recurringly the line about the inapplicability of Western standards. Usually it was invoked by someone, without alternate standards, trying to excuse himself from standards altogether. What is important is standards. Westernness is secondary. We must learn to distinguish between conventions and standards in this regard. I can scarcely imagine any advice to emerging nations worse than the notion of their being exempt from standards because these are Western and not for them. The attitude is downright patronizing toward newcomers to in dependence.

ON NOT ONE CENT FOR TRIBUTE.

Someone just spoke up for helping emerging states to realize their aspirations, whatever they may be, and not trying to impose our own views. That would amount to paying tribute. The idea is impracticable, anyway. Our resources do not equal demand. Hence we must discriminate in allocating aid around the world. This means applying preferences. Whose? Either ours or others'. If we apply theirs, we make them our own.

ON ECONOMISTS AS A GENUS.

Most intellectual endeavor consists of tracing either the unseen complicacy of simple things or the ungrasped simplicity of the complex. Economists devote themselves to embellishing the obscurity of recondite matters. They do not understand economy of words. Thomas Carlyle, mistaking their pursuit for a science, called it dismal. Edmund Burke said: ". . . the age of chivalry is gone. That of sophisters, economists, and calculators has succeeded; and the glory of Europe is extinguished forever."

From eighteen man-hours of empanelled expertise only two points have emerged: (a) it is easier to speed up from a walk than from a gallop; (b) spending and saving both come easier to the rich than to the poor. Like physicists, economists say *increase* or *decrease by a factor of two* instead of *double* or *halve*—either a time-padding habit carried over from classroom lecturing or a device signifying vocation and authority, like wearing a Roman collar or a Homburg hat.

ON A FAMOUS FRENCHMAN.

How fatuous to persist in portraying Charles de Gaulle as an erratic and obstinate elder! He is fobbed off as of another century. What galls is that he is a factor of this century.

Under the aegis of the Roosevelt-Churchill collaboration, there emerged the greatest consolidation of governing authority ever. Over an enormous span it assigned ships, allocated resources, scheduled production, set prices and deployed forces. France—or a residuum personified in de Gaulle—was client, not participant. In the sequel, what counted mainly for European nations was not colonies or forces at their command but rapport with the U.S.—now banker, supplier, prime mover. Thanks to wartime connections, the United Kingdom had an inside track. Suppose the U.K. had been overrun. Suppose France had stayed in the ring. Then things would have been different. So what?

Recovery for France meant redress for that part of the past— first by trying vainly to bid in as an equal to the U.K. and then by trying to pry out the U.K. as teacher's pet. The Nassau pact—with America and Britain agreeing on terms to offer client France—negatived the second. Now, third, France is seeking a rival concatenation, excluding the United Kingdom, along lines of Bonaparte's continental system. Obstinate? Perhaps. Erratic? Of course not.

ON MAINTAINING A GOING CONCERN.

Just voiced was another appeal for citizens to spend more time to make themselves fully informed on foreign policy and national security problems. I, who spend my professional time doing just this and yet fall hugely short, can scarcely imagine anything less probable or more futile than to get everyone engrossed over things so intractable—when there are children to rear, mail to deliver, bread to bake, streets to sweep, sick to attend, and myriad other things to do to keep us a going concern.

Besides, on close acquaintance with the diffuseness and obduracy of foreign affairs, most people might renounce the problems out of ennui. That, rather than engulfment in right-wing obscurantism, is the danger. I explained to an earnest German who queried me recently on how to rate the menace of things like the John Birch Society. As Byron put it:

> And the heart must pause to breathe,
> And love itself have rest.

I have no answer. I offer only an unsolution—that of not having too many conferences.

NATIONAL INTEREST AND

NATIONAL RESPONSIBILITY

Assailants of the idea of the national interest as a basis of foreign policy characteristically employ two quite different lines of argument. According to one line, the idea of the national interest serves to draw state power into matters of no general concern. It is but a façade commonly used for concealing a zeal for profits or some other quest of particular advantage and to deceive the public into acquiescing in use of public resources in support of endeavors bearing no relation to the general good. The result is to get the United States into problems where it does not belong. The idea is too broad. Its effects are too entangling. According to the differentiated line of argument, the idea of the national interest seems too confining. It keeps the nation out of many endeavors in which it ought to be involved. The idea is not entangling enough. Thus, according to these two lines of argument concurrently employed, the nation, by putting aside the national interest as a goal, would be out of trouble and into everything.

The nation is an entity capable of having interests transcendent over particular group interests. The nation is an entity greater than the sum of its parts. Those in positions of authority in the governing apparatus must be constrained to maintain the nation as a going concern. This obligation makes a difference in the calculation of dangers, opportunities, and requirements both

From *The Annals of the American Academy of Political and Social Science*, July, 1952. Copyright 1952 by the American Academy of Political and Social Science.

Also from *The Commonweal*, October 1, 1954, and *Worldview*, September, 1959.

within and beyond the span of national jurisdiction. In this respect, the idea of national interest is something verifiable and justifiable in its own terms. It is valid and essential.

Moreover, the world, though one, is not all of a piece. The relationships between a nation's interests and other nations' interests are variegated. Sometimes they coincide. Sometimes interests of different nations are compatible without necessarily coinciding. Sometimes the interests of one nation and another differ without coming into serious tension. Sometimes the interests of respective nations, as they see them, are mutually exclusive. From these variations between identity and incompatibility comes the nature of international life. It does little good to deplore the variegation and to meditate upon preferences for a world less complicated.

In a world as diverse as this one, a nation has to look after itself as best it can. It is good, therefore, to have the idea of the national interest restored to respectability. The rescue is not yet complete, but headway has been made, and the effect is a gain for straight thinking about foreign policy. To Hans Morgenthau as much as to any other, perhaps more, belongs credit for the effort.

I concur in his view that "a foreign policy guided by moral abstractions, without consideration to the national interest, is bound to fail." [1] Subject to some qualms about the absoluteness with which he clothes the thought, I even accept his injunction: "And, above all, remember always that it is not only a political necessity but also a moral duty for a nation to follow in its dealings with other nations but one guiding star, one standard for thought, one rule of action: The National Interest." [2]

Even so, I have some reservations to state. The significance and usefulness of the phrase are limited. It begs more questions than it answers. Whatever its utility in resolving tensions between the United States' world position and claims of particular domestic interests, the idea of national interest gives little guid-

[1] Hans Morgenthau, *In Defense of the National Interest* (New York: Knopf, 1951), pp. 33–34.
[2] *Ibid.*, p. 242.

ance for choosing among possible lines of action in the field of foreign affairs. A question whether or not to pursue the national interest may arouse debate within some group preoccupied with abstract good but has no material relevance to any practical decision in the line of policy. There the question must be not whether, but how, to serve the national interest.

That last question is characteristically subtle and complex in relation to actual situations. The reason for this is simple. The national interest does not inhere in any one aim. It is interwoven with an array of aims. Each of the following purposes might qualify as a constituent part of our national interest: avoidance of active hostilities, security in the military sense, a prospering economy, strong allies, access to strategic waterways and air spaces and to markets and to sources of raw materials, protection of American nationals' property and safety abroad, and grounds of mutual confidence with various nations newly come to independence and to a share in determining the course of world affairs. Such a list might be easily extended by dozens of items. Any matter of foreign policy pertaining to realization of only one of them would present no issue whatever in deciding on what policy to pursue. No one would have to work his brains overtime to seek an answer. No protracted debate on nuances and contradictions of purpose would occur. The policy decision would crystallize spontaneously.

The national interest is not singular. Rather, the national interests are plural. Difficulties arise from conflict between one interest and another—for example, a clash between the goal of peace and preservation of some access abroad, between a strong defense and a prospering economy, between protection of American rights and property abroad and some fledgling regime's amity, or between the goodwill and friendship of one nation and of another at loggerheads with it. Again, the list might be indefinitely extended.

A policy-maker's job is to work out, within limits of what seems feasible, a combination of actions best to serve multiple national interests in their total relation to each other. Those involved in decision may well differ as to the quotients of value to be accorded to multiple interests at stake at some juncture. It is scarcely conceivable for them to argue whether or not to follow a foreign policy conceived to be in the nation's interest.

The reference to moral duty in the injunction quoted from Morgenthau about following the national interest deserves close examination. In this connection, the term *interest* itself requires logical analysis quite apart from its meaning in regard to any particular issue. Even as an abstraction it is charged with ambiguities. First, the term may be taken in its most subjective sense —that of a concern felt for some object. The value ascribed to the object in question may be of one's own determination, or it may be intrinsic to the object. Second, the term may refer to the object of concern as well as to the concern aroused by that object. The object, moreover, may represent values other than merely utilitarian. They may be such as to exert moral demands for concern. In such a case, the meaning of interest merges with that of responsibility—a proper sense of the term, according to the dictionary. The distinction makes a difference when applied to the function of the idea of the national interest in foreign policy—a difference significant enough to deserve examination.

The first and simpler construction takes as implicit a very high degree of autonomy on the part of the entity whose concern is aroused. The concern is of a take-it-or-leave-it character. The benefit identified with the object is one to be enjoyed or foregone at the virtually absolute discretion of the entity. No reproach attaches to a choice to renounce its interest. Indeed, renunciation may imply selflessness of the noble sort traditionally ascribed to saints and the like.

Those prompted by what they regard as idealistic considerations to inveigh against pursuit of the national interest, as a basis of foreign policy, and to favor loftier and broader goals characteristically adhere to this narrow, subjective, and materialistic construction of interest. Accordingly, defining goals of policy in terms of interest seems to them mercenary, mundane, and reprehensible. They reason by a sorites: to be free of interest is to be disinterested, to be disinterested is to be unbiased, to be unbiased is to be uncorrupted, to be uncorrupted is to be righteous, and to be righteous fulfills a spiritual duty. Armored with righteousness, the nation would be in position to go about doing good everywhere.

According to this view, tension and conflict arise only from the debasing circumstance of having interests. By the same token, all tensions and conflicts are easily resolvable. All interests are expressible in calculations of material gain and loss. Rational balances are always susceptible of being arrived at. Self-abnegation provides an egress from every contest. The nation can find the path to safety and progress by applying deference to rivals much as a prudent motorist learns to minimize the hazards of the highways by not being insistent on the right-of-way.

Obviously, the joining of interest with the idea of responsibility, which adds a moral ingredient, greatly complicates the frame of thought. One's autonomy in extending concern to an object or withholding it is impinged upon. Voluntarism in selecting one's interest is seen as too simple. Obligation enters as a factor. The take-it-or-leave-it implication no longer holds. The simplistic line of argument in favor of renouncing interests is disrupted. Eschewal of interests can be made to sound good. The idea of abandoning responsibilities cannot be. Disinterestedness and irresponsibility echo quite differently in our minds.

A theologian with whom I once found myself in debate—an earnest and eloquent advocate for a national policy of abjuring the national interest—correctly and immediately discerned my intention in suggesting *responsibility* as a substitute for *interest*. The effect, as he saw, would be to close off a verbally facile avenue to adjustment and peace by making it not necessarily right always to give in to the opposed party. In rejoinder, he cited perils to the notion of casuistry in presuming moral content to its interests. The ideas of interest and responsibility must be disjoined, he argued, and the only morally secure course would lie in assuming our view of our interest to be reproachable and in undertaking accordingly to define our interest only as a step preliminary to a decision to abandon it in event of any opposition.

The theologian was half right. The peril of casuistry does confront a nation as it confronts any other human entity, but the difficulty is one to be faced rather than avoided. It would be no more becoming to a nation than to an individual person to abdicate responsibility in fear of possibly being wrong or to adopt submissiveness as a way of life merely to stay out of trouble.

Far from simplifying or reducing the problems of policy, employing the term *responsibility* as a synonym for *interest* only serves to complicate and to multiply them. I suggest it not as a solution but only as a way of understanding problems as they are. Moreover, like the idea of interest, this abstraction is better understood in plurality rather than singularity. The nation has a diversity of responsibilities. In view of limitations of means, one responsibility may come into tension or conflict with others, just as when one chooses to call concerns interests. Then, and only then, a problem in policy is posed—invariably a problem of having to make do.

The key term thus bears yet another meaning relevant to the situation of the nation making its way in world affairs. It implies possession of some powers for attending to its concerns—but only some powers, definitely short of omnipotence. In indigence, with no resources whatever to bring to bear in support of its preferences, the nation would be without responsibility. With such a fullness of power as always to be able to have its way, the nation also would have transcended responsibility. The actual situation falls between those theoretic extremes. The nation is a finite entity not subordinated to others' wills, not exempt from them either, and not endowed to prevail in every circumstance.

In such a situation the necessity of dealing with factors beyond the national jurisdiction is ineluctable. On the other hand, foreign policy can give no promise of arrival at some calculable moment when we can say that all our troubles are behind us, that everything henceforth will be tidy and easy, and that we have crossed the one last river. The broad goals of foreign policy are not susceptible of being accomplished as facts. They are purposes to be everlastingly worked at. The same is true of all the great ends of the state. The aims listed in the preamble of the Constitution—the more perfect union, justice, the common defense, the general welfare, domestic tranquility, the blessings of liberty—are not matters as to which we shall ever be able to say that we have got them tidy, firm, and final so that we can retire or find other things to do in their place. To the contrary, they are ends for indeterminate effort—purposes to be sought and maintained rather than accomplished. Their validity will depend on our going on reaching for them and doubtless would languish if we should ever come to feel either that we had them at last in our grasp or that it was useless even to try any more.

For some Americans it is difficult to face up in the present to what the nation's historic experience tended to conceal: to wit, that a great state, even their own, however huge and awesome in scope and power in comparison to an individual person, is a limited and contingent entity when measured against the scale of all that lies beyond its span in time and space, and that its way of dealing with forces beyond its jurisdiction—in other words, its foreign policy—is inherently a contingent set of purposes in which its own will, far from being absolute, is conditioned continuously by forces and events beyond its ordaining.

Probably the experience of no other people has paralleled that of the Americans in having to face drastic reduction in their security at the very peak of power, suffering impairment of freedom of action at the summit of success. With as much aptness as to be found in any metaphor, one may liken the nation's experience to that of a novice golfer who with his very first swing scored a hole-in-one. Though wonderful at the time, the experience carried a heavy deferred penalty. Even while gaining in proficiency and power, the man was probably fated never again to enjoy the beginning moment's success. Initial perfection of performance must only have made more exasperating the lessons yet to be learned about golf and about himself. So with Americans, their difficulties in their rendezvous with a stubborn and vexing world are aggravated by having a level of expectation—a standard of performance—derived from fact, yet intrinsically fictitious.

A failure of events to fulfill expectations would at least suggest something wanting in the expectations. Many Americans have not looked at it that way, however. To their view, the fault lies obviously in the actualities. With various expedients they try to rectify them to fit the preconceptions of the simpler, less vexing epoch, when the span of one sovereign's jurisdiction about covered the range of national concerns. The effects of the peculiar American past in world affairs have thus been reflected in the viewpoints of two seemingly quite different but inherently quite similar approaches to world political relations—radical nationalism and radical internationalism as exemplified respectively in such seemingly diverse proposals as the Bricker Amendment and schemes for a federated world.

Radical nationalists—I prefer the phrase to the term *isolationists*—shrink from the speculativeness of national policy in the frame of world politics. They find it too taxing, too uncertain, to have to work through the multiple factors involved in dealing with relationships among a collection of diverse political entities. They take comfort in thinking of the absoluteness of a field of concern embraced in only one state. These things are exactly true also of advocates of a world political organization to subsume nation states.

Radical nationalists have boundless faith in a constitutional formula as a means of resolving every political difficulty and are disposed to skip over the factors of power. Here too the shoe fits the radical internationalists. In this sense both groups reflect an American habit of thinking that our national future was disposed in the stately prose adopted in 1787 and of overlooking the simple fact that force, in the American Civil War, was the arbiter of destiny even for our nation.

Both groups think along lines of meeting our problems by divesting the nation of power to deal with external realities— the one by shrinkage, the other by absorption. Both groups think it possible to command the future in tight plans and prefer to speak of policy in terms of illimitable ends, avoiding the hard empiricism of means. In this sense both are utopian. In advocacy of their respective formulas both groups are wont to squint and to overlook half the facts in regarding both the past and the present. Both groups simply elide the differences obtaining in the scene of politics as between 1787 and now.

Both groups err—at least I think they do—in vastly overestimating American efficacy in relating ourselves to the world about us, in postulating a world responsive to our will if we but exercise it. The one group regards an absolute immunity from the effect of things beyond our jurisdiction as ours for the taking. The other group assumes a mission to transform the world as ours for the claiming. The radical nationalists cherish the notion that no danger would have befallen us except for a few paragraphs unwisely agreed to at Yalta. To balance this misproportion I would cite a recent magazine article by a great scholar reproaching the United States for having omitted to establish world government in 1945.

Devotees of simple happy answers to huge and complex problems, diverse as their answers may be, have more in common with each other than with those who put little trust in formulas, who see the broad past for what it was—largely a series of ordeals for those experiencing it; who are not dismayed to find our present much like the general experience of nations in that respect, and are not dismayed by thought of a future likely to turn out to be much the same also.

Keeping in mind the idea of responsibility with its connotations of capability subject to limitation, one can understand foreign policy as belonging among the performing arts as distinguished from the enduring arts. The distinction and its implications are important. They may be illustrated by a metaphor— not to prove, but only to illustrate, as metaphors never prove anything.

Consider the distinction between a symphony as in the mind of Beethoven and as in the mind of an orchestra conductor. Beethoven could produce a *Fifth Symphony,* put it behind him, move on to a *Sixth,* then to a *Seventh,* and so on. One by one, the symphonies were moved from the realm of concept and established as lasting actualities. To the conductor, production of music is quite different. Interpretative insight, discipline, precision of time and pitch—all determinants of an orchestra's quality—are not susceptible of this sort of achievement. The conductor could never say that he had accomplished them and so ask himself what to do next.

Music in its static aspect can have enduring greatness. Music in performance does not. Thus a certain composer might be said to have abounding greatness without having produced anything good lately. One could never say the same of an orchestra or its conductor in a parallel situation. Their greatness passes the moment that effort sags and insight dims. There is nothing more perishable than greatness in the performing arts. The payoff is the box office, not the royalties. In the performing arts—and foreign policy is one of them—the determining question is never: what do you think you are doing, or what would you like to do? It is: what are you doing, and how well are you doing it? It is not: what are you, or what would you like to be? It is: what are you becoming?

A view of foreign policy as a performing art enables us to get rid of a good deal of fallacy about means and ends. Surely one of the main sources of hypocrisy in foreign policy is a habit—manifest widely and at high levels—of treating them separately. They are not things apart. They are integral to each other. They are simply two ways of looking at the same actuality. Our ends are the measure of what we intend to do. So are our means. A nation's foreign policy unfolds in a progression of events, with achievements in one phase becoming means for successive phases so that the degree of success at one juncture in part governs opportunity for subsequent achievement. I use advisedly the qualifying phrase "in part." This nation exercises some franchise in its destiny but never fully controls it. Precision in this matter is impossible and unimportant. What is important is to do our best in every phase with whatever fraction of control is vouchsafed us—to see what options we have and then to try to exercise them rightly. Obviously—so much so that it is banal to say it—the way in which what we do in one phase leads into what we can do in the next can apply to a downhill as well as to an uphill course. Bad decisions father bad decisions just as good ones give rise to opportunity for further good ones.

I stress that last point because the lessons of moderation too can be learned in excess. The theme herein is the counsel of patience and self-restraint but only as auxiliary virtues. Patience is a grace when it attends perseverance. Self-restraint has value as a qualification upon exercise of power, but not as a substitute for it. As true now as ever, nothing succeeds like success.

MAKING FOREIGN POLICY

ON THE NEW FRONTIER

Among policy-makers and executors, coordination is a word
of art standing, first, for methods and efforts to resolve cross
purposes in great undertakings and, second, for the resulting
quality of coherence. Here the concern is with the function and
the attribute in relation to recent conduct of United States foreign policy. Their central importance in this field scarcely needs
lengthy laboring.

States—and in this generalization one might substitute *peoples* or *governments* with equal appropriateness—relate to each
other in many ways: for example, in respect of intimidatory or
reassuring effects, one to another, of their capabilities for force;
interplay of their capacities to help or to hinder each other in
production of goods and income; reciprocal effects of their currency systems; their influence on one another regarding the arts
and training, interchange among them, or withholding, of organized knowledge about natural phenomena; interactive effects of
different prevailing concepts of values, standards, and ends of
public life; efforts to sway each other's outlooks, purposes, and
wills through public discourse; and direct touch between their
ruling establishments through official and confidential channels
and within public organizations created to facilitate interchange
and collaboration among them.

Those aspects—military, economic, monetary, cultural, sci-

From the *Annals of the American Academy of Political and Social
Science*, July, 1962. Copyright 1962 by the American Academy of Politi-
cal and Social Science.
Also from *The New Republic,* December 25, 1961.

entific, doctrinal or ideological, propagandistic, diplomatic, and organizational—form a representative but by no means exhaustive list of activities and relationships tending to overlap and to interact and requiring continuous care to prevent conflict between lines of endeavor. In the view of fanciers of administration, achieving this sound aim is mainly a question of arranging jurisdictional boxes on organization charts and prescribing procedures for decision.

Something additional and more basic is entailed. Coordination is possible only among elements in a relationship of parity —a term such as to make complete logical sense only in relationship to some antecedent faculty or quality. An indispensable question relevant to coordination is: with respect to what? That *what* is most important. Only with the filling in of that element is coordination likely to turn out to be more than a way of keeping in balance while going in circles.

In foreign policy the *what* concerns the standards, the goals, of the United States as an entity in world affairs. It must rest, as Charles A. Beard once pointed out, on "a view of the world and of the nation as a part of the world." Beard added, "However disconcerting the thought may be, it is also an interpretation of all history, out of which all nations, provinces, and empires have emerged, in which they now have their being." [1] Supplying this central premise and purpose—as to which to orient the multifarious activities pertinent to foreign policy and by which to set perspectives for judging their relevance and usefulness—falls to political authority in the best sense of both terms.

The sensitivity and complexity of both aspects of coordination—namely the articulation of goals and the realization of operational coherence—have advanced virtually in geometric progression in recent years in consequence of developments in the external situation. This trend and its implications have been examined repeatedly of late, with many resulting designs for rationalizing and stabilizing the relevant structure of author-

[1] Charles A. Beard, *A Foreign Policy for America* (New York: Knopf, 1940), pp. 4–5.

ity—notable among them an attempt by Congress in the National Security Act of 1947 to establish a framework of procedure and consultation in great decisions bearing on external affairs, an instance illustrative of the difficulty of formulating satisfactory and enduring solutions in formal terms.

The search has gone on for answers to questions supposed to have been settled in the Act. In large part, the focus has been on relationships between the President and the Secretary of State and, implicitly or explicitly, also on the place of the Department of State in the bureaucratic firmament. These matters of relationship and place have been widely variant—a matter of the times and the personalities of the men in the two offices—from one administration to another.

The discontinuities were of little moment in more relaxed times, with the United States on the margins of world affairs, with the Secretary's job one mainly custodial of the treaty power and supervisory with respect to a diplomatic apparatus running more or less by habit and inertia. The discontinuities have persisted, however, with perhaps untoward results, even after the nation's approach and accession to world power, with involvements in problems of greatest scope, difficulty, complexity, variety, and potential for danger.

In the first Roosevelt's time activism in the presidency proved compatible with eminence and authority at the State Department under two successive Secretaries. With Taft as President, foreign policy subsided into routine in both establishments. Wilson's successive Secretaries of State were respectively overruled, overshadowed, and overlooked. As Secretary, Hughes had enjoyed pre-eminence in foreign policy while serving an uninterested Harding. An indifferent Coolidge had given the lead to an indifferent Kellogg. Serving a distant and irritable Hoover, Stimson experienced frustration and scarcely enjoyed presidential support. Hull as Secretary was a respected figure more or less out of the mainstream. His sucessor's tenure was unimportant and brief. As Secretary, Byrnes did not hit it off with Truman, but Marshall did, and Acheson did also to an exceptional degree, with high mutual deference and confidence marking relationships between him and the President, both disposed to collaboration and sharing similar views of the prerogatives of the respective offices, and neither overshadowing the other. Dulles' ascendancy, during Eisenhower's presidency, was akin to Hughes's, but over a greater scope and with a far more active approach to a role as formulator, chief spokesman, and principal agent as well as directing head of negotiations in foreign policy—a personal pre-eminence scarcely reflected onto his department.[2] His successor, though not heir to such broad scope, did strengthen identity between himself and the establishment at State.

The approach of the end of the Eisenhower tenure heightened interest in foreign policy organization. Senator Henry M. Jackson's Subcommittee on National Security Policy was diligently churning up testimony and turning out reports looking to improvements.[3] As chairman of the President's Advisory Committee on Government Organization, New York's Governor Nelson Rockefeller broached a plan for having a First Secretary of the Government as the President's coadjutor in foreign policy with status as executive chairman of the National Security Council.[4] Senator Mike Mansfield favored granting the Secretary of State fixed authority over all departments and agencies with respect to international aspects of their functions.[5] A report for the Senate Foreign Relations Committee by the Brookings Institution proposed a super Secretary of Foreign Affairs to wield authority over the Secretary of State, the Director of the

[2] For an account of the varying relationships between Presidents and Secretaries of State in this century, see Norman A. Graebner (ed.), *An Uncertain Tradition: American Secretaries of State in the Twentieth Century* (New York: McGraw-Hill, 1961).

[3] *Organizing for National Security: Inquiry of the Subcommittee on National Policy Machinery, Senator Henry M. Jackson, Chairman, for the Committee on Government Operations, United States Senate* (Washington: U.S. Government Printing Office, 1961), 3 vols.

[4] *Ibid.*, Vol. I, p. 945.

[5] Don K. Price (ed.), *The Secretary of State* (Englewood City: Prentice-Hall, 1960), p. 179.

United States Information Agency, and the director of foreign aid, to be seconded by an integrating staff in the Executive Office, and to be designated as Vice Chairman of the National Security Council.[6]

A report of recommendations from sixty-nine individuals, described as "interested citizens," meeting under auspices of the American Assembly at Arden House, in Harriman, New York, on October 6–9, 1960,[7] is of special interest here because of the inclusion in the group of a number of persons destined—though this was not known at the time—to figure prominently in foreign policy in the upcoming administration: one to be Secretary of State, another an Under Secretary, three Assistant Secretaries, two ambassadors at major posts, two prominent consultants, and one a member of the State Department's Policy Planning Council.

The statement of views, addressed to the then as yet undetermined victor in the presidential contest in progress, focused on the office of Secretary of State—office being construed broadly to embrace the establishment under his supervision and his and its relations to other executive organs, Congress, and the public. The statement disavowed discussing the Secretary's office "in terms of the men who have occupied it," but matters not discussed were not necessarily out of mind, for in effect the views emanating from Arden House favored stabilizing and institutionalizing relationships between President and Secretary in more or less the Truman-Acheson pattern.

In language hortatory and hopeful for the future rather than uniformly descriptive of past practice, the statement emphasized a Secretary's role as surrogate to a President holding "ultimate Executive responsibility"—"the agent and confidant of the Pres-

[6] *United States Foreign Policy: The Formulation and Administration of United States Foreign Policy, Study Prepared at the Request of the Committee on Foreign Relations, United States Senate, by the Brookings Institution (Pursuant to S. Res. 336, 85th Congress and S. Res. 31, 86th Congress) No. 9* (Washington: U.S. Government Printing Office, 1960), p. 3.

[7] Price, *The Secretary of State*, pp. 191ff.

ident," moreover, "the President's principal aide for the formulation of foreign policy and the conduct of international affairs," and "chief advisor to the President."

"More than ever the role of the Secretary of State is central," the statement continued. This officer "should have primacy in advising on international policy." Interposing of "any official between the President and the Secretary in the field of international affairs" would be inadvisable. The Secretary "must bear major responsibility for the formulation of all aspects of national policy bearing on our international interests and security." His "first task . . . is to identify the crucial international problems which the nation must face and devise the general strategy to meet them. This is a matter of analyzing the basic forces . . . shaping the future of the world, of framing policies by which these forces may be influenced . . . , and of identifying the means. . . ."

The statement accorded the office commensurate scope with respect to achieving coherence within the government. The Secretary "must take the lead in integrating our military, economic, and cultural programs with our diplomatic efforts into a coherent foreign policy" and "should have the opportunity, authority, and staff to guide foreign policy aspects of all national policies."

The cited use of *ultimate*—a word meaning farthest, most remote in time or space, or last in a train of progression—as modifier to the President's "Executive responsibility" was interesting. *Primary* would perhaps have been more apt. It surely would have been more prophetic.

Presidential primacy in foreign policy inheres in the American constitutional order. It has manifested itself in various ways in successive administrations. Invariably the styles and methods applied reflect the Chief Executive's preferences. This is obviously so with respect to any President disposed, in keeping with a stock expression, to be his own Secretary of State as in the instances of Jefferson, Polk, Wilson, and the two Roosevelts. It is no less so in times of presidential recessiveness, with the conduct of foreign policy left to be dominated by the Secretary —a relationship operating at the President's option.

In the Kennedy administration, presidential primacy in foreign policy is exercised actively. Presidential authority takes a principal, pervasive, constant hand in coordination, operating not only with respect to setting the main direction of endeavor but also in the daily routines of working things out among the departments and agencies. The keys to this in the President's aptitudes and personality have been pondered by innumerable publicists—restless curiosity, a large quotient of vigor, unusual capability for absorbing empirical data, a desire to make his authority felt throughout the executive establishment, and a disposition to emphasize personal relationships as distinct from institutional structures. This last attribute presumably bears some connection with a pre-presidential experience in public affairs mainly in the legislative branch and in the conduct of political campaigns, where relationship between the central figure and staff is highly personal.

The campaign itself gave small intimation of the sort of presidential emphasis to be imparted to foreign policy. Beyond the issues of Quemoy and Cuba, debate dealt with generalizations about manners of standing up to adversaries, national prestige, the importance of vigor and celerity in the conduct of great affairs, and the value of initiative and dynamism.

The first clear indication of the new style came during the interim between election and inauguration in the order and manner of the President-elect's selection of foreign policy aides: an Assistant Secretary and an Under Secretary of State and a chief representative at the seat of the United Nations designated before the choice of a Secretary of State, clearly setting a mode of direct presidential superintendency of staffing in the foreign policy establishment; [8] enhanced roles pledged—usually in a phrase regarding "a post second to none in importance"—for those designated before the Secretary as well as others selected

[8] During the Hoover Administration, Secretary Stimson deferred to the President's choice of an Under Secretary—to the Secretary's subsequent regret. Thereafter Stimson resolved that, while recognizing the President's right to veto any proposed appointments to major positions, "he would vigorously oppose any attempt to select his subordinates for him." Graebner, *An Uncertain Tradition*, p. 171.

later, implicitly prefiguring the President-elect's intention to be directly accessible to a number of second-echelon subordinates. Subsequently the new approach has been variously manifested and widely celebrated, and misgivings about it have been confined generally to private expressions within the bureaucracy. One aspect concerns structuring of interdepartmental collaboration at what is called the working level. The new administration has drawn a stringent line against proliferation of committees—as if viewing committees as bad per se and not distinguishing between unnecessary and useful ones. Committees are, of course, an inevitable part of bureaucratic routine. Many of those formally extinguished have perforce resumed a more or less surreptitious existence. The committee-destroying effort, moreover, has worked like a dual-purpose garden spray, promoting some growths while abating others.

Task forces—a name implicit of purpose and energy—have burgeoned in place of committees. Task forces are not a recent invention. Previous administrations have used the phrase to characterize committees with extra oomph. It would be misleading, however, to characterize every current task force as a committee under an alias. A regular participant describes the task force device in these terms: "Task forces really are committees, of course, but they operate with a consciousness of having a mandate, often from the President himself." The rubric gives them a feeling of special responsibility to get something finished —a way of enabling the bureaucracy to function with a feeling of transcending itself. What makes a big difference is representation of the President's authority through every stage of deliberation by the presence of at least one member of the White House staff. "That's true of all the important ones," he adds.

Vicariously, the Chief Executive's dominion is exercised not merely in passing on the final product but in forming it. For departmental bureaucrats this has a perplexing side. "When the President's man says something, you don't know whether he is speaking for himself or for his boss," according to this evaluator. "The effect can be, and often is, to cut off discussion too soon." The weight of authority lies heavy in argument.

This comment points to another aspect—an enhanced role for the White House staff, now more in the limelight than formerly, with its members carrying the implicit power of being reputed close to a highly personal-thinking President. What is apparent is that the President finds it more congenial to rely, as he can, on assistance by his own staff. Coupled with this is apparently a disposition—presumably derived from long experience at the Capitol—to regard departments and agencies of the executive branch not simply as instruments but also in a measure as adversary forces, faintly and figuratively alien. At least in foreign affairs, the presidential establishment thus seems to cap the executive branch in a new sort of way, as a kind of fourth branch of government exercising authority not only *through* but indeed to some extent *against* the echelons below.

The State Department has been getting its lumps—perhaps deservedly—for slowness and negativeness. Yet speed is not always the pace of prudence. Twenty-four-hour deadlines for responses to questions of many facets and much subtlety may only foreclose the consideration necessary for producing right answers. There can be too much emphasis on the positive. In prescribing the Commandments the Lord was not averse to being negative seven out of ten times. Blocking a mistake or correcting a superior's misconceptions may often be more valuable than merely being submissively agreeable. To regard the executive structure in foreign affairs as designed to be wholly compliant to directive and to be remiss in airing its doubts and taking time—and to try to use it as messenger and servitor in foreign policy, in derogation of its potential as a source of insights and admonitory wisdom—is to miss some of the main reasons for having a foreign office.

Appraisal for an outsider in these matters is difficult, because of discrepancies between what is publicly affirmed and what is privately confided. The version of departmental people differs, moreover, from that of members of the White House staff. Granting even a fraction of truth to allegations by departmental people, one must conclude that the staff at the apex interposes not only in channeling, expediting, and sorting but indeed in originating, rectifying, and diverting matters for decision to the extent of sometimes duplicating and other times pre-empting functions hitherto regarded as departmental. Presidential staff assistants go off to survey requirements in exigent areas and to deal with policy issues at international conferences, and the President's press secretary negotiates in Moscow over exchange of information.

Such presidential staff activity in the nexus of foreign relations has an interesting implication for the constitutional principle of accountability in that the President's assistants are exempt from even indirect congressional inquiry—a position of privilege not accorded those in the regular bureaucratic structure. No serious issue has as yet arisen over the point, however.

Of the staff at the apex, a principal characteristic is an extraordinary preponderance of academic men—writers and professors, honorable professions both, but still professions preoccupied with words, prone to regard verbalizing as completed action. One recalls Burke's words regarding men once elevated in France: "Among them, indeed, I saw some of known rank; some of shining talents; but of any practical experience in the state, not one man was to be found. The best were only men of theory." [9] One recalls and wonders what became of the attribute—"a passion for anonymity"—enunciated a generation ago in connection with the original undertaking to provide adequate staff resources for the White House.

It would be interesting to know for sure, if we could, what connection there may be between the cited characteristic and an almost immoderate success achieved in verbalizing on the New Frontier, with a result of producing an appreciable gap between declaratory and efficient intentions. There may be some connection also with an unfortunate tendency toward what John Hay once described as the practice of shaking first a fist and then a finger.

A certain disorderliness of administration and organization

[9] Edmund Burke, *Reflections on the Revolution in France* (London: Oxford University Press, 1950), p. 44.

inheres in all this—not necessary to allege because it has been conceded. A philosophy of creative confusion has been voiced in a presidential press conference. Creation had always been associated with chaos, and so assertedly chaos was linked with creation. The evident *non sequitur* recalls a girl—in a Mary Roberts Rinehart story, I think—who declared herself artistic because like an artist she kept her room in a muss. As Genesis tells us, chaos is the situation on which creation acts but is not itself creative. I wonder whether the helter-skelter theory of creativity bears any more validity than its opposite—the humdrum, neat notion of creativity entertained by the Eisenhower administration.

The theory of creative disorder reflects preoccupation with alleged secrets of Franklin D. Roosevelt's presidential successes, encouraged by Richard Neustadt's highly interesting book on the uses of presidential power.[10] Yet one must recall that F.D.R.'s ventures in foreign policy were not unexceptionably successful, and that some of the shakier episodes bore a relation to overlapping assignments and duplicating authority. I wonder in general whether perhaps such successes as he achieved as President came despite rather than through his penchant—perhaps his weakness—for topsy-turvy organization.

A relevant lingering characteristic of the scene is an energetic sort of empiricism—devotion to day-to-day concerns, a merging of high policy and trouble-shooting, so that the moment's major exigency tends to be a function of the moment's pressures. They call it the pragmatic approach. The continuously evident high level of activity is not necessarily a sign of a lot being done. The bustle may sometimes signify that a great many are pressing into the act of the moment, and that much time at levels of primary authority is being spent on secondary concerns. A State Department man expressed the thought to me the other day: "Never before have desk officers' problems been so thoroughly attended to—all the way up."

Staff activity in the process of policy formulation and in some

[10] Richard E. Neustadt, *Presidential Power: The Politics of Leadership* (New York: Wiley, 1960).

aspects of United States representation abroad reflects a bent of the President—a probably unprecedented concern in planning and operational details combined with emphasis on direct personal contact with the principals of other governments.

It is important to view these trends in relation with some basic concepts about foreign policy—returning to the insights quoted from Charles Beard, whose point about foreign policy as deriving from a view of the world and of the place of the nation in the world, is fundamental. John Stoessinger's book, *The Might of Nations*,[11] dwells upon the impossibility of anyone's gathering into his consciousness all the material and relevant aspects of any major topic or problem of foreign policy or the essence of any nation. The emerging nations, the Iron Curtain, the Atlantic Alliance, the nuclear stalemate, the Free World, Southeast Asia—one could continue indefinitely such a list of expressions having currency in foreign policy—all elude complete cognition. The empirical data never cease emerging. The mind never gets a final appreciation about any foreign policy question except, perhaps, in diplomatic history. The best one can do is to try to form some workable order of basic notions about the world environment and reciprocal effects between it and the nation—a cluster of remembered statistics, some knowledge of situations, evaluations of personalities involved, a set of general assumptions or rules-of-thumb about historical movements and a sense of what counts, a hierarchy of values, pertinent to the problems at hand.

Perspectives on such matters tend to differ from one part of the governing apparatus to another, and indeed from one individual to another. Matters in the forefront of an ambassador's mind in dealing with another government may be seen in a different scale in the State Department. Drawing upon knowledge of situations acquired over long years, specialists are likely to see a problem differently from a superior made only recently knowledgeable of specific background but disposed to see the problem in broader context. Attitudes prevailing in a permanent

[11] John G. Stoessinger, *The Might of Nations* (New York: Random House, 1961), pp. 406ff.

bureaucracy are likely to vary from those near or at the center of political leadership. Moreover, the apex of authority provides its own perspectives for those who, being there, are disposed to use their vantage.

A most important question pertinent to organization in the field of foreign policy concerns the level at which the prevailing view of the world, and of the place of the nation in the world, is formed. A strong and successful foreign policy requires, within the limits of feasibility provided by the press of time and the multifariousness of the problems, sound comprehension of the external situations dealt with. It also requires a firm, workable, unified, authoritative view of the interests and purposes of the United States—such a view as requires bringing to bear the powers of the President in constant concern and effectiveness. The creative periods in American foreign policy have invariably been associated with strong use of presidential resources.

From this premise, the depth and steadiness of presidential concern in foreign policy are reassuring. At least the degree of zeal and attention necessary to a renewal of creativity in foreign policy are being supplied. Concern, zeal, and vigor are not themselves sufficient to guarantee success, however. Effectiveness also requires a strong, proper view about the nation's place in the world and a willingness to bring this view to bear in the risks and uncertainties of the external situation. Such a view is probably not to be derived merely through churning up the processes of government and winnowing through masses of empirical data.

Interim evaluation of basic effectiveness is difficult for a number of reasons. To be sure, the Kennedy administration has enjoyed, for the time being, public support at an unsurpassed level. The suspension of critical judgment characteristic of public opinion under the preceding administration has continued and perhaps been accentuated. The prevailing disposition is to give an A for effort.

In this circumstance, the administration has been afforded unparalleled opportunity to present its case. Its case has dominated the field of public information. As one would expect of any administration—this one has not been reluctant about self-approval. On the level of personal appeal, it has proved winsome. Its spokesmen have repeatedly met the press, faced the nation, and told youth what it wants to know—all with remarkable articulateness. So far both its popularity and its problems have endured.

On the question of central premise and purpose in foreign policy, the New Frontier has yet to prove itself. The style is impressive. Style counts for a great deal but is probably not determinative in the broad test. A basis for reservations has been developed by Hans Morgenthau.[12] The gist is that the process followed on the New Frontier is, paradoxically, both elaborate and casual. Elaboration pertains to the pervasiveness and proliferation of empirical inquiry, to a tendency to bring all manner of questions—especially secondary questions—to the apex of authority for decision. Yet the seemingly opposite characteristic derives from the same circumstance.

The process, Morgenthau argues, disregards

> the natural relationship that exists between the gravity of the issue to be decided and the level of authority that decides it. Thus some paramount issues will remain unattended or will be ineffectually attended to by lesser officials lacking sufficient authority, while the President will concern himself with secondary issues which could be more effectively disposed of by subordinate authorities.

Joseph Alsop has described the United States foreign policy apparatus as seen from abroad: "not as yet . . . a unified, coherent, purposeful instrument. . . . It appears, rather, as a whole congeries of groups, and subgroups, and committees, and personages all relentlessly traveling in their own directions. . . ." He cites instances of decisions concerning particular problems made without proper regard for interactions on other problems. He professes to find in such phenomena "the root of

[12] Hans Morgenthau, "The Trouble with Kennedy," *Commentary,* January, 1962, pp. 51, 53.

the problem," and he adds that "until it is overcome the
. . . Administration is bound to go on running into bad
trouble overseas." [13] Alsop locates the fault in the State Department, that traditional whipping boy. I suspect this version over-
simplifies matters and misidentifies the trouble.

The disarray described by Alsop must be a result rather than a
cause of deficiency. If policies move in diverse directions, it
must be because of a lack of paramount decision on what directions should prevail, just as—to hark back to Morgenthau's
criticism—a tendency of secondary matters to crowd out major
concerns at the apex indicates lack of an authoritative scale by
which to weigh quotients of importance.

The trouble lies not in the lack of mechanism by which to bring
coherence to policy. That exists in abundance. The trouble lies
rather in some lingering lack of central premise and purpose
guiding foreign policy. The integrative function and authority
recommended by the Arden House group seem not yet to have
become fulfilled on the New Frontier.

[13] *Washington Post and Times-Herald,* May 23, 1962.

II.

ALLIANCE
AND CONFRONTATION

INTRODUCTION:

THE RISKS OF SOVEREIGNTY

Here I summon a recollection from a third of a century ago. As a young reporter, trying to grasp the kernel of a complex and important civil suit, I sought the court's guidance. After hearing my opening recital of what I understood so far, the judge, a rugged Texan, inquired whether I had been talking to counsel. I had. He gave me some advice derived from many years on the bench. I should be wary of ever taking as conclusive a lawyer's word for the state of the law, he said, for in his experience, one lawyer or the other had always been wrong on every legal issue argued before him. The judge extended his line of thought beyond the point of lawyers' fallibility at law. An unsightly building usually had some architect's name on the cornerstone. Bad paintings were customarily the works of painters, and composers had often composed unplayable or excruciating music. A bad haircut was usually the work of a barber, and blunders in statecraft were invariably the works of statesmen. The moral was simple: never let your judgment be pre-empted by a consideration of status.

That moral has relevance to foreign policy. Watchfulness from the sidelines is indispensable to proper government, in external as in domestic concerns. The worst situation for a government to be in—whatever those in authority may feel—is that of having no one around to find fault. That observation states only half the matter, however. The other half may be illustrated by a recollection drawn from a war-gaming weekend only a few months ago.

War-gaming is a sophisticated version of charades much in vogue in certain quarters. It does not have to concern notional warfare but can be focused on a variety of policy questions. The participants divide into walled-off groups and attempt to think and to make decisions as if they were governing authorities. One group, in control at the center of things, propounds a hypothetical problem and rations out relevant information among the supposed governments. These latter respond by making decisions. Information about the various decisions is collected and rationed out for the next stage, and a new batch of decisions is produced. From time to time the control group throws in a monkey wrench. Stage by stage an incident unfolds into a crisis and then mounts to catastrophe or eases off into anticlimax.

In one sense, the exercise resembles real life about as reading a bridge column resembles playing a real hand: that is, no penalty is entailed for being wrong. In another sense, the parallel is not apt. It is far easier to play a hand when one can see all the other players' cards. The opportunity is not vouchsafed in war-gaming. The participants have to act. The information forming the basis for decision is imperfect, contingent, refractory. The decisions formed on such a basis are inexorably subsumed into the data for the next stage. The participants are thus stuck with the consequences of their acts—at least in theory. In this regard, the exercise simulates life—save that in the latter situation the consequences would be actual rather than putative.

On the occasion concerned I served as one-fifth of the notional United States government. My President for that weekend was a distinguished writer on world affairs—a man of broad knowledge and sharp insight. The United States prevailed against all hypothetical enemies that weekend. The simulated President acquitted himself admirably. He was sobered by the experience, however: appalled by the goadings of Destiny in the guise of a control group, baffled by having to act in face of debatable data, shaken by a sense of the irrevocability of every act, and disconcerted, moreover, in finding himself—an inveterate and accomplished critic of responsible magistrates—expressing himself and acting in the manner of the objects of his criticism. Assuming the role had made a difference. He was conscious of sworn obligations. The burden of the past was upon him. He became gravely aware of limits of choice and of fateful potentials for error.

My colleague's response was a reflection of the risky side of sovereignty. His proper portion of empathy, felt at least momentarily, for our spokesmen, agents, and magistrates in the conduct of policy would befit all of us. One should not judge their action, without trying to imagine himself in their shoes. This observation applies especially with respect to that portion of state business concerned with marshaling force and focusing its intimidatory potential abroad. This onerous and often intractable part of state business—concerned with distinguishing between adversaries and allies—is surely the most sensitive part, the one most weighted with risk, and also the part farthest removed from a private person's ambit of judgment and experience. Yet, paradoxically, this part of state business is the one most likely to be a focus of vehement cavalier judgments by laymen. The temptation is not so prevalent among laymen of humbler station as among those well reputed and highly accomplished in their callings, disposed to think of themselves as of the elite, and inclined to overconfidence beyond their limits.

An instance from a meeting devoted to problems of armament and disarmament comes to mind. An affluent psychiatrist present expounded with point and certitude. The problems of force in world affairs had no objective basis, he contended, but arose from some derangement in the minds and spirits of those disposing authority. He catalogued assumptions made and measures taken in dealing with adversary forces on the present scene. Any psychiatrist discovering such patterns of thought and action in a private patient would at once recognize them as symptoms of illness, he affirmed—and so hope lay in healing our magistrates or replacing them with balanced persons who shared his own insights. "What you are saying," came a voice across the table, "is that anyone disposed to suspect his next door neighbors of being a Hitler and a Mussolini should be given not credence but psychiatric help." The psychiatrist agreed. The challenger then scored his rejoinder. Taking actualities for illusions, he said, was on a par with taking illusions as actualities; disregarding a real menace was no more sensible than fleeing from an imaginary one. The depicted situation—that of having a Hitler and a Mussolini for neighbors—had in fact been France's fateful predicament a quarter century back.

The aspect of contemporary world affairs involving calculation of external danger and action to cope with it—the aspect involving alignment, adversariness, and alliance on a grand scale and commonly called Cold War—is the one most taxing for the outsider intent on forming clear judgments. The problems undulate in one's consciousness—first recessive and then intensified, by turns sharp and clear and then obscure. The volume of wordage compulsively produced on all sides is enormous. The actual material factors are often shrouded. Our magistrates at once deplore the contest and rally us to the cause. The occasional reports of an ebb are invariably succeeded by warnings of undiminished danger. At one moment cleavage between China and the Soviet Union is portrayed as a windfall. At the next, we are counseled to be wary of any assumption of advantage. Cuba is by turns a solved problem and an unremitted menace.

My purpose is not to fault our hierarchs for inconsistency. They, like the rest of us, cannot see very far ahead. They are often baffled by events. Thereby they are led to compound bafflement, for they feel obliged to discourse, and what they say takes its place in the stream of events. Contemporary facilitation of communication only serves to aggravate the effect. Another incremental factor rises from proliferation of international organizations with obligatory periodic meetings—occasions requiring statesmen to speak whether or not there is anything needing to be said. I know no way out of the difficulty. Perhaps in the disarmament discussions at Geneva it would be helpful for the confronting powers to agree to a reciprocal reduction and limitation of public pronouncement, confining themselves, say, to some moderate amount like 5,000 words per month of utterance on the great international issues—a thought more utopian than disarmament itself.

Amid the flood of wordage, a private person needs some comprehensible and more or less enduring points of reference.

The pieces selected for this section attempt to suggest a few. A thought basic to all of them is that our adversary is quite correct in attributing authorship of the Cold War to our side. The adversary has never liked the Cold War, which rises out of resistance put up by others. The adversary's preference is for accommodation to his purposes—peaceful coexistence. The Cold War is ours, not his.

THE PROBLEM OF

INCOMPATIBLE PURPOSES

In international affairs, as in other fields, simple terms are used to communicate about hugely complex, shifting, multifarious situations and relationships. There never would be time enough to think, to remember, or to discuss if one had always to describe fully the phenomena concerned. So to keep tabs on ideas, we put tabs on them. The tabs then tend themselves to become legal tender in the exchange places of ideas as if they had independent meaning and validity. This leads to a great deal of fallacy, and it becomes necessary from time to time to refresh comprehension of the processes for which the tabs are only symbols—in a shift of metaphor, to restore the edges of words dulled by ill usage.

A number of words and phrases in the common lexicon of international affairs come to mind as illustrations—*the Cold War, balance of power, the rule of law, the battle for men's minds, containment, liberation, the free world, aggression, peace with justice, alliance,* and so on and on. Anyone can make his own list of the poster words which publicists, professors, and practitioners use often with careless regard for the complex actualities. Just now an overworked tab is *negotiation,* closely attended by *disengagement* and *relaxation of tensions.* It is to negotiation that I wish to give academic attention. A catalogue of the vapid, inapposite things said with high solemnity during the last few months' debate on negotiations on

From *East-West Negotiations,* Arnold Wolfers (ed.) (Washington: The Washington Center of Foreign Policy Research, 1958). Copyright 1958 by The Washington Center of Foreign Policy Research.

both sides of the Atlantic would be as long as your arm. I can deal here with only a few of them.

"What harm would there be in our talking to the Russians?" is a question put by a midwestern newspaper. The same issue contained two long news items demonstrating that in fact our government was doing just that already, and being talked to voluminously in turn. The idea that negotiation is necessary to cure Washington or Moscow of being tongue-tied is obviously specious. Has there ever been a time of fuller communication between adversaries than the present?

"Negotiation at least might lead to better understanding even if it did not produce agreements," a professor said at a dinner meeting. One hears this idea repeatedly. It is as if a reservoir of reconciliation were secreted in the rock waiting only to be smitten by negotiation, whereupon it would gush forth in abundant streams. The nub, I suspect, is that in fact our government and the one in Moscow actually understand each other quite well.

One current notion about negotiation attributes to it qualities of an intercollegiate debate—an exercise in histrionics and logic, with the decision going to the side scoring best in presentation. It is as if at a certain point in the argument across the table Khrushchev might say to Mr. Dulles, "All right, you've got me! I can't answer that one. So what are your terms?"

Another notion attributes to negotiation the characteristics of a one-shot business deal. Let us call this the haggling theory of negotiation—or the Yankee trader theory. One can imagine the American and the Russian arguing about prices and the quality of the goods—Mr. Dulles making for the door in feigned scorn with Mr. Khrushchev turning around with a shrug to put the fabrics on the shelf and then each turning back to renew the bargaining until at last the price is right.

A third notion conceives of negotiation in terms of a Quaker meeting—as if the spirit of togetherness descends upon a gathering, bringing new insights, new efficacy, and a new spirit of reconciliation through the interaction of souls in propinquity. This view of negotiation let us label as the inspirational theory.

In searching for illustrations of these views of negotiation, I happened to come across all three in one context. It is an item in a recent issue of *Saturday Review*. It refers to a speech by Alf Landon to a teachers' meeting in Kansas and characterizes him as sounding "more like a yeasty young liberal than a former Republican candidate for President." The article then quotes him as urging "that we should use our Yankee ingenuity in a summit meeting," continuing, "Instead of saying no-no-no to the Soviets' proposal for a summit conference, why don't we sit down and start arguing?" The quotation then goes on: "The Secretary of State says we can't trust them. Who wants to? Americans were famous once as Yankee traders who always got their money's worth. They didn't bother about the religion, the political philosophy, or sincerity of the other party, just so the deal suited them." The *Saturday Review's* writer endorses all that and adds on his own: "The time seems ripe for a fresh, imaginative, and inspired approach to international relations."

There we have the three—sit down and start arguing, get your money's worth and don't worry about sincerity, and finally get inspired.

According to my dictionary, *negotiate* means "1. To treat for, obtain, or arrange by bargain, conference, or agreement. 2. To transfer for a value received, as a note, bond, or other written obligation. 3. To accomplish or cope with successfully, as to *negotiate* an obstacle. 4. To treat or bargain with others." Negotiation embraces then the process of talking about terms, the achievement of terms, and the terms.

Clearly we are already in the midst of negotiations, and long have been, if we mean only the process of talking about terms— at least about the terms for talking about terms. The Russians have been busily propounding the conditions for a spider's feast. Mr. Eisenhower and Mr. Dulles have been assiduously—and properly—rejecting these. In this Mr. Dulles has been accused of inflexibility—which is the pejorative word for firmness.

The reason why negotiations have not progressed to the achievement of terms (in this case even the achievement of terms for trying to achieve terms) is not a lack of inspiration or yeastiness. It is not even a lack of understanding.

We do understand the Russians.

Basically, and quite clearly, the Russians do seek world domination. A great many experts on Russia may deny this. They will point to the remoteness and theoretical character—and hence the supposed irrelevancy—of the ultimate aspirations of the Marxist ideology and contend that there is no active desire whatsoever in the Kremlin rulers really to subjugate Western Europe, etc. This is really not the point. The point is that the Russian rulers do set as their goal and actively pursue the condition that all problems exterior to Russia deemed important to them are to be settled their way. This does not mean that the Russian rulers aspire to see the Red flag over the Quai d'Orsay or Whitehall. It merely means paramountcy for Russian purposes when the issues are drawn.

On the other hand the Russians understand us quite well. I can state this only as a supposition. I cannot give personal assurance about it. Our own purposes and interests make unacceptable to us the condition of world relations coveted by the Russians.

This mutuality of understanding is what impinges upon negotiation in the sense of achievement of terms. In a negotiation which advances to terms, each side seeks ends and brings means. Each side conceives its ends in terms of means to be tendered by the other. In a one-shot deal—the Yankee trading sort of negotiation—means and ends settle out in an exchange if the price is right, and the seller awaits other customers while the buyer takes home the goods or goes to other markets. This has no bearing on the sort of negotiation which the U.S. is being exhorted to undertake. The point at issue is the conditions for a continuing relationship. Whether at the summit or elsewhere the basic bargaining must be on how in broadest terms the entities concerned are to relate themselves to each other. If we wish to draw a metaphoric parallel, the most apt would be the sort of negotiation which took place between the U.A.W. and General Motors in 1937. Here the issue was whether the company and the union would thenceforth relate themselves to each other in a continuing bargaining relationship. That issue settled, the other elements in contention fell into place more or less readily.

The conditions of successful collective bargaining shed some light on the problem of negotiating with the Russians. In collective bargaining that works, the adversariness of the parties is limited by their recognized need of each other. Their ends are not the same. They may even be opposite, but they are compatible. Each side seeks satisfaction of its own ends at a minimum practicable expenditure of means to satisfy the ends sought by the other, but neither hates or fears per se the ends which the other seeks, and so neither feels compelled to suspect or to distrust the use which the other might make of a success. Between the Russians and us such conditions do not exist. Debate is not likely to convince either party to the contrary. A basis for Yankee trading is lacking. The inspiration of tête-à-tête is not likely to cause either side to forget the facts.

In this perspective the argument about locus—whether to negotiate at a mysterious summit or along even more mysterious corridors of professional diplomacy—becomes as derivative and arid as a question whether Neville Chamberlain or Nevile Henderson was the best man for doing business with Hitler. If a universe of discourse making for compatible ends were shared, negotiations at whatever level might be productive of the longed-for solutions. If this were so, moreover, the problems and dangers which men of good will wish to abate would not exist.

This brings us to the vaunted relaxation of tensions. One hears that the Russians harbor thoughts of bringing this about and need to be met only half way. If by the phrase one means a sag along our side of the confrontation—a disengagement, an abatement of the challenge which we carry to Russian purposes —then the answer is that, of course, the Russians are ready for it and want it the worst way. If it means that the Russians are in the mood for modifying the intensity and constancy of their own desires, one can only answer that the mood is deeply concealed, and its existence a matter of guesswork.

This does not mean an endlessly static situation. The material relevancy of certain means may alter from one stage to another, and problems may move up or down in the scale of negotiability; particular impasses may become unblocked, as occurred, for instance, in the case of the Austrian Peace Treaty. The time when it will become possible to transform the situation by putting means of high importance into the bargain and to reconcile ends seems remote, however.

If there is to be relaxation of tensions otherwise than on terms of capitulation, it will be only in the inward sense: a reassertion of captaincy over our own spirits and resolving to live calmly in danger for a long time to come. I am not hopeful that this will be done easily. I can almost hear the yeasty throngs chanting:

> One-two-three-four
> Terminate the Cold War!
> Five-six-seven-eight
> Hurry and negotiate!

The problem is how to restore balance to our side, how to dispel the beguiling notion that negotiation of itself is a means of redressing dangers and achieving harmony of interest, rather than merely an avenue along which one may proceed to success, impasse, or catastrophe, depending on the ratios of will and resources between the adversary parties. To counter the surge of demand for negotiation under conditions of high disadvantage to our side it will be necessary to abandon the secondary and unattractive propositions that clutter up the American case and to concentrate on a few basic and sound propositions: a proper insistence on the baleful character of the adversary, the necessity of American interposition, in fact and not merely in promise, on the continent; and the indispensability of NATO. Above all, it will be necessary to correct our imprudent strategic reliance on a thermonuclear weapon that frightens our friends more than it cows our putative enemies.

THE U.S. AND THE U.S.S.R.

IN THE UNITED NATIONS

Alexander counted among his achievements the gathering of the world together under one rule after extending dominion over a span less than that of South America. The Romans thought of themselves as approaching the limits with an empire about equal to present Indonesia in scope. The ancient dream of organizing the world through conquest testifies to the circumscription of geography in those epochs. In any event, the idea of organizing the world through subordination of its parts to one center of authority differs from that of organizing it through free association among juridically equal components. This latter notion had to await the emergence of modern nation states. So long as such states were phenomena exclusively or preponderantly European and so long as power in world affairs remained concentrated in the same area, the notion of world organization was reflected in various schemes for institutions of ordered accommodation among Europe's rulerships—academic projects dreamed up by such figures as William Penn, the Abbé de St. Pierre, Jean Jacques Rousseau, Jeremy Bentham, and Immanuel Kant, and poetic speculations such as Tennyson's. As an undertaking pertinent to the policies of governments, world organization has less than a half century of continuity—brought to life in the circumstances of World War I, given form in the Treaty of Versailles, and recast as the United Nations in 1945. In age as an active political idea, it is among the newest.

From *The Strategy of Deception*, Jeane J. Kirkpatrick (ed.) (New York: Farrar, Straus & Company, Inc., 1963). Copyright © 1963 by Farrar, Straus & Company, Inc.

Here the concern is with the place of the world organization in the policies of two governments, the great adversary powers of the contemporary world scene, namely, the United States and the Soviet Union. The approach is one emphasizing the effect on the world organization of trends and forces having sources outside it—as distinct from an approach emphasizing the forms of the organization. In formal terms, the world organization has developed so far in two stages—the League of Nations and then its successor, the United Nations. From a standpoint emphasizing the play of politics rather than the function of form, the League went through four distinct stages, and the United Nations has experienced three and now confronts an issue over entering a fourth. It would be appropriate to consider the whole development as a succession of seven Leagues, and a possibility of yet another.

The first phase of the League proper might be called the Wilsonian phase, reflecting the idea of permanent participation by the United States with other powers, especially those of Europe, in keeping constant watch over the problems of order, stability, and peace. The American President did not precisely invent the idea—though his name was graven on a tablet at Geneva as the founder. It had been talked about unofficially for some years. Lord Grey, the British Foreign Minister, broached it first as a policy proposition in the summer weeks of 1914 during the vain efforts to head off the outbreak of war. The concept took hold among sectors of public opinion first in Great Britain and then in the United States. Woodrow Wilson put behind it the force of his personality and office. Not as a matter of proof but at least as a reasonable speculation, the League would scarcely have materialized otherwise. To this extent it is just to refer to Wilson as the founder.

Justice to the proponent's practical sense requires mention of a linkage in intention, if not in form, between the League project and a collateral treaty anticipating the North Atlantic Treaty by thirty years in committing the United States explicitly to the security of Western Europe—an undertaking put aside after the Senate's rejection of the League. Thus Wilson, however much pressed to it, at least came to recognize need of a foundation in regional security for a projection onto a world scale of the premises of a democratic and constitutional order. In his estimate, moreover, realization of the project would be worth a high price in compromise and expediency with respect to other considerations. The imperfections could all be corrected in due time after establishment of a framework of constant, open interchange. Communication was a key to reason in world political relations. Community would be discovered through discourse. Rivalries would eventuate into accommodation if the parties would but hear the issues out—given a framework of obligations and principles to which all were plighted.

Germany, too, would be brought into the conclave—though this, instead of being immediate on the return of formal peace as at first projected, came to be deferred until after a period for rehabilitation. Save for a few exceptions, the door otherwise was to be left open wide. The most significant exclusion was that of Soviet Russia, a new revolutionary power nursing an expectation of creating a world order in another pattern, imagining itself as destined to be the model-maker of a world organization, and scornful and hostile toward the emerging League as an instrument of its adversaries marked for early failure and bound to be superseded when the dream of world revolution should come true. It was a case of mutual antipathy.

The League coming into reality differed in a signal respect from the Wilsonian project—a difference such as to make the League basically different from what had been planned. The withholding of United States participation was the obvious factor making the difference. The organization took shape on a basis of a hegemony of the European victor powers—a hegemony too limited, fragile, and doubtful to serve the purpose for long. This was the League in its second phase.

A third phase began in 1924—the phase of the Locarno Pact signaling reconciliation between the European victor powers and defeated Germany. This brought the League to the height of its promise. Its tenth anniversary in 1929 was the occasion for a great array of congratulatory speeches, hopeful essays, and assured books hailing the apparent fact of the League's having overcome its initial disabilities. It seemed to be succeeding in making do without United States collaboration. It appeared to be making a place for itself as the instrument of a concord wider than that of the victor powers. While by no means exclusively European, it remained a Europe-centered institution, but Europe still enjoyed ascendancy in world affairs and seemed for the moment to have achieved a durable basis for collaboration almost as wide as the celebrated concert of European powers of the preceding century.

During this phase both the United States and the Soviet Union, while maintaining formal aloofness, took tentative steps toward collaboration in work of the League, especially with respect to disarmament. The United States moved a long way from the attitude characteristic of an earlier time when communications from League headquarters were left unanswered. The Soviet Union modified its earlier approach of discount and diatribe. This mellowing of aloofness by both powers at least implicitly added to the brightness of the time.

The hopefulness of the broader prospect was of short duration. Just when it ended is difficult to say. The economic depression of 1929 and subsequent years and the related rush into economic autarchy revealed the basic weakness of the European hegemony. The durability of German cooperativeness with the victors appeared increasingly dubious. The earlier hopes lapsed with the collapse of the Weimar Republic and the reversion of Germany to militant defiance—a course already undertaken by Japan, whose example in withdrawing from the League Germany followed in the same year of 1933.

With Germany and Japan off on paths of intransigence and Italy veering in a like direction, the League entered a fourth phase, coincident roughly with the vogue of the United Front in European politics and marked by ambiguous approaches to cooperation between the Western European powers and the Soviet Union—ambiguous because each side in the ventures had fingers crossed and each suspected how it was with the other. For Soviet Russia the development brought transient vindication. It entered the League in 1934, not at its own request but on the bidding of the organization from which it had been proscribed. For a few years, represented at Geneva by Maxim Litvinov, it was among all governments the most vocal and active advocate of collective security—at least in discourse and probably in other respects, for the Soviet regime was sensible of its infirmities, alert to resurgent German aggressiveness, and anxious to stave off danger.

The year 1936 marked for all practical purposes the end of gestures toward collaboration between the Soviet Union and the West in the League—the year when things began definitely to go to pieces, the year of the reoccupation of the Rhineland and the abrogation of the Locarno Pact, of Italy's official annexation of Ethiopia and of the League's ignominious recision of sanctions placed against Italy for aggression there, of the outbreak of Spain's Civil War, of the formation of the Rome-Berlin Axis, and of the German-Japanese anti-Comintern pact. It was a year of foreboding also with respect to intensification of the purge within the ruling Communist party in the Soviet Union—a circumstance bringing into grave question the Soviet Union's internal strength as a factor bearing on its reliability in international affairs.

This last point has relevance to evaluation of the respective roles of the Soviet Union and the Western European powers in the breakdown of European security and the advance toward war. Basing judgment solely or primarily on declaratory policies uttered at Geneva may bring one to a highly affirmative appraisal of Soviet policy. Soviet attitudes on countering Axis aggression were unequivocal, while those of the Western powers were halting. In his generally authoritative *History of the League of Nations*, F. P. Walters thus comes to a high estimate of the Soviet approach with blame clearly falling to the Western powers for failing to take at face value and to act on the Soviet proffers of cooperation in defense. Implicitly, by this version, things would have turned out well and the debacle have been avoided if the Western parties to Locarno had made other assessments and joined hands with the Soviet Union. One is liable to fall into fallacy by accepting declarations in an international forum as conclusive. The West's statesmen had reason enough to be wary of the Soviet Union's solidity and reluctant to bring Soviet weight to bear in Central Europe. The course they elected turned out badly. This does not prove the alternative better. What confronted them was a dilemma. History is full of examples of getting caught between a reef and a vortex.

In any event, after 1936 the eclipse of the League never really lifted even briefly. Collaboration in security between the West and Soviet Russia became a dead letter. Geneva became less and less a place for making great decisions or even attempting them—an institution where important affairs were watched, occasionally commented on, but not dealt with seriously. The center of events moved elsewhere—to Nyon, Berchtesgaden, Munich, and then to Moscow itself for the signing of the Hitler-Stalin Pact, which opened the way to World War II and the partition of Poland. The League had but one more decision within its capability—that a negative one. In December, 1939, its Council declared the Soviet Union no longer a member—an action of symbolic punishment for the Soviet Union's attack on Finland. It was the sole instance of expulsion of a member in the League's unhappy and futile history and a last act of clearing up an anomaly before the League itself went into caretaker status for the duration of the renewed world war.

The League had begun with forty-one member states. Cumulatively over twenty years the members totaled sixty-four. By 1939, forty-three remained—four of these being countries actually under annexation and only nominally participating. The European component of membership totaled sixteen at the outset, rose cumulatively to twenty-eight, and declined to a final twenty. The Latin American group began at fifteen, rose cumulatively to twenty-one, and declined to nine. The Asian members began at five, rose cumulatively to eight, and ended at seven. The African states began at three and rose to four. The balance consisted of three British dominions, two in the South Pacific and one in North America. Non-European participation was proportionately even less in interest and influence than in numbers. In sum, the League never really succeeded in fulfilling the design of a world organization. Through much of its practical life, and especially toward the end, the League was characterized by instability of membership—both a cause and a symptom of its weakness.

It is a commonplace to describe the pervasive effect of World War II as a transformation in the pattern of power in world affairs. The transformation was worked in many ways. Some countries were depleted by efforts beyond reasonable capacity. Some suffered social disintegration under enemy occupation. Some experienced the ordeal of being fought over once and again. Some were brought low by defeat. The broad consequence was a draining away of capacity to achieve. Power being relative, what is lost by some passes to others. The United States and the Soviet Union were the receivers—the two major nations to emerge aggrandized in power. The first was stronger even in absolute terms than before the war. The second was certainly stronger in a relative sense despite huge losses in an absolute measure. Large portions of the Soviet land were still devastated. Its economic situation was precarious in the utmost. It had sustained huge losses in manpower. Its place in the world, nevertheless, was aggrandized by the abstract factor of prestige in having won through in the bitterest and most extensive fighting of the war and by the concrete factor of positions occupied by Soviet forces in the wake of retreating and collapsing Axis armies.

The central question bearing on the prospect for world tranquility thenceforth involved the future relationship between the two now major powers. In the circumstances, the question of a resumption of effort in world organization—and the form for it to take—lay with these two as with no others. Each, in distinct ways, was deeply affected in its approach to the question by experience and recollections related to the League in its various phases.

With the United States, a primary consideration was a fault of conscience over having forsaken the League. That act set the precedent of being cavalier about League membership—an example all too widely copied later on. The withholding which fated the League to remain a mainly European institution had been an American action. Advocates of the League, Wilson pre-eminent among them, had based their case on the essentiality of a strong League to preservation of peace and the essentiality of United States participation to a strong League. With the United States' strength withheld, the League had remained feeble and unfulfilled, world war was renewed, and the United States was again drawn in—a sequence seemingly corroborative of the warnings disregarded by public opinion and other forces of American politics at the time of the decision to stand aloof.

This argument from experience was neither empirically demonstrable nor logically conclusive. No one could ever know whether United States participation in the League would have made a determining difference between peace and renewal of war. Perhaps the forgotten treaty on Western European security was even more important among might-have-beens. The collapse of the structure of peace might in any case have been an inevitable consequence of the economic debacle following 1929 —a set of circumstances as to which the question of United States membership in the League had little bearing. Such conjectures were beside the point, however. After two decades, the predictions of dire consequences of the United States' default seemed amply confirmed on the face of the evidence. The record suggested a set of compelling syllogisms regarding United States participation in world organization henceforth.

On this second opportunity, United States public opinion was amply affirmative. This time no party issue was posed. In the prevailing mood, the United States was to outdo all others in devotion to the renewed cause. The undertaking was plighted in the Atlantic Charter even before the entry into belligerency. This time the planning effort for organizing peace began virtually with the onset of hostilities. The act of organizing was not to be postponed until the sequel but persevered in to completion even in the course of war. The organization, though successor to the League and modeled after it in many particulars, was to represent a new start juridically and to be rooted in, and to derive its name from, the coalition of powers against the Axis.

Naming it the United Nations was a triumph of public relations, perhaps unconsciously contrived. Unity was explicit in the title. Unity means concord; and concord, peace. The tendency would be to foreclose argument in regard to issues arising over courses set in the emerging organization. Such a psychological advantage would surely not have obtained if it had been called the Assorted Nations, the Various Nations, or even the Assembled Nations.

The chosen name reflected, moreover, an assumption—at least a hope—of a continuation in the sequel to hostilities of the sharing of purposes taken to characterize wartime efforts against common foes. The official as well as the public disposition at the time was to overconstrue community of purpose and, as a corollary, to discount divergencies among the wartime collaborators. The differences among them, while not obscured, were certainly not highlighted. It is human nature to make the best of an ally while confronting still unvanquished enemies, and it should not be amazing to find human nature reflected in foreign policy. Policy, moreover, must be grounded on hope. The hope of finding a basis for working things out between the two powers of pre-eminent importance to the chances of peace had rational roots. As Inis Claude, Jr., has pointed out in his *Swords into Plowshares*, what was assumed was not an infallible prospect of post-war cooperation between the great powers but its indispensability to a peaceful order. Circumstances of the time rather than perfectionism of hindsight provide the best perspective for judging United States policy in that phase.

International as the frame of the new organization was to be, it was an American project in essential aspects. The thought— echoing Wilson—that realization of the project might be worth some compromises along the way was strictly an American attitude. One can scarcely imagine the Russians withholding their weight on an issue in hope of promoting thereby the achievement of a new world organization. Americans might entertain the idea—again echoing Wilson—that any imperfections necessarily acquiesced in could all be adjusted in the long run within the framework of the organization, but for Russians to have acted on such a premise would scarcely be imaginable. Irked over Russian obdurateness, the President could, as he did, warn the Soviet Foreign Minister that the United States might change its mind about wanting Soviet participation. Surely the Russian official was in no position to hint at the retaliatory possibility of excluding the United States.

With the Soviet Union, it was a case of going along with a project of others' devising. It did go along, notwithstanding rumors, persisting to the last minute, of a design to stand aside from the conference at San Francisco, where the Charter was put into final form and signed. The idea of Soviet reluctance to join was to prove a durable myth. It presumably stemmed from Marshal Stalin's intermittent professions of velleity and doubt— made with intent to elicit concessions as a price for the Soviet Union's consenting to embrace an opportunity which it is scarcely conceivable it would have renounced in any event. On this score, President Truman was surely nearer correct than his predecessor. The Russians must have been in a mood to be deterred by a prospect of being kept out rather than requiring to be humored into going along. Going along, however, did not entail identity as to understanding and purpose. This circumstance, discernible at the time and amply demonstrated since, gives rise to a question whether the Soviet Union was devious or sincere in the action —a question worth dwelling upon with care.

As an American Secretary of State was to put the matter sixteen years later, the Soviet Union, while having signed and ratified the Charter, never really concurred in it. In Leland Goodrich's telling phrase, the Soviet Union made its subscription to the Charter subject to a unilateral amendment entertained in its own intentions. The amendment, if the term applies, was of a most basic character. On one occasion—it happened to be at the Danube Conference in 1948—the Soviet Foreign Minister proposed what he called a procedural amendment: to insert a *not* before every verb in a draft under consideration. The reservation regarding the Charter entertained in the Soviet view might seem to be of that sort, involving mental insertion of a negative into some of the propositions fundamental to the document, at least as those propositions were understood by the proponents.

Care is called for in applying this notion of a mental reservation. One may too easily construe intended deceptiveness from Soviet discourse and actions. Moreover, the assumption may mislead one into unfulfillable hopes. To assume mental reservations on the Russians' part in regard to the Charter implies their recognition of the authentic meaning, colored by preference for knowingly substituting an invalid interpretation as a basis for playing a double game to serve their own ends. From this assumption there seems to flow a possibility of the Russians' some day owning to error, confessing to having known what was right all along, and promising to desist from further waywardness. These things will happen when shrimps whistle. Individuals and groups with divergent concepts of meaning and truth are likely to regard each other as prevaricators even when doing their respective best to be sincere. In any dialogue, it is important to recognize linkage between sense of truth and grasp of reality as these are revealed in terms. To attribute untruthfulness to a person having hallucinations and reporting the presence of objects not actually at hand is no more appropriate than his counter attribution of the same malign quality to someone denying their presence—notwithstanding the question of validity as between their respective views. An Englishman using *billion* where we would say *trillion* no more intends to deceive us than do we him in saying *billion* for his *milliard*. This injunction against construing deceptiveness from deviant usage of terms applies to international dialogues in general and to that with the Soviet Union in particular. The point to comprehend is that Soviet discourse does not necessarily involve flouting of truth in interpreting and using terms differently from us, asserting as real things which we do not discern, and denying matters of which we are certain.

Such differences are not likely to be manifest in relation merely to tangibles. They may not emerge in any dialogue about values, purposes, and principles as abstractions only. They are almost inevitable, however, in relation to any question linking tangibles and abstractions—as political dialogue essentially does.

I have heard individuals of scientific bent remark on the harmony prevailing between themselves and Russian counterparts in interchanges confined within the limits of a precise, verifiable common discipline and construe therefrom an idea of rendering all issues negotiable by translating them into terms of the mutual specialty. On the other hand, I have heard idealists comment upon the community of ultimate goals entertained by the two political societies concerned—both the United States and the Soviet Union affirming justice, progress, peace, and other such abstract goods. The conclusion drawn was that apparently intractable political issues might be resolved by concentrating on final desiderata. Such simple, hopeful propositions are correct enough on a basis of inadequate premises. It is invariably futile, however, to suggest alleviating a difficulty of combination by reducing the problem to one term, as one does in proposing to solve political issues by treating them as if they were of some other sort. The rub is that politics—meant here in its broadest, most dignified sense—involves not merely tangibles or ultimate and indisputable goods. It involves linking the one sort of thing to the other in courses of action. It embraces not merely means or merely ends but means and ends. The focus of politics is what to do to promote the good society. Its issues do not impinge so long as talk is directed merely to the self-evident goodness of a good society or to things to do without reference to their effects in retarding or forwarding realization of one concept or another of such society. Means take on another dimension of value when linked to ends. Ends cease to be mere abstractions when linked to means. Then it is that issues are quickened and complicated by what one calls political characteristics.

Persistent differences with the Soviet Union within the United Nations, as elsewhere, have been in this realm of combining means and ends—not ever questions of means or ends pure and simple. Soviet divergence from our views about implementing the Charter does not signify Soviet dissimulation in signing and ratifying it or even Soviet cynicism about its high purposes. It is indicative rather of a discrepant view of what the ends involve in relation to means. The discrepancy rises from basic differences about reality, the relation of will to history, and so on. Consideration of what this implies as to limits of usefulness of discussion as an avenue to solution of issues may be deferred for the moment. The focus here is on questions of Soviet motivation and sincerity in going along with the Charter.

It is unnecessary to account for the affirmative action by negative or subsidiary explanations—a presumed anxiety to avoid diplomatic isolation and to widen contacts, recollection first of long exclusion and then of punitive expulsion from the League and a linked desire for vindication, or reassurance due to the titling of the organization after a wartime collaboration of proved convenience. Beyond such marginal considerations, the Russians in all probability heartily accepted the Charter as they understood it in a frame of understanding cognate with a world outlook, a view of history, known as Marxism-Leninism.

World politics, according to this outlook, inherently polarizes around two sets of opposed purposes. Since 1917, when the state of Russia was taken over by those adhering to the Communist conception of world socialist revolution, the Soviet Union has been one of the essential poles. This is so because it is the exemplar and agent of an ineluctable truth of historic development, in the view of its proponents. The opposite pole, at any stage, has represented whatever outlooks, interests, and purposes were deviant from and opposed to those of the Soviet Union. The polarized situation in a world thus divided into a Communist camp and that of the others is taken not to be merely an object of preference, a working of policy, but an ineluctable characteristic of historic development. At some junctures the division into two camps may be blurred by the presence of third forces not identified explicitly with the Soviet Union or its adversaries. In some phases, interests and purposes may tend to overlap as between the Soviet Union and others not under its control or aligned with it. These are temporary situations—mere passing exceptions to a general course, breathing spells in historic progression. What seems aberrant to us is normal in the Soviet view, and vice versa.

An idea pervading the Soviet outlook is a total claim on the future. The law underlying the Soviet conception of what is rightful and what is not is taken as a law of history. It is conceived of as ordaining the universal triumph of Communist interests and purposes. Those interests and purposes are asserted to have an exclusive access to legitimacy, and all other interests and purposes are regarded as deviant and illegitimate. Peace to the Soviet regime, as it would mean to anyone, means a legitimate order free of violence. Since in the Soviet view, however, legitimacy stands for whatever favors Communist interests and purposes, peace therefore stands for a nonviolent situation favorable to those interests and purposes. Whatever tends otherwise is by definition deviant in the direction of war. Peace, then, besides entailing an absence of war, means essentially a situation free of impediment to Communist purposes. To promote peace thus necessarily, in this view, entails frustrating all interests and outlooks standing aside from or opposed to those of the Soviet Union. Progress is defined from a similar set of premises. The same is true of justice. World affairs—interpreted in terms of a quest of these abstractions—are seen as a struggle between the Soviet Union and its adversaries. The conflict is regarded as one between ultimately irreconcilable opposites.

In Alexander Dallin's apt summation, the "presence of a superpower with a deeply engrained 'two-camp' view in a 'one-world' organization presents a challenging problem." With respect to this problem, as with other difficulties rising from the combination in the Soviet Union of great scope and power with an adherence to irreconcilability, some persons seek a hopeful way out by postulating a doubt of the Soviet rulers' belief in their own stated theory of history. The phrase "believe in" stands for the mind's function in ascribing some quality to an object. To test the phrase in a particular context requires filling in the attribute. Thus the quality concerned in believing in a weather report differs from that pertaining to belief in free enterprise, and that involved in believing in a religious doctrine differs from that pertaining to belief in, say, the integrity of a friend. Those hopefully skeptical of the Soviet rulers' belief in their own asserted dogma are usually at a loss when called upon to specify the qualities supposed to be inwardly withheld or when asked to explain in what, as an alternative, the Soviet rulers are supposed to believe. Clearly enough, those in the Soviet rulership do accept and use their assumptions as a framework for interpreting realities.

How, then, can this be squared with believing in the Charter? The problem of squaring would present no difficulty to one habituated to dialectic. The Charter and the pertinent organization are viewed in the special perspectives of Marxism-Leninism. Their reality is accepted. They are to be interpreted or participated in as may befit Soviet interests. In these senses they are believed in just as are the state system, the institutions of bilateral diplomacy, the pattern of world trade, or any other frame of action on the world scene. The dogma is not a basis for denying or withdrawing from a differentiated world but a way of coming to grips with it, interpreting it, and acting on it. To have subscribed to the Charter in a way involving abandonment of basic framework for interpreting political reality would have been beyond the capability of minds attuned to such dogma. To have accepted the Charter as a summation of final principles governing international relations in keeping with our premises and professions would have entailed their putting aside their own way of viewing the world and taking unto themselves outlooks of quite another sort. Such renunciation, such a reversal of habits of thought, sometimes accompanies religious conversion and may sometimes occur in consequence of purely intellectual persuasion, but to have expected it of the Russians as an act of political accommodation was simply unrealistic. The idea of Soviet mental reservations regarding the Charter thus misses a point. It was not a case of withholding some part of their minds. It was a case of giving adherence consistent with their dialectical way of thinking. That some Americans assumed otherwise—and that some still look hopefully for evidences of transformation—

is evidence of the innocence of pragmatic minds when confronted with dogmatic resoluteness.

The Russians, moreover, have remained true to the Charter in their fashion. That is to say, they have fitted its meanings into their outlook on politics. In their own way, they have regarded it as an instrument for peace—but with an approach quite different, as the power situation and the circumstances of power are different, from the necessitous time of the Soviet Union's attempts at leadership in collective security at Geneva during the United Front period when Moscow was anxious for allies. In the United Nations, as elsewhere, peace pure and simple is seldom at issue. Either side in any confrontation is most likely to wish to prevail without violence. Issues turn rather on the conditions of peace. As one should expect, the Soviet regime has sought to interpret and to invoke the Charter in a way to promote conditions tending toward triumph of its own outlook, interests, and purposes and to impede, as it could, the fostering of an order based on any differentiated concept of legitimacy that is to say, peace on other terms. The endeavor has been constant. Methods have been elastic—adapting to conditions prevailing at one phase or another in the organization's course.

A brief account to distinguish among these phases is appropriate. The first phase was that of the United Nations as projected in plans at Dumbarton Oaks and confirmed at the San Francisco Conference. In the chronicle of world organization in relation to political forces rather than documents and forms, this might be considered the fifth League, with a character derived from conditions and suppositions pertaining to the wartime coalition. That coalition had had five principal members. They varied widely in relative importance. As to two of them, major status was more a recollection or a hope than a current fact. Whatever the gradations among them, the five became the permanent hierarchs of the reincarnated and revamped world organization. Their collective authority was to be shared in a Security Council with six other governments serving in rotation on election by the member states at large in a General Assembly. Subject only to a requirement of support from two among the seven adjuncts, the permanent five would be arbiters of legitimacy on questions of peace and war. A requirement of unanimity among the five reserved control to each of them, namely the United States, the United Kingdom, France, the Republic of China, and the Soviet Union—an arrangement theoretically advantageous to each but peculiarly so to the Soviet Union as the single one with a concept of legitimacy antithetic to all the others.

As the fact of intransigent singularity prevailed over assumptions of concord, the Security Council became a center of inaction from the start. Its effectiveness has revived sporadically under special circumstances aligning the Soviet Union's *ad hoc* interests with others, but in respect of the primacy of the Security Council the United Nations as originally designed can scarcely be said to have materialized—a result generally recounted as a tale of frustration, though not so by the Soviet Union, still devoted to the primacy and exclusiveness of the Security Council on the grave questions of peace and war.

Not the hoped-for harmony among the five great juridic equals but the hegemonic position of the United States was the main political circumstance affecting the United Nations as it emerged into reality. The components of the position were many—among them a productive plant protected by distance from the impact of war and indeed greatly expanded by the war effort to form an unrivaled source of supply, transport capabilities both relatively and absolutely greater than ever before despite wartime attrition, unimpaired resources for credit, and a temporary monopoly of nuclear capability. These elements of ascendancy, long in development, were coming into full play about the time of the end of hostilities. The need of using this ascendancy on behalf of national policy came into reluctant recognition with mounting evidences of the Soviet Union's true purposes in Eastern and Central Europe, the Eastern Mediterranean, Iran and East Asia, in Soviet performance in the United Nations, and in attitudes of Moscow-oriented Communist parties around the globe.

In this phase the United States turned significantly to frames of action outside the United Nations. It renounced the United Nations Relief and Rehabilitation Administration as a channel of assistance abroad—thereby recovering control of its aid as an instrument of policy. It moved on to imaginative undertakings for bolstering Greece and Turkey against Communist penetration and for the economic rehabilitation of Western and Central Europe. It adopted a program for military strengthening of areas under Communist pressure. As a matter of high importance, the United States turned to the creation of structures of collaboration for security apart from the United Nations—first with the Organization of American States and then notably with the North Atlantic Treaty Organization, an updated counterpart of Wilson's abandoned project to contract the United States into the security of Western Europe. As at Locarno a generation before, Germany, so much of it as was politically accessible, was brought into the security arrangement—now in concrete form rather than being an expression of intentions on paper. Rapprochement was established with the other erstwhile principal enemy, Japan.

United States hegemony was operative during this second phase within as well as outside the United Nations. The main events revolved around Korea. The United States turned to the General Assembly, first, to try to bring about the reunification of the country divided along the 38th parallel by the Soviet and United States occupations and, second, to set up a frame of legitimate government in the southern part as a prelude to the withdrawal of United States forces. On June 25, 1950, forces of the Soviet-oriented northern part attacked the Republic of South Korea. The United States spearheaded resistance carried out under the United Nations' emblem and authorization.

In the first instance the United Nations' aegis was granted by the Security Council—thanks to the Soviet Union's inability to impede with a veto because of absence in a purported huff over an earlier decision against transferring China's franchise from the refugee regime on Formosa to the Communist regime now ensconced on the mainland. The absence has often been attributed to inadvertence—an implausible explanation quite at variance with the substantiated premise of long preparation for the attack on South Korea. The opportunity for veto was missed on purpose—a miscalculation rather than oversight. Copies, later captured, of operational plans in Korea gave a clue; success in the attack was expected to be so prompt as to foreclose riposte even if the idea should be entertained. The Soviet Union must have wished to save itself the unnecessary embarrassment of vetoing an action supposedly futile in any case. Probably no riposte, even a futile one, was expected. This view was implicit in a discourse some months later by the Soviet Foreign Minister to a neutral diplomat. His theme was American perfidy. The United States had withdrawn its forces from Korea without leaving in their stead so much as a detachment with a flag. It had created only minimal military strength among the South Koreans. It had made no pledge of defense. It had conveyed responsibility to the United Nations—something scarcely compatible with serious intentions, according to the spokesman. The United States had suffered its forces within reach to go slack on household duties. It had dawdled on economic aid to South Korea. Short of an open invitation, it was hard to imagine clearer signals for forces from the north to clear up the anomaly of a divided Korea, said Vyshinsky, but the United States had responded to the resulting attempt by making a war of it and summoning the United Nations to its side. The account closed with sharp observations about inconsistency and irresponsibility.

With the Russian return on August 1 blocking further use of the Security Council as a channel for United Nations authority in the Korean action, the United States led the way in asserting a substitute authority in the General Assembly. An alternative way was conceivable, that of carrying the Korean action to conclusion without further color of United Nations authorization and in company with such partners as might choose to see the enterprise through—an awkward course involving risk of diplomatic isolation and loss of moral advantages implicit in having the United Nations identity. These difficulties appeared forbidding. By the letter of the Charter, the Assembly could not

command but only commend in such matters—and this by affir-
mation of two-thirds of the members voting. In essence, the
view according the General Assembly the desired authority tried
to rise above literalness to construe the United Nations as a
body politic and the General Assembly, by virtue of being the
plenary group of such an organic institution, as appropriately
and inherently empowered to act in event of the Security Council's being incapacitated by procedure. This conception of the
United Nations as an organic entity and of the General Assembly as its capstone and as a body politic has been the kernel of
the enduring central issue ranging the United States and the
Soviet Union on opposite sides thenceforth.

Details regarding subsequent use of the Assembly as a source
of symbols of legitimacy in the Korean experience may be
elided here. The parliamentary device for shifting issues of war
and peace from a blocked Security Council to the Assembly did
serve to preserve a United Nations color to the operations. It
was employed again to produce a resolution "endorsing all appropriate steps to ensure conditions of stability throughout
Korea" coincident with the fateful carrying of military operations north of the 38th parallel. An adequate majority for a
resolution condemning aggression was pressed forth in the sequel to Chinese Communist interposition. Eventually, after
more than two years of exasperating battle and toilsome negotiations, hostilities were brought to abeyance, with the Chinese
still holding the positions gained by the action labeled as aggression and with the United Nations and the United States, here
interchangeable, willing to settle for a standoff. This set off a
baleful precedent for interpreting stalemates as achievements.
The foul-up over moving into North Korea and the subsequent
complication of issues by the Chinese entry had helped induce
another development within the United Nations—the neutralist
trend—with India as bellwether.

The second phase in development of the United Nations—
that of United States ascendancy and the direct confrontation of
Communist power—corresponded approximately to the tenure
of Trygve Lie as Secretary General. The beginning of a third

phase coincided more or less with Dag Hammarskjold's succession in 1953. This is not to imply a cause-and-effect relationship beyond the circumstance of the second Secretary General's celebrated talents and energy, characteristics conducive to accentuation of his office—a main trend of the period. A companion trend was a growing vogue of neutralism—its exponents prefer to call it nonalignment—within the organization. This in turn related to far-reaching changes in the membership concomitant with the rapid decline of the colonial order and the proliferation of new states in the close of the 1950's and the opening of the decade of the 1960's. All of these developments bore closely upon adaptations in the approaches both of the United States and the Soviet Union to the world organization. The complex of changing circumstances makes it not amiss to think of the period as that of the seventh League.

A comment on neutralism, or nonalignment, as a phenomenon of the period is fitting. Neutralism is distinguishable from neutrality as abstract nouns ending in *ism* are generally distinguishable from cognate terms ending in *ity*—as for example, moralism differs from morality or nationalism from nationality. The distinctions derive from differing degrees of self-consciousness, zeal, and desire to project. Neutrality denotes a policy of standing aside and withholding one's own power from the determination of outcomes. Neutralism is a way of pitching in, exercising power, and seeking scope—in sum, a cause. Like neutrality, however, it has to have a referent. About either abstraction a pertinent question is: with respect to what?

The new governments expanding in numbers within the United Nations in recent years are not indifferent on issues in general. They tend to be thoroughly committed, thoroughly aligned, on issues counted important to themselves. Their assumption of nonalignment pertains to a complex set of problems antedating their existence as national entities. These governments had no hand in their making. The problems involve questions of power and strategy foreign to their backgrounds. The understandable response is to wish to override them, to get them out of the way, to bring to the forefront of concern causes rooted in their more limited experience and attuned to their ambitions. Neutralism is not a way of standing in the wings but a way of pushing to the center of the stage. It generally reflects not a simple meekness but the sort of meekness expectant of inheriting the earth. A spokesman for one of the new African governments stated the case in a speech in the fifteenth General Assembly. Put in compressed form, his line of thought equated newness with inexperience, inexperience with innocence, innocence with purity, purity with righteousness, righteousness with rightness, and rightness with moral title to determine what should count in the world.

The cause typically closest to the hearts of new governments burgeoning in the United Nations is anti-colonialism—an attitude having affinity to anti-imperialism in terms of which the Soviet Union articulates its distrust, grievances, and ambitions toward the non-Communist world. On the other hand, the new states generally incline—at least in some parts of their discourse —toward viewing the United Nations as a body politic, attributing to it corporateness, a general will of its own, an authority inherent in the structure, a capacity to ordain beyond the strict letter of the Charter. It would be excessive to credit them with absolute consistency in this respect. Their endorsement of this view of the organization depends in some degree on their appraisal of the issue at hand in relation to their interests. In the degree of their adherence to the view, however, they tend to support the theory of the organization advocated by the United States rather than that maintained by the Soviet Union.

The stalemated outcome of the United Nations' military endeavor in Korea bears symbolic significance for the subsequent approach of the United States in relation to the organization increasingly weighted toward nonalignment. For a season this government voiced objections to the trend—exemplified in the late Secretary of State John Foster Dulles' abjuration of neutralism as immoral. The attitude still shows through in American discourse from time to time, but the policy of the government accepts, even as it came to accept in Mr. Dulles' tenure, neutralism as a force to be recognized as legitimate and to be turned to useful purposes where possible. In exceptional cases, as in the Soviet attack on Hungary in 1956, a requisite majority may be generated in favor of an expression of disapproval, as distinguished from action. In the main, the United States has settled for an attitude of "if you can't help me, then please don't help that bear." United States policy has discerned in the United Nations, gravitating toward a neutralist stance, a considerable utility in providing buffers between the great adversaries in the confrontation called the Cold War. This form of usefulness was exemplified in the United Nations' interpositions first in the Suez crisis of 1956, then in the Lebanon crisis of 1958, and again in the Congo crisis of 1960 and forward.

This concept has involved emphasis on two parts of the organization—the General Assembly as a collectivity preponderantly desirous of peace and the Secretary General as the executive arm of a discerned world community and an instrument of what has come to be called preventive diplomacy. A concept of an executive authority presupposes existence of some corporate entity or body politic on behalf of which to exercise such authority. The Charter contains no reference to executive authority. In Mr. Hammarskjold's case, such power was implicit in style, and the style was the man. Having a Secretary General with endowments for ministerial initiative fitting for a premier encouraged assumptions of the existence of an underlying body politic. In recent years the concept of executive authority in the Secretariat has appeared increasingly in United States discourse about the United Nations, and a like assumption of executive power was articulated in statements by the late Mr. Hammarskjold in the closing part of his tenure. In Karl Mannheim's perceptive generalization in *Ideology and Utopia*, "The fundamental tendency of all bureaucratic thought is to turn all problems of politics into problems of administration." In the shift of emphasis toward the United Nations Secretariat in this phase, the broad tendency remarked upon by Mannheim was abetted by a felt need for finding a path around political cleavages within the representative bodies of the organization. It was a case of enlarging administrative scope and construing executive attributes not on a basis of political consensus but in place of it—a reflection more of what is missing than of what is present in the world organization considered as a body politic.

As for the Soviet Union, its approach to the United Nations has appeared more subtle and resilient from 1953 onward. This change in tactics has sometimes been accounted for as a result of the passing of Josef Stalin and the advent of more flexible and resourceful leadership in Nikita Khrushchev, more inclined to take initiatives to mold opinion and to court favor in the exterior world. This personifying interpretation is probably too simple. It overlooks a number of important collateral circumstances. One of these circumstances was that economic recovery, accompanying political stabilization, and progress in the Atlantic Alliance had gradually made Central and Western Europe less subject to pressures of the palpable sort previously exercised by the Soviet Union. A second circumstance was the progressive modification of political relationships through the world with the breakup of empire and the emergence of numbers of new states, presenting both new problems and new opportunities for Soviet policy. An accompanying circumstance was the Soviet Union's success in getting over the worst of the tasks of recovery from the ravages of World War II and generating some capability for competing with the United States in economic assistance to the emerging countries. In other respects, too, the ascendency once enjoyed by the United States— so important as a factor underlying its challenged but unrivaled leadership within the United Nations in the preceding phase— had eroded. With progress in economic recovery elsewhere, exigency for United States assistance had lessened or ceased. To some extent amenability to leadership eased off with dependency for aid. Perhaps most importantly of all, United States monopoly in nuclear weapons was fading out.

The Soviet Union has never abated its juridic objections to the use of the General Assembly as arbiter on questions of legitimacy concerning peace and war. It has stuck to the letter of the Charter assigning authority in such concerns to the Security Council, subject to the Soviet Union's negative control as one of the permanent members. It has opposed consistently all tendencies to treat the United Nations as a body politic endowed with a mystique of inherent authority. In the Communist view the realization of a world community must be reserved for the time, still asserted to be within view and drawing closer, of a general triumph of the Communist outlook, purposes, and interests in world affairs. Only the Marxist-Leninist outlook has real legitimacy, in this view. Only a gathering of nations harnessed to this dogma could amount to a legitimate community by this tenet. A group of governments gathered together under the Charter's principles can be only a contingent rather than a final expression of the idea of community. Expression of executive power emanating from such a gathering is a presumption, unwarranted by the law of the Charter or the facts of historic development, in this view.

At the same time, the Soviet approach has been resilient with respect to dealing with the drifts and realities. The Communist leaders of eighty-one countries meeting in Moscow in the autumn of 1960, Nikita Khrushchev addressing Communist organizations of the Soviet Union in January of the following year, and the Twenty-second Party Congress in the next autumn all made articulate the Communist abjuration of neutralism, asserting a historic obligation and destiny of all nations to come at last into the Communist fold. This has not stood in the way of taking all possible advantage of the neutralist trend, exploiting it for support with customary Communist phrases inveighing against imperialism. While standing against the idea of inherent corporate authority in the General Assembly and the Secretariat, the Soviet Union has been intent upon ensuring against a possibility of having a requisite majority in the Assembly and the capacities of the Secretaryship brought to bear against Communist purposes and interests. This much it wants—the assurance that lies in being able always to count on the amenability of one-third plus one of the Assembly. Beyond that, Soviet policy aspires to pluralize the Secretary Generalship and to make its powers contingent upon agreement among three elements representing, respectively, Communist interests, avowedly non-Communist interests, and neutralism, thus to subject the office to the negative control that operates with respect to the Security Council.

This last proposition—commonly called the troika—projects another phase in world organization, a sort of eighth League. The proposition was formulated by the Soviet Union after dynamic events in the Congo for a time brought the late Secretary General athwart the line of Soviet purposes and interests. It was articulated vehemently by Premier Khrushchev at the General Assembly in 1960 but put in abeyance when the Soviet Union agreed late in 1961, after long delay, to the selection of U Thant of Burma to fill out the term left unfinished by Mr. Hammarskjold's death. The issue still hangs over the United Nations in its seventeenth year, counterpart in chronology to the year 1936 in the life of the predecessor organization.

The seventeenth year since origin finds the United Nations on surer footing, in certain measurable respects, than the League was twenty-six years before. The act of belonging has settled on the members. The fad—so troublesome in the League—of quitting under the spur of pique or convenience has not been manifested. Perturbation has occasionally led one member government or another to mutter about getting out, but none has ever given effect to the threat beyond ostentatious withdrawal of delegates from sessions. Stability of membership and, even more importantly, the burgeoning of new states attending the decline of the colonial order give the organization scope of membership never approached by the predecessor, though comparison is less impressive, because of the absence of the mainland Chinese, when made on a basis of proportions of world population spoken for. Bureaucracy has proliferated beyond anything dreamed of in League days. Magnitude of physical plant and bustle of activity exceed the experience of the predecessor. Yet the issue arising from projection into the United Nations of two antithetic sets of ideas concerning its future and the courses of world politics hangs over the world organization.

There remains something to be said about putting the issue in perspective. The issue tends to take on an appearance of compelling importance because it reflects contrasting basic ideas between a Soviet government disposed to interpret all world affairs in light of its dialectic and a United States inclined to see the United Nations as a reflection on a larger screen of some elements of national experience in the development of its federal system. The constitutional doctrine of implied powers has a loose counterpart in efforts to construe greater scope for the world organization. The American tradition of executive authority, including the constitutional doctrine of inherent power, has a psychological link to current interpretations of the role of the Secretary General.

One cannot dismiss as wholly illusory the urge to visualize a true body politic representing a world community. Success in any such course must depend less on logic than on what events may produce. If enough governments and peoples should be persuaded to accept and to abide by certain premises of public conduct expressed in the Charter and properly interpreted, then the idea will work—a conclusion pre-empted by use of the word *enough*. The rub is that *enough* would have to include the Soviet Union and, of course, Communist China as well in order to amount to a world community transcending the present divisions.

Even in face of the reality, significance, and depth of these divisions, it is appealing to some to fashion hopes of accommodation of more modest dimension—perhaps a community effective at least as to issues outside zones of confrontation between the major antagonists. How this might be done has been dwelt upon by Inis Claude, Jr., in an essay in a book titled *The United States and the United Nations*. It is scarcely fitting to describe Professor Claude as an enthusiast for this idea. "I am not sanguine about our prospects for convincing the Soviets in these matters," he says realistically. Nevertheless, he postulates a possibility of persuading the Soviet Union to greater amenability with respect to issues in such marginal situations. In dealing with such instances, he points out, "The Organization may (A) take pro-Western action; (B) take impartial, neutralizing action; (C) take no action at all; or (D) take pro-Soviet action. In general, our preference runs like this: A-B-C-D. The Soviet preference . . . runs in reverse: D-C-B-A." He takes for granted the incompatibility between the two sides of the confrontation with respect to extremes in the orders of preference. He focuses instead on the importance of the middle members— B and C. Much could be accomplished, he argues, by getting the Soviet Union to accept our order of preference, placing neutralizing action ahead of no action. The avenue recommended is that of "persuading the Soviet leaders that they have a stake in preventing the Cold War from getting so desperately out of hand that it might precipitate World War III, and in convincing them that the United Nations can function impartially in forestalling such aggravation. . . ."

The formula for abatement is based upon an interpretation of the confrontation as delimited rather than pervasive—an undemonstrated assumption. It also assumes that issues in marginal areas, if such areas exist, are significant as to the danger of letting the Cold War get out of hand. This seems to make them at once both marginal and central. These points of doubt, however, may be put aside for something more basic. The suggested approach entails persuading the Soviet Union to concede impartiality and authority to a consensus beyond its control—thereby giving up on the essence of its dialectical view of world affairs. This seems to me to amount to alleviating problems of the Cold War by construing them out of existence. What I should regard as most useful and important in Professor Claude's views is the idea of influencing the Soviet rulers by pressing upon their minds the follies and penalties of letting matters get out of hand. In this respect, he enters upon sound ground and puts our relationships to the adversary and to the United Nations into good perspective.

It is difficult for Americans, whether for or against it, to see the United Nations in proportion. This is so merely because of its physical presence. It stands far larger in the public life of the United States than in that of any other country. Its activities are concentrated at the originating terminals of United States communications—press, radio, and TV. This can be said of no other country. Its delegates congregate in our midst. The debates resound in our ears as in no others. In so far as it is a forum of propaganda, it acts upon Americans as on no others. The responsibilities of being host fall peculiarly upon this government. Concerning no other government would one be likely to hear, as here, references to a team of ambassadors operating at the United Nations. These circumstances add to the apparent dimensions of importance. It becomes easy to imagine the fateful questions all being centered at Forty-second Street and First Avenue.

The tendency is abetted by a disposition both of apologists and of critics to attribute more, for good or ill, to United Nations authorship than warranted by reality. Just as two decades ago it was easy to attribute immense evil consequences to the simple fact of our having stood aloof from the League, so now it comes easy to imagine that the world situation is either as bad as it is or else not a whole lot worse solely because of the existence of the United Nations. The United Nations gets blamed for military frustration in Korea. Actually the choice of settling for a standoff was primarily an American choice taken, however reluctantly, in full account of all the factors. The United Nations is credited with having stemmed the Communist thrust in Korea. Symbolically this can be asserted. Actually the action depended on our own national will to meet the challenge when it arose. The United Nations is often praised for unique virtue in providing facilities for confidential diplomatic approaches— notably the contact leading up to the Korean armistice talks— implicitly as if such contacts would not otherwise be possible, or as if such things had not occurred innumerable times before the origin of world organization.

The United Nations often is blamed for loosing floods of propaganda into channels of international politics and debasing the value of words in international affairs—tendencies well along before its creation and inherent in the development of modern communications. It is credited for having frustrated Communist designs in the Congo and having saved the world from something tantamount to the Spanish Civil War, whereas the determining factor seems clearly to have been logistical inaccessibility—a matter of enormous hindrance to the Russians in any case, given a will to contest them. The United Nations is praised for having brought about the surge of colonial peoples into independence and blamed for having thereby diluted the essence of responsibility through helping bring about too much independence too soon—but none can demonstrate that the collapse of the imperial-colonial structure would not have occurred in any event. All this adds up to what Senator Henry M. Jackson has expressed as "a tendency to believe the UN makes more history than it really does."

Alexander Dallin's wise words are in point: ". . . too much must not be anticipated or asked of the United Nations. . . . The UN can be expected to alter neither the fundamental power relations among states nor the motives of their rulers." This being so, the world organization will continue to be affected by forces of politics beyond its scope and control rather than being the determinant of those forces. Thus it has been for the decades since the beginning of the experiment. Thus it is likely to be for the calculable future. There will still be occasion for heeding Niccolò Machiavelli's advice: "That deliverance is of no avail that does not depend upon yourself; those only are reliable, certain, and durable that depend on yourself and your valor."

DÉTENTE: EFFECTS
ON THE ALLIANCE

THE ALLIANCE IN
THE PERSPECTIVE OF TRADITION.

Judged on the factor of expanse, the United States' security commitments have no match in history. This nation ranks pre-eminent among all as an undertaker of contractual obligations to protect others. Judging by measure of time, one gets a contrasting impression. Our engagements of this character have all taken form during roughly the most recent tenth of the nation's history—the first venture coming in 1947 with the establishment of the Organization of American States, the second two years later with the North Atlantic Treaty Organization, and thereafter a considerable proliferation, especially from 1953 on, with Secretary of State John Foster Dulles in his collector's phase.

A change so wide and drastic seems indubitably permanent when looked at from one point of view. Yet one wonders whether zeal may not have outdone itself in trying to make up for deferment and whether so vast a structure, put up so hurriedly, is likely to endure. Rather than trying to answer that question in general, I intend only to examine some of the considerations bearing on it in application to one range, the great-

From *Changing East-West Relations and the Unity of the West,* Arnold Wolfers (ed.) (Baltimore: Johns Hopkins, 1964).

Also from addresses delivered at Harvard University, Cambridge, Mass., on July 17, 1963, and at the University of Denver, Denver, Colo., on December 2, 1963.

est, of our commitments—the range engrossed by the North
Atlantic Treaty.

Tentatively—the reason for that modifier will become clear
as I proceed—I should describe the undertaking of that commitment in 1949 as the great watershed in United States diplomatic history. Others assign such pre-eminence, as a turning
point, to the decision made during World War II to commit the
United States to a world organization, namely the United Nations. It is worth taking a moment to distinguish basically between these two events: the one reflecting a hope for a pervading harmony of interest in world relations; the second—in such
close sequence—facing up to the fact of deep conflicts of purpose in the world and to a requirement of combining strength
with others to counter adversary intentions. In comparing them,
we may get some clues to the problems confronting the Atlantic
Alliance.

The idea—reflected in the United Nations—of a harmonized
world purged of power politics runs back in the American consciousness to a time even before the national foundation. It was
an American habit of long standing to look askance, as at something inherently reprehensible, upon any combination of interests
and purposes on a basis narrower than universal. The isolation-
ist attitude was rooted in a desire to stand apart from a divided
world—to avoid taking sides in rivalries and animosities. A
better sort of world was supposed to emerge someday, one
made up of nations brought to enlightenment concerning the
folly of enmities and opposed interests. The United States
would consent to full partnership then. Meanwhile, the Americans would stand aloof. What was wrong was not inclusive
partnership with others but exclusory partnership.

Woodrow Wilson's project for a League of Nations reflected
such a dream of all-embracing partnership. All nations were to
be eligible, once having established their qualifications by becoming self-governing—a term indicative of government accountable and representative as well as autonomous in the
Wilsonian lexicon. A peaceful ethic would be generated by the
partnership—and woe to any nation defying it. The wayward

one would be borne down upon by the others in retribution. It would be impossible to identify any malefactor, and therefore to plan concerted action, in advance. In event of a transgression, however, the collectivity, rallying to the side of the offended party, would make up its mind what to do to prevent or to redress evil. Collective security is the name for this concept—a principle entailing a commitment of every government to take whatever action necessary against any nation whatever found transgressing in whatever circumstances.

Within modest limits, the scheme as embodied in the League seemed to work for a time. Upon my entry into the study of international relations, a little more than a third of a century ago, the theme prevailing in relevant literature was of the new light emanating over the world from Geneva. Europe, at last and at least, with some collaboration from abroad, was said to be setting an example of reason, mutuality, and authority in intergovernmental relations, and the model was presumably slated to win universal emulation. As an underlying reality, that historic collaboration of the powerful known as the Concert of Europe was temporarily back in operation. This circumstance provided the light. The League apparatus only reflected it. In face of small problems of order the League seemed efficacious. With Europe riven again, and with great problems to be dealt with, the idea inevitably proved evanescent.

Having been principal protagonist, the United States had led the way in renouncing the League. The failure to join, leaving that collectivity to make its eventually futile way without the Americans, became strongly imprinted on the national consciousness as a default against our own interest as well as against the world's welfare—especially so after the advent of another general war following only two decades of surface tranquility. The League project was revived, brought up to date, and reincarnated as the United Nations in late stages of that second world war, this time with a contrite United States as a committed, hopeful, and enthusiastic leading member.

Though much like the League in some respects, the new venture differed in others. It was premised on an expectation of continuity, as a basis for an enduring peace, of the coalition prevailing in the war. Issues regarding conditions of peace over the globe would be handled by a Security Council inclusive of the principal elements of the victorious combination—namely, the United States, the Soviet Union, the United Kingdom, France, and China—as permanent participants. In essence the scheme involved applying on a world scale an analogue to the historic Concert of Europe, with great powers joining hands to guide lesser ones, to restrain irresponsibles, and to tranquilize the Balkans wherever located. Resolving and acting in unison, the permanent members would presumably dispose power enough to pacify the world, but under the organization's rules this power was to be checked and mitigated by a requirement of concurrence by two of a quota of six other and lesser governments taking turns as members.

It was a collective security system of sorts—with central direction, calculable resources, and a presumed capacity to make joint plans for meeting contingencies—a collective security arrangement with teeth, in a phrase of art. Like the Concert of Europe, the scheme depended on a huge prerequisite—that of unanimity among its major elements, and in particular between the pre-eminent two, in this case the United States and the Soviet Union.

Hope, however, had apparent grounds even beyond that optimism perennially disposed to discern a dawn of universal reason. In confrontation with common foes, the major elements had had experience in disposing political, military, and economic power to agreed ends. Repeatedly agreement between the United States and the Soviet Union had proved determinative, and the others had been impelled to go along. Problems of handling erstwhile enemies would provide an irreducible necessity of continued collaboration. The agony of war, moreover, was believed to have been enough to drive the world sane. Ideologies were supposed to have burned out under the searing effect of battle. Concurrence in seeing the ultimate folly of risking another such holocaust would provide a solvent for animosities and impel the leading members to work together as allies.

With no longer a common foe to confront in battle, the assumed unity proved to be a fragile reality. At once cracks began to show in the foundation. Relations with ex-enemy countries, notably Germany, gave rise to divisive issues rather than unifying interests. Improvisation has saved the organization, but the original design for the Security Council has not been fulfilled in practice.

Following disappointment in this second venture to organize peace globally, the United States' policy has had to adapt to a view of possibilities more finite than the dream of a universal solution. It has done so without retreating to a simple and circumscribed view of responsibility like the one reinvoked in the sequel to World War I. The venture has involved reconciliation to a role as a leading protagonist in a deep and persistent contest of and the putting aside of a traditional inhibition about alliances—a part of the national psyche reaching back to a time when Americans, as yet colonial subjects of the Crown, were anxious both to enjoy protection åfforded by British power and to avoid embroilment in the mother country's quarrels and rivalries.

Among terms associated with international affairs, *alliance* is a good way from being the most precise. In eighteenth-century usage the term broadly denoted an arrangement for mutual benefit and limited participation among states.[1] Later usage narrowed its meaning to a contract between or among governments more or less explicitly obliging at least one of them to use military force beyond its own domain, under certain defined contingencies which indicate the purpose and scope of the obligation, against an adversary or adversaries, whether or not specified, external to the undertaking. One might appropriately apply the term in this sense to the organized unity among permanent members of the Security Council predicated in the Charter as the foundation for universal collective security. An alliance thus conceived as a central frame of collaboration in ministering a world assumed to be basically harmonious well

[1] Felix Gilbert, *To the Farewell Address* (Princeton: Princeton University Press, 1961), pp. 44–45.

suits an old American dream. Combinations against adversaries in a tense and contentious world are a quite different matter. Alliance in this version is alliance undiluted, alliance in the balance-of-power motif, alliance charged with perplexities warned against in Washington's and Jefferson's famous admonitions to America.

At the inception of the subject Alliance, most of the countries concerned across the Atlantic were only beginning to rally from the depletions of war and the indignities of occupation. Their public life had suffered impairment. Their economies still faltered. Their military establishments were in bad order or, in some cases, even virtually nonexistent. A formidable Soviet military presence, which held mastery over Eastern Europe and pushed well into Central Europe, pressed heavily upon them. The Communist attachment of Czechoslovakia by coup stood fresh in their minds as an example of what they might expect in event of having to face Soviet power alone. The Berlin blockade demonstrated the intransigence of Soviet designs. The internal programs of indigenous Communist parties indicated the extent of adversary intentions.

With U.S. assistance, these countries were just under way in a combined effort of economic rehabilitation. The corollary of a common effort in military security followed as logically as the idea of a fence goes along with the idea of a cornfield. A purely European combination—exemplified in the Brussels Pact of 1948 among the United Kingdom, France, Belgium, the Netherlands, and Luxembourg—simply did not add up to enough to do the job, for it only combined factors of weakness. An arrangement of mutual defense—one spanning the Atlantic and embracing initially the United States, Canada, Iceland, the United Kingdom, Norway, Denmark, Belgium, the Netherlands, Luxembourg, France, Italy, and Portugal—followed in natural course. The fundamental character of the shift from striving to organize peace on a basis of world concord to trying to realize and to protect it by regional combinations was obscured, however, in the United States government's appreciation and interpretation of its own actions.

True enough, the scheme in the Charter had not panned out —the circumstance accounting for the new undertakings. "Whenever a powerful minority repudiates the basic principles and uses the procedures to accomplish directly contrary purposes or to frustrate the organization, then obviously it will not work as intended," Secretary of State Dean Acheson explained in the hearings on the North Atlantic Treaty. This, however, was no reproach to the concept—a sound fraternity with, alas, some bad brothers in it. The Secretary's rationalization dealt with the United Nations as a mechanism rather than a society. The machine was ideal, irreproachable. The whole fault was in wayward hands put to the wheel.[2] The dream was valid in every respect save relation to reality.

To explain regional defense as an auxiliary to, rather than a substitute for, universal collective security, much was made of Article 51 of the Charter itself as a provision countenancing regional defensive pacts and of parallels of language concerning goals contained in the respective basic documents. These links to the Charter were cited in answer to a Senator who sought rebuttal of charges "that this is a military alliance" and assurance against any similarity to "balances of power and things like that in the old world . . . commonly denominated military alliances." [3]

The United States' representative to the United Nations, Warren R. Austin, labored the denial with considerable explicitness:

I have been asked whether the North Atlantic Treaty is not the resumption of the practice of setting up a power equilibrium. . . . My answer is "No."

The ancient theory of balance of power lost its potential utility through the voluntary association of states, on the basis of sovereign equality and universality. The old veteran, balance of power, was given a blue discharge when the

[2] *North Atlantic Treaty: Hearings before the Committee on Foreign Relations, United States Senate, 81st Congress, First Session* (Washington: Government Printing Office, 1949), p. 7.
[3] *Ibid.*, p. 14.

United Nations was formed. The undertakings of the peoples of the United Nations to combine their efforts through the international organization to maintain international peace and security, and to that end, to take effective collective measures, introduced formally the element of preponderance of power for peace. And out went old man balance of power.[4]

Reaffirming a view that "Military alliances are not in the tradition of the United States," the Secretary of Defense, Louis Johnson, described the North Atlantic undertaking as "not a foreign military alliance in the customary sense." This denial, representing an attempt by officials to assure themselves as well as the public against the fearsome idea of acting in a mode from the bad old world instead of the good new one, was a recurring theme in the exposition. The olden and alien alliances, as to which the new project was presented in favorable contrast, were not specified or analyzed. The substance of the distinction was left unclear.

All split hairs notwithstanding, the North Atlantic Treaty was, and remains, a design for maintaining security by working on and combining factors of armed power within an exclusory scope. In Secretary Johnson's own words:

> From the military viewpoint, the basic objectives of the collective defense system are to deter war and to attain maximum military effectiveness in war, if war cannot be prevented. The North Atlantic Treaty will form a basis for improving United States security by improving the military potential of all the member nations. This potential will be improved in terms of collective action as well as individual armed strength.[5]

An obligation to respond in event of attack on any party in its homeland or in insular positions in the North Atlantic was made pervasive and explicit upon each member. Each was left

[4] *Ibid.*, p. 97.
[5] *Ibid.*, p. 146.

free to determine its own response. The principle of collaboration in strategic preplanning was avowed and institutionalized, however, among members not equal in potential—some contributing significant positions rather than appreciable manpower or other deployable military resources. The strategic anchor was the United States' monopoly of nuclear weapons, then deliverable solely by bombers. Of a relatively rudimentary type, these weapons were numerous enough for inflicting huge damage though not enough for annihilating the enemy establishment in event of general war. The cover afforded by their capacity for retaliation was extended to the selected parts of Europe as well as North America. This capability was to be supplemented by conventional forces generated mainly in Europe, with some American subvention, to provide a respectable impediment to attack from the East. Operational facility was to be enhanced by drawing the participant lands together into one area for planning, maneuver, and operations.

The European participants were thus to be restored in confidence by being assimilated into a strategic going concern—by knowledge of having now, westward across the Atlantic, a reserve area of great potential—while the United States in turn added great depth to its territorial defenses. The aim was redress with respect to capabilities for bringing force to bear and the reassuring and intimidatory effects of these capabilities on friends and adversaries. Even a Humpty Dumpty might find it difficult to make words reflect a significant differentiation between this focus and the balance-of-power concept.

Besides revealing an inhibition about departing from tradition, the asserted distinctions between the new undertakings and old-time alliances, examined in context, reflect a purpose to disavow belligerent intentions and to stress peaceable aims. The Alliance was originated to support peace in a minimal sense—meaning absence of destructive use of force—and to save participating governments from the baleful necessity of having to choose between submission and hostilities. Beyond that aim, the Alliance was conceived also as a step toward peace in its broader sense of a reliable legitimate order—meaning a disposition of authority and jurisdiction enjoying general acknowledgment of its rightfulness and enabling all affected by it to feel confident of its unchallenged continuation into a long calculable future.

The Alliance was to do its work in this last respect by laying a basis for bringing the adversary to an accommodating disposition in a prolonged process of conversion. Confronted by situations of strength, in the prevailing phrase of art, Communist power would presumably be rendered amenable eventually to settled arrangements compatible with outside interests—that is to say, the United States' and its allies'. The Communist side was to be persuaded by irreducible realities to see matters in perspectives which had been hopefully attributed to the Soviet regime in the engrossing design for an enduring peace developed in World War II and embodied in the Charter. Thus the Alliance would fulfill its purpose by remedying the conditions giving rise to it. By frustrating the adversary, it would transform him. These goals inherently involve a question of how—by whom and in accord with what criteria—to decide when they have been reached.

As part of the supreme law of the land in the United States the Alliance was given place along with a quite distinguishable scheme for establishing security on a chimerical basis of a global concert of power. Rapport and collaboration between the great powers of the Atlantic area, especially the United States and the Soviet Union, were conditions necessary to realization of the global concert. The absence of these conditions was what necessitated the regional Alliance. The obligations entailed by the latter undertaking, however, were made absolute only for a term of twenty years—this in deference to the United States' preference as distinguished from the European allies' wish for a fifty-year period [6]—so that any member may leave on a year's notice from 1969 on. In contrast, the Charter has no terminal date. The solid, measurable reality was thus made contingent, whereas the dream was made enduring.

[6] *Ibid.*, p. 87.

THE ALLIANCE'S COURSE
WITH RESPECT TO REGIONAL SECURITY.

Three states of mind, broadly speaking, are relevant in measuring the avail of the Alliance as a military undertaking for preserving peace in its minimal sense—the putative opponent's, our allies', and then our own. Confidence on our side is a function of doubt on the Communist side, where, obversely, the estimate of opportunity varies in proportion to disbelief among the allies in the efficacy of the Alliance. All parties concerned must go through a sort of continuous notional warfare involving calculation of interrelationships among these states of mind. The United States' primary concern necessarily focuses on adversary estimates, because basically the other side holds the franchise on the question of success or failure of the deterrent design. Yet this adversary's estimate is inseparable from calculation of will within and among Alliance members. This brings us to the relationship between the concept of deterrence and strategy—two aspects of the same matter. The deterrent design is to render unlikely the occasion for having to put the military strategy to a test. Deterrence can work only on a basis of high estimate of the effectiveness of the strategy in event of a failure of its primary aim of deterrence. Thus, one is not excused from burdens of military analysis by hope of never having to test relevant capabilities against adversary forces.

In the instance of the Atlantic Alliance, these rudimentary considerations are complicated by certain characteristics of contemporary weaponry, which does not quite match anything in other and more familiar lines of experience. Analogies recurringly drawn between the deterrent-strategic link and poker, football, or the operations of fire departments, and so on, never quite fit. Even the now familiar metaphor about deadly scorpions coexisting in a bottle is inadequate. The problems must be understood in their own terms. The novel problems in calculation revolve around the prodigious destructive capabilities of contemporary weapons of top-level potential, their instant readiness, and great radius of feasible delivery. Effects and counter-effects cannot be tested in experience. There is no really adequate way of running maneuvers with them. So men are left to compute and to theorize about them.

Computation and theorizing, moreover, must struggle with problems arising from an enormous and continuous multiplication of offensive power—that is, of prodigious capabilities in contemporary specialized weapons for destruction in carrying on attack as distinguished from suitability for interdicting attack. The advantage of the offensive over the defensive was a primary feature of World War II in contrast to World War I. With the release of the first two atomic weapons the trend rose drastically higher. It has been that way ever since—with a consequence of unprecedented degrees and an unprecedented range of anxiety in international affairs. Until and unless some way of redressing the imbalance—enabling defensive power to shorten the gap—is achieved, the easier sort of relative stability experienced in past epochs will remain beyond reach. Each side in the great confrontation is aware of possibilities of reaping great advantage by being first to develop techniques for nullifying the other side's offensive power while holding on to its own absolute offensive capability. Each side must also be aware of the vital importance of keeping up with the other in this respect and of finding ways figuratively to flank any temporarily efficacious defensive technique developed by the opponent.

Meanwhile, the pre-eminent adversaries in the competition have to rely primarily on weapons intrinsically unsuitable to defensive operations in that they can only be turned against an adversary's homeland and are of no use for intercepting attack—in contrast to the double capabilities for attacking and for warding off attack generally characteristic of weaponry in other epochs. Neither side can feel confident of escaping ruinous damage. Each relies for security on inculcating a like consciousness in the other. I wish neither to deplore nor to celebrate these factors but only to trace their unfolding effects on the Atlantic Alliance.

The assumption initially reflected in Alliance strategy was to prove highly impermanent. Two fairly close occurrences overturned them. The first was the Soviet Union's achievement of capability in atomic fission in the latter part of 1949, considerably ahead of the time anticipated on this side. The second was the launching of an attack southward across the 38th parallel against the Republic of Korea in June of 1950—a portentous occurrence followed by less than a year the notable aggrandizement of Communist dominion in the winning of mainland China. The Soviet atomic achievement brought into close prospect an end to the United States' monopoly of prodigious weapons and opened a prospect, moreover, of early Soviet progress in weaponry of hugely greater potential, namely the hydrogen weapon. The implications of the second event seem less certain in retrospect—a point worth a moment's consideration.

Unequivocal advance assurances of protection had not been given South Korea. Accordingly, some would emphasize, Communist willingness to use force in testing for opportunity to establish dominion over that area and to reunite Korea under Communist aegis did not necessarily betoken a disposition to defy protective guarantees respecting other regions. According to this line of argument, the United States reacted excessively to the challenge in Korea, and the drastic responses undertaken with respect to Atlantic defenses were uncalled for. The argument is not convincing, and hindsight is not always a better judge than the insight of a crucial moment. The potential for erosion of confidence in Europe in the wake of the attack in Korea seemed enormous and menacing, though its actuality and extent would have been verifiable only under conditions of a failure to take compensatory measures. I venture—and no one is entitled to a more assertive verb with respect to a question of what would have happened if the things that really happened had not happened—that if a stand had not been made in Korea, a sharp, and perhaps determinative, turn for the worse in the Atlantic framework would have been unavoidable.

The Korean War provided an occasion and a stimulus, but

the need for revaluation and revision of strategy was derived
from now manifest Soviet progress in the nuclear field, for under contemporary conditions a sudden advance in invention
tends to reverberate in the same way a seizure of strategic territory did in past epochs. As custodian of the strategic anchor,
the United States decided to press on with development of a still
more prodigious weapon array in the hydrogen fusion bomb and
with improvements in delivery systems and in techniques for
early warning of attacks directed against the American position,
lest determinative advantages should fall to the Soviet Union.
Within the framework of the Alliance proper a number of important steps were proposed, with variant results.

One step was establishment of a supreme and engrossing
military command structure to provide the Alliance greater
coherence in plans and operations. This was done. A second
step was inclusion of Greece and Turkey, so as to add important positions and manpower resources and to give the Alliance
scope on the southern flank through the eastern Mediterranean.
This was done. A third step concerned deployment of sizeable
American conventional forces in Europe to serve as an increment of posted strength, to encourage the European participants to marshal will for greater effort, and, most importantly,
to provide hostages as an earnest, to adversary and allies, of the
absoluteness of the American commitment to European security. This was done. Fourth was conversion of occupied West
Germany into a participant in the Alliance and its councils as a
military resource rather than a liability. After long and futile
dalliance with the intricate concept of a supranational European
army, this was finally done—subject to conditions subordinating
all West German forces to the Alliance's command and barring
West Germany from domestic manufacture of certain types of
sensitive weapons, including nuclear. The fifth item called for
more military contributions by other European principals. This
was debated, resolved about, hedged, and, in final analysis,
not really done. The propensity of togetherness for promoting
big talk is well known. Collective frameworks almost invariably

tempt governments into declaratory intentions far in excess of their wills to perform. With respect to this last item, the Alliance proved no exception.

A third phase in Alliance history opened with a decision in 1954 to substitute tactical nuclear weapons—under United States possession and control—for increments of manpower at the European bulwarks, a development logically in keeping with a concurrent phase in American military policy of preoccupation with trying to load missions onto prodigious weaponry, a phase identified by such phrases as "the new look" and "more bang for a buck."

The next phase is, broadly speaking, one still in progress in 1964. The technical developments bringing it about were cumulative. Soviet achievement of hydrogen weapons was revealed as early as 1953—even a little ahead of the United States. Conjecturally, the realization of this capability was accompanied by advances in bomber developments adding a portion of danger for the United States. Dire portents of the trend, however, rose signally in men's consciousness after the launching of Sputnik in 1957, with its corollary implication of missile systems capable of vaulting warning networks and outracing interception. Strategically, in this phase the United States has been brought unequivocally within the target area. This circumstance affords considerable potential leverage to the adversary. Theoretically, in event of full-scale war, the Soviet Union would have an option between directing its attack on the United States while sparing Europe or vice versa. Thereby a considerable doubt is engendered, a doubt repeatedly denied and allayed but still persistent in many minds.

The United States' current emphasis is on laying a basis for plausible conduct of hostilities in event of war. This calls for non-nuclear strength sufficient to make a contest, at least for a while, in event of an attack in kind; a reserve of tactical nuclear weapons to enable our side to raise combat to that level if necessary, a strategic array of nuclear strength capable of gravely and decisively impairing the adversary's retaliatory nuclear capability in event of our being forced to take initiative in that kind of strategic war; and, finally, a further nuclear capability to inhibit adversary nuclear initiatives through its power to inflict unacceptable retaliatory damage. This strategy would make Central and Western Europe, in extremity, an area to be fought over—a dour prospect for peoples and governments of the area.

One must refer back to the 1954 decision—prompted by frugality rather than strategic theory—to deploy tactical nuclear weapons to Europe. Men are impelled to bridge, one way or another, between theory and practice. By the concept eventually fashioned in this instance, the big thing was not to fight a war rationally, in event of having to fight one at all, but to forestall war altogether, an aim to be served more convincingly by nuclear weapons for the battlefield, with an implicit threat of immediately having to raise the level of combat to prodigious heights, than by an increment of men and weapons of lower potential. By an opposite argument, a prospect of having to go at once to such drastic and unknowledgeable lengths of destruction might more readily paralyze one's own resolve than deter a challenger. Whatever the merits, the former line of hypothesis has taken firm hold among the European allies. Their preference is for a strategy to obviate even a small calculable probability of ever having to be employed: a strategy involving high probability of an early nuclear exchange in event of hostilities and, as an implicit corollary, a high probability of making the United States, in dire event, the adversary's prime target.

Whether the United States would honor its commitments is a question basic to the North Atlantic Alliance, for any answer short of a firm affirmative would fail of the necessary degree of deterrence to the adversary and of assurance to partners. The United States' six divisions remain in West Germany as a concrete guarantee supporting the pledge of involvement in event of attack from the east. Their presence crowds the restricted maneuver areas of West Germany, so that the latter government must shop around in France, Spain, and even Scotland for room to train its soldiery. It reflects no military necessity, for troops of equivalent number would be readily enough deployable to scenes of action in extremity. The United States' forces are there to foreclose any presumption of a possibility of default. The U.S. is at a loss as to how to withdraw or even substantially to reduce them without weakening that assurance. Yet their presence seems to inhibit additions of conventional strength among European participants fearful of hastening the day of withdrawal—and thereby precipitating a detraction from the assurance—by providing substitute forces.

The United States' commitment remains pre-eminent as a factor in the military efficacy of the Alliance. The deployment of forces to substantiate warnings against transgression is in one direction—from west to east—across the Atlantic, and the nuclear resources essential to sustain the defenses are under United States ownership and control. The arrangements are inherently asymmetrical, with the United States, as from the beginning, in the role of main and essential determiner of Alliance strategy. This special role, with its related prerogatives and burdens, has been a source of recurring tensions within the Alliance, but the issues have not impinged upon the integrity of the strategic structure. Whatever its unresolved differences, the Alliance has worked and continues to work as a military undertaking. The continuous exercise in notional warfare has sustained the allies' confidence; the unremitting query as to the probable character and course of hypothetical war, on a basis of factors presumably apparent to the adversary, has brought an assuring answer of the improbability of real war.

Because of its inherent preventive character, one cannot prove the effects of the Alliance. We shall never be able to ascertain, but can only conjecture, the course of events that would have obtained in the absence of such an alliance. How far the compact may have stayed adversary purposes, what desperate straits may have been averted, are questions susceptible of no proof. The past does not reveal its alternatives. This observation bears on a recurrent fallacy, which I have sometimes heard in high places. By this fallacy, dire possibilities which one has anticipated and taken pains to ward off and which thereupon failed to materialize were never really in the cards anyway—like counting the hire of a watchman as needless because, in all his time on the job, no thief has come in the night.

THE LINGERING PROBLEM OF ACCOMMODATION WITH THE ADVERSARY.

Unlike history, policy does not subsist on the past. Whatever its accomplishments up to now in marshaling force to forefend against war and its intimidatory shadow, the Alliance is troubled and its future clouded. Doubts and difficulties pertain both to defining conditions for a settled legitimate order in succession to the menacing confrontation which gave rise to the Alliance, and to determining the frame of authority for defining those conditions. These problems, involving questions of value and the locus of decision and falling, therefore, in the catchall category called political, have a bearing on the future cogency of the Alliance as a military undertaking.

The factors of difference between the obvious successes and the apparent frustrations in the Alliance's record pertain in an elementary way to the degree of the Alliance's autonomy with respect to problems concerned and, conversely, to the degree and character of response required from the Communist side. Even the minimal aim of forefending against war and related intimidatory gestures is contingent, obviously, on decisions and actions taken on the Communist side. Reluctant or otherwise, Communist compliance in desisting from the launching of force is a condition necessary to success. The power of decision in supplying means of insuring this compliance, however, in so far as marshaling of force and manifestation of will can serve to insure it, lies with the Alliance members.

The Alliance enjoys no such autonomy with respect to achieving peace, conceived as a pervasive and reliable legitimate order. Settled arrangements reflecting reciprocal confidence and assent would be necessary constituents of success in this purpose. Such arrangements would have to be contractual in form and spirit. Explicit mutual steps would have to be negotiated. The course would be contingent upon Communist—specifically Soviet—intentions in every phase.

The idea of coming to terms with the Soviet adversary over relevant issues of dominion, jurisdiction, and security respecting Europe, far from having been neglected, has been a focus of diplomatic interchanges of unmatched thoroughness and persistence dating back to World War II. The protracted exercises have got no closer to substance than exploring possibilities of negotiating about points of substance, with each side testing notional alternatives to the confrontation, without as yet achieving agreement. Concerning conceptual possibilities for settlement, as distinguished from calculable probabilities, the redundant negotiations about negotiating have only confirmed in experience what should be inferable by logic.

The possibilities—four in number, two of them with one side prevailing and the other giving in, and the other two reflecting stalemate—are: retraction of Soviet power in acquiescence to the Alliance and to the United States' interposition in Europe; withdrawal of United States power and thus liquidation of the Alliance with Soviet sway left undiminished; reciprocal retraction of United States and Soviet power; and indefinite continuation of present alignments with both sides reconciled and assured of reciprocity.

Deliberately designed and documented changes are not the only ones possible. The pattern, as I am aware, might be changed by unraveling as well as through planned intention. Here, however, discussion is focused on the idea of coming to terms—not that of losing control. The aim is to examine the entailments for a settled order encompassing Europe and to examine, as well, how these entailments bear on problems confronting the Alliance. Whatever their content, such arrangements, if validly realized, would signify conditions amounting to a renewal of the Concert of Europe in some form. The conditions would presumably be susceptible of being extended from Europe, as a base, to the world in general and would provide, at least in concept, a workable foundation for a collective security system as predicated in the Charter. As a postulate—one can scarcely assert it as a fact—arrangements settled on in Europe would be reflected globally. Retraction of Soviet power accompanied by Soviet acquiescence in United States interposition in Europe would indicate a Soviet disposition to accommodate everywhere. Unilateral United States withdrawal from the confrontation, leaving the adversary position intact, would signal a disposition to knuckle under in general. Reciprocal retraction of United States and Soviet power from the European arena would signify an easing of opposed purposes in other theaters. Mutual reconciliation along present lines would similarly project as a sort of tired standoff elsewhere.

Beyond a purpose to avoid an outcome leaving Soviet power intact and triumphant in Europe, and beyond what may be construed from the twenty-year span of obligation, the treaty gives no clues to the character, timing, and other circumstances of the hoped-for easement. Whether the Alliance should continue in effect afterwards or be phased out as a condition thereto—a matter obviously beyond the Alliance members' autonomous power to ordain—is not specified. Hope is pinned on nothing more definite than promoting—to borrow George Kennan's phrase—"tendencies which must eventually find their outlets in either the breakup or the gradual mellowing of Soviet power." [7]

The advent of the Eisenhower administration produced, besides the military modification noted, an attempt to bring about a more specific political focus, with *liberation* the watchword and Secretary of State John Foster Dulles the articulator:

> What we need to do is recapture to some extent the kind of crusading spirit of the early days when we were darn sure that what we had was a lot better than what anybody else had. We knew the rest of the world wanted it, and needed it, and that we were going to carry it around the world. . . .[8]

[7] George F. Kennan, *American Diplomacy, 1900–1950* (Chicago: University of Chicago Press, 1951), p. 127.

[8] John Robinson Beal, *John Foster Dulles* (New York: Harper, 1957), p. 310.

Soviet power would retreat. As to means of compelling this outcome, "Those who don't believe results can be achieved by moral pressure, by the weight of propaganda, don't know what they are talking about," Mr. Dulles told Senators at his pre-confirmation hearing.[9] Less than four years later, the United States and its allies, short of will and appropriate capabilities, stood by during the episode of Hungary and drew consolation from moral condemnations and an exercise known as mobilizing forces of world opinion, and the season closed on the Dulles prescription for liberation.

Attempts at settlement and accommodation, however, were not foreclosed by the verbal devotion to a liberation strategy characteristic of the Eisenhower tenure. These were pursued in a series of ministerial meetings, produced one tangible result in the Austrian State Treaty, and engendered two seasons of general, superficial promise in connection with direct encounters at the supreme level of authority at Geneva in 1955 and then at Camp David in 1959. Prospects glowed in discussions focused on generalities of peace and good intention but faded at contact with specifics. The contradictions of parleying about peace while prosecuting opposed purposes set the stage for a grand anticlimax, at Paris in the spring of 1960, involving a Soviet Prime Minister in dudgeon, an American President in wordless distress, a British Prime Minister in tears, a French President in preoccupied contemplation, and all four in predicament. The quest was suspended thereupon to await a changeover in Washington.

Achievements, officially asserted, from the resumption and reinvigoration of efforts toward accommodation during subsequent years include installation of a Moscow-Washington teletype link for quick communication in dire emergency, a nuclear test-ban treaty, agreement in principle on law for outer space, joint acceptance of a United Nations' resolution banning weap-

---

[9] *Nomination of John Foster Dulles, Secretary of State-Designate, Hearings before the Committee on Foreign Relations, United States Senate, 83rd Congress, First Session* (Washington: Government Printing Office, 1953), p. 6.

ons in orbit, suspension of Soviet jamming of the Voice of America, a transaction for sales of wheat to the Soviet Union, and concurrent decisions by the two governments for proportionate reductions in production of uranium and plutonium for nuclear weapons—with additional progress claimed in negotiations toward a consular convention and a new cultural exchange program.[10] One's appraisal of the extrinsic significance of such a list is likely to turn on one's inclination as between interpreting events in light of hopes and construing expectations by measuring events.

The test-ban treaty serves as an example of relevant ambiguity. By it, in Senator Fulbright's hopeful interpretation, "each side in effect assured the other that it was prepared to forego, at least for the present, any bid for a decisive military or political breakthrough." [11] A contrasting interpretation would stress the perseverance on each side in testing to a point of marginal utility before the shutdown. It would stress the failure to include in the agreement the one environment requiring on-site inspection as a means of verification and involving, therefore, a point of difference basic to issues in the confrontation with the Soviet Union. Such an interpretation would emphasize, also, the inclusion of terms for abrogation of the agreement at the convenience and discretion of the parties—something like a marriage contract with a protocol for divorce—a point justifying a purist in regarding the undertaking as a treaty only in name.

So it goes with the other items. Equipment for instant communication does not affect substance to be communicated. Agreement on law for outer space is marginal to agreement on legitimacy in Europe and over the globe itself. An orbital-weapon ban forecloses something not yet known to be feasible and probably redundant strategically. The Voice of America permitted to be heard, for the time being, is bland. The wheat deal mainly serves, at a subsidized price, to succor the Soviet Union from consequences of improvident policies and has no impact

[10] *Washington Post and Times-Herald*, January 3 and April 21, 1964; Press Release No. 328, American Embassy, Bonn, February 18, 1964.
[11] *New York Times*, March 26, 1964.

whatever on the Soviet Union's use of exterior trade as an instrument of politics and strategy. The announced reductions in uranium and plutonium increments are like swearing off on third helpings of ice cream. I should concur with Hans Morgenthau's estimate: "None of these . . . changes has any bearing on the substance of the cold war, while only one of them bears upon its modalities, and in a way . . . detrimental to the interests of the United States." [12]

Official discourse concedes the smallness of the steps taken, but alleges great portent: "Small steps . . . worth taking because we may find them to be the key to larger ones," according to the Secretary of State.[13] Thus—to quote Morgenthau again —does policy "search for the swallow which will make a summer." The assumptions and attitudes reflected in the pressing of negotiations are ones long established in the American approach to world affairs: a habit of extolling peace in tones of invoking policy, a postulate of basic harmony of interest among all nations derived from a common stock of reason, and faith in transforming issues by talking them over—a concept of an inherent efficacy of negotiation as an avenue for finding agreement. The mystique of negotiation has been summed up by a spokesman for United States foreign policy:

> The essence of a normal business transaction is that each party, from his own point of view, makes a gain. There is no reason why, with proper caution and much patience, we cannot arrive at agreement of this kind with the Soviet Union.[14]

The hope in which such attitudes converge is that of achieving détente. Circumstances abetting such hope include the current style of Soviet discourse under Premier Nikita Khrushchev's spokes-

[12] Hans Morgenthau, "Peace in Our Time?," *Commentary*, March, 1964, p. 67.
[13] *Washington Post and Times-Herald,* January 3, 1964.
[14] Press Release No. 328, Embassy of the United States, Bonn, February 18, 1964.

manship, deepening cleavage between the Soviet Union and China, and cumulation of nuclear striking power in American and Soviet possession. Brief elaboration and analysis of each of these circumstances is fitting.

Notwithstanding George Kennan's appeal to Americans not to be "put off by the angularities of Mr. Khrushchev's personality," [15] the subject personage's peasant rotundity gives an essentially subtle operator an advantage of not appearing subtle at all. An item in the Khrushchev armory is his custom of parading every purpose, however inimical, as peaceable. His success in winning wide acceptance, as a synonym for accommodation, of his favored formulation of the Soviet version for peace— peaceful coexistence—epitomizes his accomplishment in attracting attention to the block letters, and away from the fine print, of Soviet intentions. Remarks by the Secretary of State, in a dour phase of his alternation between somber and bright outlooks on world affairs, put a proper measure on the protestations of peaceful purpose:

> No one has to convince us that when Khrushchev said communism will bury us he was proclaiming not just an alleged historic inevitability but an objective toward which Communists work relentlessly by all means they deem effective. No one has to convince us that peaceful coexistence means to them a continuing attempt to spread their system over the earth by all means short of the great war that would be self-defeating. No one has to convince us that the contest . . . is for keeps.[16]

The quarrel between Moscow and Peking is rated as a windfall in coping with Communist power—a factor to temper Soviet intransigence if not to convert the adversary to amicability for all practical purposes. In a manner recently exemplified by the Secretary of State, these assumptions may be projected to

[15] George F. Kennan, *Russia and the West Under Lenin and Stalin* (Boston: Little, Brown, 1961), p. 394.

[16] *Department of State Bulletin*, September 3, 1962, p. 343.

taking sides, more or less, with Moscow in its rivalry with Peking.[17] I should accept Morgenthau's summation: "The issue . . . is in the short run the leadership of world communism; in the long run it is the same issue that currently divides the United States and the Soviet Union: who shall inherit the earth?" [18] The proposition that *ipso facto* one's enemy's enemy is a friend of sorts led to great fallacies of policy in World War II and is little likely to serve us better now. In choosing among opponents so disposed, relative armed potential is a criterion as plausible, to say the least, as militance of current tone. Whatever opportunity may be offered by division within the Communist camp could be exploited against the stronger element as plausibly—here I understate purposely—as against the one more wayward for the time being.

In commonplaces of the time, the potency for destruction represented in nuclear striking power divided between American and Soviet possession has rendered war impossible and unthinkable and peace inevitable, nuclear weapons useless for supporting sensible policy, and the idea of winning obsolete. I am often at a loss whether to concur in such propositions before knowing whether they are offered as mental shorthand or as conclusive concepts. Though using them myself, I question some of the significances attributed to them. Shared belief in high probability of war under calculable circumstances, which the respective sides are loath to bring about, underlies current strategic stability. The high probability of avoiding a contest at arms stems from the thinking done about war—a prudential consideration, not something inherent. Notwithstanding the often declared impossibility of using nuclear arms to support sensible policy, capacity to use them and the companion possibility can serve a sensible policy. War is avoided by generating knowledge of its imminent potential. Peace persists through attentive effort growing out of recognition of its tenuousness. Such peace as is realized represents scant concord beyond a shared desire to avoid hostilities—an agreement not produced

---

[17] *Washington Post and Times-Herald*, December 17, 1963.
[18] Morgenthau, "Peace in Our Time?," p. 67.

by negotiation. The cliché about the obsoleteness of winning is easily tested. The term in question is not necessarily absolute. It may stand for making headway with one's purposes—maintaining them as valid and solvent—in face of what opposes them. Events have not superseded the idea of winning, and they will not supersede it until, in some unimaginable circumstance, the opposite possibility, losing, has been eliminated.

The workings, rather than the intrinsic validity, of the notions dealt with concern us here. The analogues to ideas shaping policy in World War II and its immediate aftermath are obvious. Khrushchev's style serves to renew and to reinforce belief in general reasonableness and belief in fundamental mutuality of interests underlying the moment's differences and bound to emerge and to transform issues—given patience and plenty of talk. The hopes for world concord in the mid-1940's were based on such beliefs. China, in the role of common adversary, is considered a sort of substitute for the Axis foemen of World War II in providing cement for entente with the Soviet Union. Shared comprehension of nuclear lethality as something bigger than both of us—a danger transcendent over conflicts of values and interests related to ideology—is viewed as a solvent equivalent to what was supposed to be provided by experiences of battle in the hopes of 1945. Bonds of understanding and shared responsibility are projected as emerging realities, if not yet full blown. They become predicates supporting an aspiration to vindicate the dream, never really put aside, of structuring world peace on a basis of general concord—a motif objectified in the Charter. In hopeful imagination, the idea of détente leads on to an entente with the Soviet Union as a counterpoise and eventually a successor to the Alliance. In effect, a framework of assumptions expressible as the Yalta pattern emerges.

Such is the aura of détente—something felt to be under way if not yet in sight of fulfillment. In one perspective, the reality of such a process as détente inheres in the assumptions of entities concerned. Views of a determining number in determining positions are determining. A change in frames of mind among those dealing with great affairs, even though a matter of imagination, rates as a change of reality, for attitudes are part of reality in foreign affairs. Yet the very subjectivity of the word puts in question any attempt at prediction. The moment's anticipation may mark a start of an enduring trend or prove as insubstantial as the nimbus of Geneva and Camp David in 1955 and 1959, when urge for accommodation boggled on specific terms. Discussion thus brings us to a consideration of the price of a détente now, to its relation to the future of the Alliance, and its connection with the questions shadowing it.

THE PROSPECTS AND
THE PRICE OF ACCOMMODATION.

Finding the Soviet Union amenable to bargaining in the mode of what a United States spokesman has described as a "normal business transaction," which enables each party to make a gain from its own point of view, is a reasonably adequate expression of favorable conditions for the Alliance as a design for a situation of strength on the basis of which a settlement could be attempted.

From adversary relationships in international affairs to normal business dealing is a large leap—one not to be accomplished merely by verbalizing. Of itself, the cited assertion of "no reason why, with proper caution and much patience, we cannot arrive at agreements of this kind" does not bridge the gap. The past has shown manifold reasons. They are not susceptible of being overridden by declaration. As a central point of difficulty in the past, the purpose of the other side in the bargaining attempts has been to eliminate the basis from which to approach bargaining on this side. By logic, the likelihood of finding opportunity for significant mutual gains in such a circumstance is ruled out. The analogy to "normal business transaction" is inapplicable. A more apt analogue would be that of a trading relationship between a gunsmith and a customer imbued with intentions of subsequently holding up the gunsmith.

So far, the idea of negotiating a way to settlement in Europe

—however attractive to American preferences and expectations —has repeatedly stranded on the circumstance of incompatible purposes. Yet hope of somehow talking a way to agreement has persisted. The simple logical difficulty of squaring hope with circumstance comes through clearly in a pronouncement by the Secretary of State: the Soviet Union's implacable hostility of intention is postulated; our policies are conceived as a formula for enabling everybody to come out ahead and specifically pointed toward mutually advantageous permanent solutions in Central Europe.[19] The hopeful good will in that formulation is unchallengeable. Doubts pertain only to logic. The effect is like multiplying a negative and a positive number and getting a positive result. Something is missing from the equation. The ideas do not fit into syllogisms. From a frame of logic, they dangle like the notion of solving large central problems by attending to small marginal ones.

One may find a supposititious way out of the difficulty by predicating conversion of the adversary. I should not presume to rule out all possibility of a transformation of outlook and conviction by action of some moral equivalent of a seizure along the road to Damascus. The question is one of evidence, not of exploration of logical possibilities. A change in manner is apparent—even a change of method—but so far not one prudently to be construed as a reform of purpose. Events in Cuba and Cyprus, for example, indicate an adversary more deft but no less inimical and resolute than in the past. In my estimate, notions of a transformed adversary reflect wish rather than reality. That is not to gainsay a real significance of heightened expectations for détente measured in effects on the Alliance.

However simple in its logical essences, the problem imposed by the double task which the United States has been essaying— maintaining the Alliance intact, or even improving it, and simultaneously seeking détente—is difficult in practical terms. The purposes tend to come into contradiction. The reason for having combined lies in the outsider's hostile intractability. To render him amicable and tractable removes the reason for combining.

[19] *Department of State Bulletin,* September 3, 1962, p. 343.

Lapse of motivation for combining relieves pressure on him to be tractable. In this sense, an alliance conceived in strictly defensive terms is inherently subject to manipulation. The reactivity may approach that of Sweet Alice in the song, "who wept with delight when you gave her a smile, and trembled with fear at your frown."

Such an alliance, moreover, is likely to be far more unified on reasons for resisting than on terms for accommodating. The locus of authority in judging the relevant considerations and in arriving at terms, whether conceived as those of détente or more definitively as a settlement, involves great potential issues. Their imminence and significance grow in proportion to the emphasis and energy brought to bear in seeking to negotiate an easement and in proportion to the degree of likelihood accorded the prospect of success.

From a determining position in alliance strategy, as custodian of the nuclear underpinning, the United States is projected into pre-eminence in quest of satisfactory permanent arrangements with the Soviet Union, and, indeed, a desire to prevent diffusion of that prerogative with respect to hopes of negotiating for arms control with the Soviet Union and of approaching a European settlement is not least among reasons for seeking to restrain the proliferation of nuclear weapons, and it is also part of the rationale behind the nuclear test-ban treaty. The principals in the nuclear cartel, reflecting a strategic equilibrium consonant with nuclear stalemate, are seen as arbiters over the future of Europe. Mutuality of understanding, assumed to be operative between the nuclear principals, takes on a character of entente. Bonds of collaboration between them are given increasing emphasis.

Ipso facto—notwithstanding the declaratory aim of holding onto and even strengthening the Alliance while pushing initiatives for easement with the adversary—considerations integral to the Alliance framework are concomitantly downgraded. The Alliance texture is affected adversely. Here it is in point to trace some of the effects with respect to allies across the Atlantic—

the main ones in the central range of the Alliance, namely the United Kingdom, France, and the German Federal Republic. The first instance presents no trouble. By reason of a modest auxiliary portion of nuclear capability that was undertaken in 1954 during the phase of alliance strategy which emphasized such weaponry for tactical uses, the United Kingdom shares in the nuclear cartel as a minor member. Moreover, on the merits of détente, the United Kingdom is so thoroughly at one with the United States as to make it unnecessary to decide which one to cast as the Don and which as the ever faithful squire in the quixotic quest.

With respect to the two continental allies mentioned, the prospect summons up remembrance. A shift of emphasis for the United States from its role of principal deterrer to that of principal bargainer in the effort to arrive at conditions for the future of Europe with the Soviet Union suggests sensitive parallels to the Yalta phase. The situation of each country is vastly different now in comparison both to that phase and to the circumstances obtaining upon entry into the Alliance. Each has experienced a recovery, in part with United States subvention. Each has undergone a transforming experience politically— France under President Charles de Gaulle's endeavor to reintegrate public life and national authority, and the German Federal Republic in being taken into the councils of the Alliance and converted from ex-enemy to ally status. Neither, obviously, has forgotten its time in eclipse—the one as a beaten ally reduced to client status and the other as a defeated enemy at the conquerors' disposal.

As to France's case, the impulsions are complex. One must take care not to misstate the matter and not to exaggerate the argument. From the standpoint of the United States' preferences, France's attitude in the Alliance appears wayward. Client status is recalled as humiliation, especially by President de Gaulle. The United Kingdom's reputed special relationship to the United States dates back to the same period. President de Gaulle recalls a vain bid, broached in 1958, to share that special relationship on a basis of parity, thus to set up a triune directorate for the Alliance.[20] His program for restoring France's importance in world affairs centers on capability in manufacture and delivery of nuclear weapons. The explicit purpose is to gain for France a franchise in nuclear matters at least equivalent to that disposed by the United Kingdom and thereby a higher rating in the striking of bargains, one to insure being listened to and to avoid being overridden or ignored.

France's avowed justification rests on doubts of the United States' constancy with respect to commitments to defend Europe. Prospects of having nuclear capability come into hands of an ally disposed to work at cross purposes raise dire possibilities. In imaginable extremity, United States' forces in Europe might become hostages to a dissentient ally's pressure. Continuation of the deployment in that circumstance would come into some question. Withdrawal of the forces would undercut the Alliance's credibility and vindicate French doubts. To that extent, France's course tends to induce the circumstance claimed in justification and exploits protection afforded by the Alliance to ends unfavorable to that protection.

The aim here is not to settle the merits of France's course but to trace the relevance of questions raised by the quest for détente—as to which, incidentally, the French government's estimates of probabilities have been as shifting and ambiguous as the American. An assumption of the adversary's imminent amenability to a measure of accommodation that would be compatible with the Alliance's integrity and purposes signally reduces the seriousness of the implications of France's bid to cut in on the nuclear cartel. Moreover, by that assumption, France's desire for nuclear credentials for entry into the bargaining circle

[20] The character of President de Gaulle's bid has been elucidated by James Reston in the following words: "In his private memorandum to President Eisenhower on Sept. 17, 1958, de Gaulle said that there must be a United States-French-British organization to take *joint* decisions on questions affecting Western strategy anywhere in the world, and specifically decisions on any use of nuclear weapons. In short, a French and British veto on the use of American nuclear power unless the United States were attacked." *New York Times*, May 3, 1964.

becomes quite comprehensible. On the other hand, one may assume, as I do, the delusiveness of the idea of an adversary at last, or on the verge of being, converted to tractability. That premise puts the United States' judgment of realities into question and makes comprehensible an ally's desire to hedge its position. In sum, the reprehensibility of France's course is inverse to belief in Soviet tractability, and it is contradictory to reprove France and to court the adversary.

Simpler but also more serious and central questions rise with respect to the German Federal Republic. Though in many ways the most successful of the European participants and, among them, the source of the greatest contribution of military strength to the Alliance, the German Federal Republic bears awareness of being incomplete—a truncated portion of the country, with the eastern portion of the land under Soviet domination and the western portion in position neither to acquiesce in nor to overturn the fact. As in the beginning of the confrontation, Germany remains the focal point of issues over the future of Europe—the locality for testing whether the idea of a reservoir of opportunities for working out mutual gains with the Soviet Union represents actuality or is diplomatic happy talk; a testing ground also for the concept, fascinating to United States foreign policy, of persevering in negotiation of small and marginal issues in expectation of thereby transforming large and central ones.

In relation to Germany, one can best understand the dilemmas posed by pursuit of détente. The German instance brings one to the bare bones of logical possibilities for settlement in Europe—Soviet retraction, leaving the Alliance triumphant; United States retraction, leaving the Soviet Union encamped; reciprocal retraction by interpositions by both sides; and reciprocal acquiescence in existing lines, legitimizing zones of authority and influence as they are.

Détente means the last—a point not to be concealed by verbal distinctions between *de facto* and *de jure* and so on. Détente means a bargain by the paramount powers, the principals of the nuclear cartel, over the sharing of Germany. The Yalta prototype rises, with implications of acute sensitivity. In being bargained over in a settlement between the paramount powers, Germany's status would descend implicitly to that of an ex-enemy country again. The Soviet Union, moreover, would be shown to hold the keys to Germany's future. Alienation of the Federal Republic from the Alliance would presumably follow in natural course. The Alliance would be hurt as a going concern. The flow of events would tend toward the second of the possibilities listed.

Yet for the Federal Republic to be associated as an ally in a decision disposing the future of Germany as a whole is logically and practically incompatible with terms likely to be conceded by the Soviet Union in circumstances short of a determinative defeat of its purposes in Central Europe. With respect to Germany, one sees how soon the course of détente comes to dead end—how soon exploration for possibilities of mutual gain must play out. Within the limitations, it may well be prudent to negotiate on small matters for their intrinsic worth, however slight, but only harm is likely to result from avowing expansive importance for the effort. Such avowal implies basic misunderstanding of the problems of dealing with the adversary, puts to doubt the United States' grasp of the requirements, and thereby is all too likely to derogate from credibility of the Alliance.[21]

[21] A report—at hand as I write—of an interview given by President Johnson to the weekly, *Quick*, of Munich, points up the difficulty of applying to the actual situation the abstractions associated with the mood of détente. See the *New York Times*, April 29, 1964. The gist is to "put yourself in the place of the Russians," to "try to understand their feelings," to "allay their concerns," and to seek "better relations" with the Soviet Union. By definition, each of the ideas has appeal. Empathy is preferable to alienation. Understanding is preferable to miscomprehension. Alleviation sounds better than aggravation. Yet the focus of issues between the Soviet Union and the Federal Republic of Germany is the fact of the latter government's having turned westward in developing political associations, having entered the Atlantic Alliance, and not having acquiesced to the proposition of the rightfulness of the Soviet-supported German Democratic Republic. Better relations, judged from the Soviet Union's standpoint, would involve reversal of these positions. Improving relations in that direction would correlate to worsening relations with the Federal Republic's allies, including the United States. Implicit in the interview is an idea of an underlying harmony of interest regarding Germany as between the United States and the other Western allies on the one hand and the Soviet Union on the other. As the central essence of the German problem, these respective interests are opposed.

The unpromising character of available avenues to settlement brings one back to consideration of an indefinite prolongation of confrontation, to acceptance of what President Kennedy in his inaugural address called "a hard and bitter peace" as the best in sight even with its tensions. This would be a morally taxing course, for "hope long deferred maketh the heart sick." The Alliance as a whole would have to remain indefinitely content with, or at least devoted to, its proximate goals. This prospect poses a question with respect to every member of the Alliance, but especially with respect to the German Federal Republic, where pressures to seek terms on its own with the Soviet Union regarding Germany's future as a whole would presumably become increasingly formidable. Not a prepossessing prospect, I repeat, but those disposed to reject it should come up with a plausible case for something better.

CUBA: AFTERTHOUGHTS

ON THE CRISIS

Seeking comprehension of the 1962 crisis over the Soviet Union's deployment of certain types of weapons to Cuba, an outsider to channels of official responsibility feels overwhelmed by the sheer bulk of information available. Governments and international organizations have produced voluminous wordage. Parliaments have added their glosses. Newspaper and magazine writers have performed prodigies of exposition, and writers of letters to editors have shown thoughtfulness as well as zeal. A succession of relevant books of varying quality has begun. In respect of range and depth of analysis stimulated as a by-product, probably no other episode of such brief span has approached the one in question. Even so, one is impressed by what is missing from the accounts available. The depth of treatment necessarily remains journalistic.

Historic analysis lies far ahead at best. Many items of information still withheld must be forthcoming before such analysis becomes feasible. Such a stage may never be reached completely. Totalitarian and authoritarian regimes do not voluntarily divulge such records as they keep. The motivations and estimates underlying their actions at particular junctures are subject to conjecture from the outside, but substantial proof becomes feasible only if and when defeat compels confession of secrets in retrospect. We know much, for example, about Ger-

From *The New Republic*, October 1, 1962; November 10, 1962; and May 25, 1963.

Also from an address delivered at a seminar sponsored by the Council on Religion and International Affairs at Aspen, Colo., September 16, 1963.

many's patterns of decision preceding and during World War II. The victors inherited the archives. Defeated functionaries talked. In contrast, little is known to us of the Chinese Communists' processes of estimate and choice during the Korean War. The reason for the deficiency is obvious. The latter struggle ended in stalemate, with the adversary establishment intact and its functionaries beyond communication. We are left to guess the course within from shadows cast on a screen.

An outsider is, and will probably long remain, only a little better off with regard to patterns of decision on this side of the confrontation over Cuba. To an extraordinary degree the government was, so to speak, in executive session in that critical fortnight. Even the few participants were not all full participants. Individuals among them with similar shares in the deliberations differ widely in their recollections of evaluations given to various factors in working ahead to a consensus.

My own outsider's curiosity focuses on one particular item among the still missing pieces—a letter from Premier Khrushchev to the President of the United States dated October 26, 1962. A companion, but reportedly quite different, letter from the same sender dated on the following day has been given out. Each of the two letters, coming at the most critical phase, proposed some basis for accommodation. The former letter was the one responded to by President Kennedy. The second letter was put aside as a basis for transaction of business. Thus, paradoxically, the public has been let in on the contents of the ignored letter, but the one chosen for response remains withheld. Published explanations attributed to government sources describe the letter in question as anguished in tone and allege a desire to avoid exposing Premier Khrushchev to reproaches within his own camp—a good deal like saying a lady's note must be burned lest it blemish her reputation.

So long as basic elements of the account are inaccessible, one should take care not to overdo enthusiasm for whatever was undertaken. What I have stated amounts to a reservation, not a dissent—a case of raising two cheers. I wish specifically to dissociate myself from three sorts of critics of what was done.

First are those disposed to deplore the course because it involved huge risk. Their reproach arises from misgivings about the dangers inherent in problems of such extremity. Choices so charged with peril are repugnant to a personal ethic, they say. Weapons have no business being so big. Strategy should not be so complex and speculative. Danger has no right to be so clear and present. They prefer righteous privacy. To a President, as a high public magistrate, it is not given to forswear a problem at hand as too ugly, miserable, and dangerous for his liking and concern, to choose instead to pass on the other side of the road, and to leave the question to the care of unbelievers. Such an instance as the missile crisis presents the President with no option between risk and risklessness. The logical debate over choices between good and evil or even between greater and lesser theoretic evils must be left to others. To a President, at such junctures, come problems of choice between admixtures, and often the best he can do is to seek the course promising the greater amount of the lesser evil. At least, President Kennedy did not choose the worst course of acquiescing in the missile deployment—the worst by any measure, including degree of risk entailed.

Criticism of another sort pertains to diplomatic method. Two items in particular have been cited: first, the President's withholding from Soviet Foreign Minister Andre Gromyko, during their discussion at the White House on October 18, the fact of our government's having come into possession of hard information concerning the emplacement of intermediate-range missiles; second, this government's omission of consultation with its allies before announcing a blockade and bringing to bear threats of further measures on October 22. A respected professor's letter to the *New York Times* illustrates the former view. It refers to "the present state of public hysteria"—a phenomenon I missed—and asks, "Was there no other way of dealing with the . . . threat than to provoke a direct United States-Soviet confrontation and thus place the two super powers on a collision course?" The answer, I believe, lies in the nature of negotiating relationships between governments in a basic conflict of interests and purposes, as the United States and the Soviet Union were and, for that matter, still are. The relevant points are so elementary as to seem banal.

Such relationships differ fundamentally from those between governments with compatible outlooks and aims. Diplomatic interchange between the United States and the Soviet Union is only a way of registering the wills and capabilities brought to bear by the opposing sides. It is a mode of conducting a power contest—not an alternative to it. This reciprocal process is exacting and risky. It calls for hardy wills and fine discernments. It is susceptible of getting out of hand and eventuating into war when one party overcommits itself to a proposition which underestimates the adversary's will to prevail or resist. Any agreement on terms of peace negotiated by adversary powers must be conditioned on their fear of the consequences of not agreeing. In this perspective, President Kennedy's favored and oft-repeated apothegm about never negotiating in fear and never fearing to negotiate seems to me quite misleading, even contradictory. Adversary powers have to negotiate in fear of what may happen in the sequel to a failure to settle on terms. A power must rationally fear having to negotiate under unfavorably disproportionate compulsion.

Whatever its precise effect on relevant military factors, the Soviet Union's deployment of intermediate-range missiles to Cuba constituted an apparent attempt to redress factors of compulsion in its own favor so as to render the United States amenable to terms more to the Soviet Union's advantage. The President's response was an initiative designed to be countervailing. Whether there was some misunderstanding regarding meanings and facts, especially with respect to content of the elusive word *defensive* applied to the Soviet armament of Cuba, is a niggling point. One can only wonder at the import attributed to the point in supposedly serious criticisms of the President's conduct of the meeting with Gromyko.

On a basis of cold words contained in snippets from the key conversation, no outsider can competently judge the state of understanding between the President and the Soviet regime. It was a matter for intuitive judgment—not a matter susceptible of being tested under the rigors of judicial evidence. As Commander-in-Chief, as primary agent of our foreign policy, and as the specific executor of the congressional resolution of intent regarding Cuba, only the President was in constitutional position to make the judgment. Only he, as our chief participant in the interchanges, was able to take into account all relevant nuances.

For the President to have taken further pains to notify and to warn the adversary regarding our knowledge of what the adversary must have known we knew could have gained nothing. To have made the prospect and thrust of our counter initiatives a topic of diplomatic interchange would in high probability have lost much. It would have deprived the contemplated actions of whatever cogency they might have, dulled the impressions of resolution we wanted to convey, and afforded the adversary opportunity to forestall or to nullify our initiatives with some more of his own.

Mere words would not have served. Too much of a past had to be overcome. Our government had bespoken determination over Laos, only to settle for the troika there. The United States had flinched on following through at the Bay of Pigs. The pattern of the call-up of reserves in mid-1961 had prefigured an addition of five or six divisions to our Army. After words of rage privately conveyed from Khrushchev, the plan had petered out. The United States had huffed and dawdled as a wall rose in Berlin. Admittedly, the problem of discoursing both to give pause to adversaries and to humor the timorous and uncommitted is not easy, but the latter aspect had long been overdone with maxims about no alternative to negotiation and about willingness ever to traverse another last mile in parleying—this last an invitation to adversaries to go on setting up mileposts along an interminable course.

Only a few days earlier the President himself had ferociously assailed a Senator for proposing, with respect to Cuba, a course involving exposure of other people's sons to risk. A prerogative to expose other people's sons to risk underlies state authority as distinguished from that of a tribe, whose powers are circumscribed by kinship. State authority endangers other people's sons when it quenches a fire, quells a riot, or defends a homeland. With respect to Cuba, the President had gone so far as implicitly to derogate from his power to perform constitutional duties.

With so much in the record to be offset, immediate and unequivocal action was called for to re-establish credit. This was not abandonment of diplomacy. It was a step necessary for reconstituting an acceptable basis for it. The same line of thought supplies an answer to the reproach concerning neglect of consultation. To have gone off consulting far and wide on next steps with three dozen allies would have vitiated the whole idea. What was to be done had to be done without regard to contingencies of support or assent from other quarters. United States determination to act thus alone in sovereign discretion had to be manifested to friends as well as opponents as a fact requiring to be taken into account in their relations with us. Advance consultation could only have obscured the fact.

A further circumstance militated against consultation. The great ranges of lands and peoples in the world are the northern and the western hemispheres. Cuba is a focus of interaction within and between them both. The United States, besides being custodian of a nuclear shield integral to the security of either hemisphere, is the only great power located in both hemispheres. It is the sole nation involved in both relevant security structures—the North Atlantic Treaty Organization and the Organization of American States. Its government alone among the American allies had appreciation of the interaction between Cuba and, say, the Berlin situation. Among the Atlantic allies the United States government alone was intimately knowledgeable of Cuba's implications through the Americas. To have gone off now on exploratory talks could scarcely have added anything to what was required for the government to resolve its will.

The cavil about consultation misses an essential aspect of alliances. I can perhaps make my point clear by an analogy to something I observed when in the Army. When a man was not up to the mark, the practice was to assign him a helper also not up to the mark. I learned to call this faulty premise the half-wit fallacy because it involved a notion of combining half-wits to form whole wits. Actually the relationship was not additive but multiplicative, producing quarter-wit results. Deficiency does not compound into sufficiency. The lesson applies to factors of heart as well as mind. Half-heartedness does not combine into courage. An alliance can be strong only as its leading elements have and show moral capacity to act alone in exigency.

The question regarding legality of our actions—here I comment on a third point of criticism—can best be left to international law classrooms. Blockade—in this instance invoked under a euphemism of quarantine—is a belligerent prerogative. If parties affected choose not to acknowledge its belligerent character, it gets by as a peaceable act. Our resort to such action and hints of worse to come were probably not countenanced by the letter of Article 51 of the United Nations Charter, for no attack to justify invocation of force in our own behalf had as yet occurred. By a purist's argument, we should have cleared our plans with the veto-bound Security Council before acting at all. The point lies with equal relevance to our *ex post facto* clearance with the Council of the Organization of American States, whose warrant to authorize forcible remedial actions is subordinated to Security Council approval under Article 53 of the United Nations Charter.

Capacity to bring about drastic shifts in force factors by sudden, stealthy, massive weapon deployments in a nuclear age simply renders obsolete the precondition of attack to the licensing of self-defense under Article 51. Facts have outgrown a concept. It is beyond law to provide a signal for transgression against one's vital interests. A government must make up its own mind on that. Goethe provides a proper answer on the legalities: "In the long run, over-great goodness, mildness, and moral delicacy will not do, while underneath there is a mixed and sometimes vicious world to manage and hold in respect."

Having said enough in praise, I turn now to an elaboration of my reservation. Only by focusing narrowly on the issue of missile deployment, it seems clear to me, could one call the outcome a retraction on the part of the Soviet Union. For the time being, pledges by the Soviet Union to shelter the Cuban regime have been redeemed. Our own government's repeated avowals of resolve never to abandon Cuba to communism remain unfulfilled. A situation "detrimental to the intellectual and emotional health of our body politic," in Hans Morgenthau's descriptive phrase, still confronts the country, and as yet no cogent remedy is at hand.

The justificatory argument has been well summed up by one of the Assistant Secretaries of State, Harlan Cleveland. It postulates a rule of economy applicable to what has come to be known as crisis management. The gist is: do not overload. By a complementary proposition, equally self-evident, one should not underload a crisis. One may readily hypothesize a cataclysm as a consequence of a different handling of the crisis in question. With equal ease, a case may be made against passing up opportunity to end a dangerous nuisance. The outcome realized was perhaps the best achievable in view of the lag in drawing the issue at all. No one will ever know for sure. The determination, as made, between what the United States would and would not insist upon requires scrutiny, nevertheless. The inquiry entails review of a longer past.

The position of Cuba, close to our shores, is a key one in relation to the multifarious lands of the Caribbean area and especially to the approaches to the isthmian canal. With a highly heterogeneous population and without a binding canon of public life, the island has gone through a succession of political and economic ups and downs in the more than six decades since the end of Spanish rule. The basis for strategic concern in Cuba is either obvious or undemonstrable—depending on whether one accepts or rejects the materiality and validity of strategic considerations. To serve that concern, Cuba's independence was trammeled until about three decades ago by treaty conditions designed and imposed by the United States. The provisions included a concession of privilege to intervene to preserve order and to prevent other foreign interposition. The abrogation of that privilege was an act of Franklin D. Roosevelt's Good Neighbor Policy, which, abjuring unilateral intervention, set a course toward making the general security of the Americas to the southward a collective responsibility of all the states concerned. That latter purpose culminated in the Organization of American States created in 1947. Americans tend to think of it as an instrument for widening support of United States strategic concerns. Among other participant countries it is often regarded as an instrument of restraint upon, rather than support of, the United States.

Whatever the grand undertakings in the wider sphere, the problem of order within Cuba persisted, along with problems arising from propinquity to a far larger and more affluent neighbor. A good many Americans have not thought through to a consistent position on intervention. Those most ardent against it in abstraction incline to belabor the withholding of intervention against the right-wing tyranny which dominated Cuba in the 1950's. Anyway, that tyranny collapsed at the close of 1958. In its wake an insurgent coalition without governing experience, but with a diversity of revolutionary aims, succeeded to power. It soon manifested intentions to flout good relations with the United States and to cultivate the Soviet Union's patronage and protection. Which was the dominant, and which the instrumental, intention is a question not susceptible of conclusive answer.

I shall not try to catalogue, let alone analyze, all the consequences of that course. The American ambassador, newly accredited to symbolize a clean diplomatic slate, was ignored. United States initiatives regarding economic and financial aid were rebuffed. A series of expropriations and confiscations involving American-owned property was put into effect, and negotiations about compensation were spurned. Cuba's new rulers derided the country's privileged quota in the United States sugar market. The United States government reduced and then suspended the quota. It clamped down on exports to Cuba in items other than medicines and food. Cuba imposed restrictions on

United States diplomatic access so drastic as practically to compel a break in diplomatic relations. The economic and social as well as political revolution in Cuba produced an exodus of refugees, with the United States a natural haven. Sorties, alarms, and recriminations were rife. Accusations of Communist penetration of the regime by dissident former participants rose through 1959. By early 1960 a Soviet Deputy Prime Minister was in Havana to conclude arrangements extending credits and contracting large-scale Soviet purchases of Cuban sugar.

President Eisenhower declared in July of that year a determination never to permit establishment of "a regime dominated by international communism in the Western hemisphere." This declaration was countered by Premier Khrushchev with an invocation of Soviet rocket power he used a cryptic qualifying phrase, "figuratively speaking"—as a protection for Cuba against invasion from the United States. The United States, however, was manifestly abiding by the patterns of collective responsibility established within the American hemisphere. In August of 1960 the Organization of American states was convoked to appraise the divisive effects, and to vote condemnations, of interference by extracontinental Communist forces—Chinese and Russian were specified—in affairs of the hemisphere.

The issues regarding Cuba's future were soon to be joined between the Soviet Union and a new administration in the United States. The Soviet propositions were stated in a speech by Premier Khrushchev on January 6, 1961—a labored discourse, circular in logic, not new in content, but important as a manifesto to the leadership about to take office here.

An idea pervasive through the text is the totality of the claim on the future asserted by communism. The law underlying the Communist conception of what is rightful and what is not is taken as a law of history. This law is conceived of as ordaining the universal triumph of Communist interests and purposes. Those interests and purposes are asserted to have an exclusive access to legitimacy, and all other interests and purposes are regarded as deviant. Peace is interpreted to mean an ordering of affairs furthering Communist ascendancy. Peaceful coexistence is portrayed as a situation or process tending toward reduction of impediments to Communist expansion, besides being free of general war. It is a program for compelling acquiescence from others. General war and local war in the customary sense are portrayed as inadmissible because of the perils inherent in nuclear warfare, but what Khrushchev calls wars of national liberation are commended. The phrase is interpreted to embrace all conflict tending to weaken the position of powers and interests— the label word is "imperialist"—differentiated from and opposed to Communist purposes.

The remarks touching pontifically and specifically on Cuba are placed in perspective against that general background of ideas:

> The multiplying of forces of the national liberation movement is due in large measure to the fact that in recent years one more front of active struggle against U.S. imperialism, namely, Latin America, has emerged. Only a little while ago that vast continent was identified by a single concept—America. And that concept accorded largely with the facts, for Latin America was bound hand and foot to Yankee imperialism. Today, the Latin American peoples are showing by their struggle that the American continent is not a manorial estate of the U.S.A. Latin America is reminiscent of an active volcano. The eruption of the liberation struggle has wiped out dictatorial regimes in a number of the countries. The thunder of the glorious Cuban revolution has reverberated throughout the world. The Cuban revolution is not only repulsing the onslaught of the imperialists; it is spreading, signifying a new and higher stage of the national-liberation struggle, when the people themselves come to power, when the people become the master of their wealth. Solidarity with revolutionary Cuba is the duty not only of the Latin American peoples, but also of the socialist countries, the entire international Communist movement, and the proletariat all over the world.

The words scarcely need elucidation. They avow Cuba as an

instrument of Soviet purposes focused on a contest for ascendancy in the American hemisphere.

During the 1960 American presidential campaign the prevailing candidate had asserted the intolerability of a Communist presence so near at hand and prefigured a venture in using and assisting political exiles in an overthrow of the Cuban regime. His inaugural address, however, stressed the collective pattern: "Let all our neighbors know that we shall join them to oppose aggression or subversion anywhere in the Americas. And let every other power know that this hemisphere intends to remain master of its own house."

The Moscow-Washington dialogue entered a new stage following the feckless invasion by exiles. Khrushchev's response to the event seemed timed to match the moment of its patent failure. "There should be," he notified the American President, "no misunderstanding of our position: we shall render to the Cuban people and the government all necessary assistance in beating off the armed attack." The immediate rejoinder from Washington was not an example of distinguished diplomatic discourse under pressure. A day or so later, however, the President had opportunity, in an address to a convention of editors, to express himself with greater deliberation. After referring to certain Cubans' determination "that Cuba must not be abandoned to the Communists," the President added, "and we do not intend to abandon it either." There was a call for "an ever closer and more realistic look at the menace of external Communist intervention and domination in Cuba." This was linked to a description of the situation as "less a threat to our survival than . . . a base for subverting the survival of other free nations throughout the hemisphere." Moreover, "not our interest or our security but theirs . . . is now today in greater peril." It was declared that "for their sake as well as our own . . . we must show our will." Further, "We and our Latin friends will have to face the fact that we cannot postpone any longer the real issue of freedom in this hemisphere itself."

The speech disavowed "unilateral American intervention in

the absence of an external attack upon ourselves or an ally," but this disavowal was linked to an admonition to "let the record show that our restraint is not inexhaustible." The tone implicit of warning was continued: "Should it ever appear that the inter-American doctrine of noninterference merely conceals or excuses a policy of nonaction; if the nations of this hemisphere should fail to meet their commitments against outside Communist penetration, then I want it clearly understood that this government will not hesitate in meeting its primary obligations, which are the security of our nation." The impression of caveat carried on into the subsequent words: "Should that time ever come, we do not intend to be lectured on intervention by those whose character was stamped for all time on the bloody streets of Budapest."

In retrospect, as at the time, the operational words are elusive of identification and analysis. Our primary obligation is stated as our national security. It is described not precisely as unaffected but rather as affected in less degree than that of others. We do not intend to act alone on behalf of that obligation, but a contingent event might induce an absence of hesitation regarding that obligation. The line to be taken in that case is not further described beyond a negative point rejecting an imputation of intervention. Resolve subtly expressed in contingencies and indecision reluctant to reveal itself may sound nearly alike. We shall probably never know which way the words were interpreted at Moscow. The vague hint of possible unilateral action may well have been taken to indicate a need for a forestalling move on the part of the Soviet Union. The elaborate framework of contingency with which the hint was hedged about may well have been taken to indicate an opportunity. The combination of hint and contingency may well have been taken to indicate an occasion for experiment to see how far it was possible to go without being unambiguously confronted.

What one of the powers in contention had avowed—a Communist base in Cuba—the other declared unpermissible. The mutually exclusive purposes expressed related not to remote and generalized futurity but to a specific, instant situation. What either might do to substantiate its position—and how much leeway either might gain for itself—was problematic. There would have been plenty for the President and the Soviet Premier to have clarified concerning this topic in their face-to-face meeting at Vienna a few weeks later, but the communiqué gave no hint of the matter. Apparently it was not discussed at all. Concerned over signs of an approaching clash over Cuba, I privately commented on the omission to a high member of the administration at the time, and was told that the danger spot was Berlin—as if there could not be two.

For relevant considerations, the record available from the ensuing months is susceptible of quick recapitulation. The United States persevered in the course of collective hemispheric collaboration. In January of 1962, the Organization of American States voted resolutions suspending Cuban participation, recognizing "dangers for peace and security which threaten this hemisphere" in continuing Communist interposition in Cuba, and recommending "such steps as seem suitable for national and collective self-defense." Meanwhile, the Cuban regime proceeded with organization of a monopolistic domestic political base styled the United Party of the Socialist Revolution. The leader avowed himself ever a Marxist-Leninist, first prospectively and then retroactively. The climactic undertakings between the Soviet Union and Cuba, unfolding in the late summer and early autumn of 1962, but presumably developed over a long period, consisted of two related but separable projects—the one publicized, the other secretively put into execution—for Soviet assistance in a general military build-up involving arms and technicians "to resist the imperialist threat" and for deployment to Cuba of missiles and bombers of offensive striking power, with ancillary equipment.

A few observations concerning the mission of the Soviet forces—technicians as they were called—and the uses of the equipment within the first project are called for at this point. *Technician* is a euphemism covering fighting men sent abroad as tactical instructors and weapon specialists to act on the military environment in another land. Such an undertaking is deep and pervasive under conditions imposed by contemporary weapon systems at any level of capability. The mission obviously was to help mold the original insurgent force and the peasant militia in Cuba into a cogent military force with a unity based on a common discipline and doctrine, thereby to lesson the likelihood of a domestic rising against the regime, and to diminish lingering active resistance. The effect would be to reduce the political import of civil discontent and presumably to strengthen the underpinning of the regime in such a way as to rule out selective assassination as a means of redress and reform. The effect was to increase the danger to the hemisphere inherent in the Communist presence in Cuba.

A defensive undertaking in this instance? The Soviet Union and the Cuban regime so termed it. The speculatively hopeful word did not tell us much. No probability of attack on New York, New Orleans, Miami, the Canal, or probably even the Guantanamo Naval Base was construable. The forces and equipment involved in this part of the program were sent to serve as mainstays of an organized position which the Organization of American States, acting at the instance and under the leadership of the United States, had officially determined to constitute a menace to the peace and security of the American hemisphere. They signalized that the Cuban regime had been finally and fully stuck with an association hostile to the environment and that the Soviet Union had for the first time formed a military front with a Communist state overseas and sitting next to the United States. With the disclosure of the treaty under which the project was contracted, and with the mounting evidence of progress in execution as the summer wore on and autumn set in, the United States turned to technical and tactical criteria for evaluating the deployment. The authors and beneficiaries of the project vaunted the undertaking as defensive. The United States, in reluctant permissiveness, concurred.

An outsider simply does not know enough about the dialogue between Washington and Moscow at that time to be able to tell whether, and in what degree, it was confused by use of different frames of reference by the respective parties in regard to the question of what was defensive and what offensive in weaponry. Whatever the esoteric details, the United States government, in employing technical distinctions, assumed a common frame of reference. The dismaying discovery of concrete evidence concerning the other part of the military program, embracing missiles and bombers capable of carrying attack over a considerable range, was what impelled the United States government to a decision, arrived at in its single discretion, to act. The clearance thereafter sought and forthwith received from the Council of the Organization of American States was expressed in a resolution recommending to member states "all measures, individually and collectively, including the use of armed force, necessary to ensure that the Government of Cuba cannot continue to receive from the Sino-Soviet powers military material and related supplies which may threaten the peace and security of the Continent and to prevent the missiles in Cuba with offensive capability from ever becoming an active threat to the peace and security of the Continent." The language adumbrated attack as well as blockade, and the language referring to blockade, if read alongside the earlier resolution concerning the threat to the hemisphere posed by Communist interposition in Cuba, might have been construed to apply to any military material in support of the Communist establishment.

The blockade proclaimed, however, was directed only to weapons and equipment of technical offensive capability. Recision followed upon the Soviet pledge to retract all such items from Cuba, subject to verification on the ground. The collateral inhibitory effects on ordinary commerce, which might have had a determinative impact on Cuba if continued a while, were alleviated. Great care to keep the issues confined to an axis between the United States and the Soviet Union and to avoid direct confrontation with Cuba was manifested—presumably out of anxiety to maintain backing from other American states. When Cuba forswore permitting verification on the ground, the United States did not insist upon this proviso but reconciled itself to substitute means. The Cuban regime's prestige was thereby spared a serious blow. In high probability the blow would have toppled it. One cannot say for sure.

Moods are basic realities in such episodes. As the United States government considered whether and how to challenge the Soviet actions, the likelihood of imminent war with the Soviet Union was gauged high. Margins were assumed to be razor-thin. The mood at centers of responsibility was one of enormous tension—an awesome feeling of standing eyeball to eyeball, as a principal participant put it. Soviet retraction on the narrow issue drawn produced sudden release. Anxiety about pressing fortune too far was succeeded for the time being by a desire magnanimously to spare a discomfited adversary unnecessary embarrassment.

By the estimate which prevailed as the basic decision was arrived at, the United States government credited its own ability to make persuasive its willingness to face risks of war over the presence in Cuba of Soviet weapons capable of jeopardizing the United States' homeland but not over the Soviet military presence in so far as it related to capability of smaller operational radius. Will was governed by estimate, but estimate was in a sense governed by will. What more might have been made persuasive if the determiners of the decision had first persuaded themselves is a matter for conjecture; the caution displayed may have been a feat of prudence or a case of missing the boat.

In any event, Khrushchev's invocation of Soviet rockets as a protection of the Cuban regime was validated. The United States' pledge against invasion—which remains effective for all practical purposes notwithstanding a *pro forma* retraction asserted in view of the subsequent default on the counterpart condition for verification on the ground—was made to the Soviet Union, whose role as a party of interest in Cuban security was, within that limit but beyond peradventure, thereby acknowledged. As a corollary, the Soviet Union's vicarious role in security and political arrangements within the American hemisphere was sustained, notwithstanding the declaratory policy "that this hemisphere intends to remain master of its own house." [1] It is in this connection that my curiosity is whetted by the still withheld Khrushchev letter referred to earlier.

The dour implications were generally ignored under the stimulus of elation as the crisis eased off. The euphoria has proved remarkably durable. In its broadest manifestation, the lingering mood sees the Cuba crisis as having worked a transfiguring effect on the great antagonists. A change in outlook and relationships giving promise for negotiating a general détente is alleged. On this premise, Communist Cuba is reduced to a tertiary nuisance destined to abate with time or to be rendered immaterial in relation to the anticipated wider accommodation. The view reminds me of an occasion when the Duke of Wellington was approached by a man saying, "Mr. Peabody, I believe!" The Duke replied: "If you believe that, you can believe anything."

Another comforting thought, often officially voiced, infers the exodus of a quarter million refugees from Cuba as ominous for the regime in Havana and as an achievement for United States policy. Communist regimes have characteristically sought the reduction of opposition. In the instance of China, where large scale emigration was not feasible, the regime resorted to massive executions. The Soviet Union, too, has used that means in the past. In general, Communist regimes have permitted or even abetted the emigration of intractable elements when this has been feasible. The drain may get out of hand and have to be stanched as in the case of the Berlin Wall. Short of that extreme —and there is no sign of Cuba's being near it—an exodus of refugees helps more than it hinders.

Another postulate, again emphasized by our spokesmen, makes a big thing of Cuba as a showcase of Communist economic shortcomings, which are supposed to render the regime unpopular at home and unattractive abroad. What Communist

[1] A news item in the *New York Times* for July 25, 1964, is relevant. The first paragraph suffices for quotation: "Washington, July 24— Secretary of State Dean Rusk was reported to have informed Latin American foreign ministers today that the United States had been pressing the Soviet Union to prevail upon Cuba to cease her subversive efforts in this hemisphere."

regime has not been such? The rub is that the showcase is all too likely to display something else—to wit, the feasibility of taking over a society, deliberately depressing consumption, and using stringency in combination with monopoly of supplies as an instrument of control. Communism has subsisted not on a reputation for general affluence but on its effectiveness in holding on to power once installed.

Whether matters will turn out thus in Cuba is the main unresolved question which survives the autumn crisis. In a favorite phrase to describe the United States' policy, communism in Cuba is said to be not negotiable. Whatever negotiating was done in regard to that position in the autumn crisis of 1962 is not to be construed as acceding to or legitimizing it. Ostracism of Cuba under Communist rule is to be encouraged so far as feasible. By suasion and pressures, the United States seeks to get others among the American states to follow its lead in cutting off commerce and political relations. It presses friendly powers outside the American system to do likewise with respect to commerce with Cuba. Hopefully, this approach, while avoiding a belligerent stance, may achieve effects approaching those of a blockade increasing the regime's troubles and running up the costs of Soviet support of its Caribbean client. Forgetting the historic ineffectuality of embargoes helps one's faith in the remedy.

The phrase concerning non-negotiability of communism expresses the opposed position as well. Each side takes its stand on the same formula. Cuba is to be restored to fellowship as Cuba is, according to the opposing case. The aim—consistent with the program of peaceful coexistence—is not alienation but acceptance. A return of Cuba to participation in the political and economic affairs of the hemisphere on those terms would signalize great headway indeed in the course for Latin America set forth in the Khrushchev speech of January 6, 1961.

The situation which is neither war nor peace is bound to be a test of resolution. If it is going to be hard for the Cuban regime to hold up, it will be difficult for the United States to hold out. Even as at the peak of the missile crisis, voices will be raised on behalf of accommodation. Abstract equity will be cited, matching half a victory for one side with half a defeat for the other. The gospel of always meeting something half way will be renewed. The regime will be described as having learned a lesson. Retreat from some of its more extreme postures will be cited. Reason will be prompted not to exact embarrassing concessions from its necessitousness. Legitimacy will be construed from the passage of time itself. Men will counsel adjustment to the realities.

DOUR THOUGHTS ON INSPECTION

Some key terms relevant to arms control and disarmament —a field of endeavor lacking an adequate frame of discourse and overburdened with ambiguities—have been mauled about by government spokesmen, news analysts, and editorial writers since the onset of embroilment over missiles in Cuba. I feel prompted to offer, on behalf of rigor, some simple definitions.

I begin with a term embracing all techniques and functions available or conceivable for keeping track of events and prospects bearing on performance of obligations under any agreement for arms control and disarmament. This term is *verification*.

One kind of verification pertains to techniques and functions susceptible of being effectuated without acquiescence or cooperation of the government whose actions or capabilities are subject to check. Included here are ranges of information available through knowledge of science and technology irrespective of intentional grant of access—information explicit in or inferable from open sources, from observations made from without or from covert operations within or over the domain concerned. An appropriate term for this kind of verification is *monitoring*. Verification further includes techniques and functions requiring grant of access by a government whose actions or capabilities are assessed. The operations concerned divide into two classes determined by character of the grant of access—a basic point of distinction.

One sort of access is that conceded by a government for a specific limited occasion. It controls the scope of ingress. Out-

From *The New Republic*, November 24, 1962.

side authority is permitted to enter an area only to confirm deeds asserted by the inviting government to have been done, without warrant to ferret unreported matters. In effect the government is host and the outside authority under circumscription is guest. An appropriate term here is *authentication*. A contrasting sort of access is one exercised on the basis of a continuing right acknowledged and submitted to by a government subject to verification. An outside authority juridically vested with powers to enter, to investigate, to measure, and to ascertain performance carries on the process, with a warrant not merely to check matters owned to by the subject party but also and essentially to determine, within limits of relevance, what may have been left undone or done covertly. The correct term here is *inspection*. Such is its sense in official parlance generally—in banking, postal operations, military outfits, and so on. An inspector comes around, welcome or not, with warrant to poke and to raise issues—not merely to nod through a prearranged checklist.

The general concept, verification, is what was alluded to in Chairman Khrushchev's offer on missile retraction, concurred in at once by President Kennedy, subject to a proviso for continuing U.S. monitoring in an interim. United States spokesmen immediately began calling the prospective operation inspection. By any feat of imagination, essential attributes of inspection were lacking. U.S. officials appeared anxious, nevertheless, to nudge arrangements toward at least nominal or symbolic conformity to standards assiduously contended for by this government through drudging years of talks on test bans and arms limitation. With matching alertness to record and precedent, the Soviets set about to attribute an invitational and *pro forma* character to whatever, if anything, had been agreed to.

For an outsider, analysis of the ensuing exercise in tactical diplomacy revolving around these opposed themes is highly difficult—much like trying to comprehend a merry-go-round by glimpsing it in motion through a fence crack or a score of counterpoint by hearing gust-borne sounds of a distant orchestra. Who and what prompted U Thant to the pilgrimage that resulted in establishing a United Nations absence at Havana? On a basis of what estimates did the U.S.S.R. propose and did the U.S. hasten to accept the impeccably humanitarian International Committee of the Red Cross as a verificative agent on matters of war technology outside its familiarity? Were Castro's dissents at the instance, by leave, or in defiance of Moscow? Perhaps the explanations of these and many other mysteries will never be known.

One matter seems fairly evident, however: both sides have been doing their cagey utmost to avoid precedents and to minimize compromising basic positions on verification in broader context. It is in point to weigh implications with respect to the question whether the main parties to negotiation remain at cross purposes or are ready to round a turn in the eighteen-nation conference on arms control and disarmament scheduled to resume at Geneva on November 12. The maneuvering is probably a much more significant augury than the fervent pieties about disarmament exchanged between Chairman Khrushchev and President Kennedy at the peak of crisis over missiles in Cuba and added to an already replete record.

Here, at risk of elaborating what is evident, it is in point to stress the identity of the main parties to negotiation at Geneva. They are the governing groups in the respective countries, namely the U.S. and the U.S.S.R. Their views of interests and requirements do not necessarily coincide—and in some aspects are not at all likely to coincide—with attitudes reflected in a still growing bulk of literature on arms control written by psychiatrists and sociologists intent upon resolving policy conflicts by dismissing them as aberrant, by physicists disposed to evaluate an adversary government's aims from sentimentalities uttered over cocktails at a Pugwash meeting, by psychologists seeking clues to the weapon riddle by analyzing chit-chat of train attendants and of concierges met during a Russian tour, or by any of various other sorts of imaginative but nonresponsible authors.

Concerning these main parties to negotiation, a shared awareness of destructive potentials and of chances for calamity and a coinciding of purposes with respect to getting armaments under control may be assumed without arguing, for on any other premise the relevant international exercises consist of subterfuge and fall beyond rational analysis. Arms control and disarmament, however, are not absolute and discrete aims. The worthy goals overlap and interact with a great range of other considerations entertained by the respective parties to negotiation. The rub is—or at least has been up to now—with respect to these other matters.

A bargain, if and when arrived at, must be consented to by each side on a basis of taking into account all the interests and preferences it must uphold not only to make the bargain satisfactory to those immediately responsible for negotiating it but also to those whose concurrent consent is required. The problem of divergence is basically a political one. That modifier is used not in a narrow and demeaning sense but in a sense involving orders of values basic to polity. Each party is under constraint to ensure terms provident from a standpoint of preserving and giving effect to an order of values. As a test of their providence, the terms must have convincing marks of being provident—convincing to constituents and allies whose concurrence is necessary as a condition to giving the terms effect. While still vouchsafed choice, while still in position to give or to withhold consent to terms, each party is constrained to seek terms consistent with other purposes reflecting the relevant order of values.

This gets close to the heart of the inspection issue. Each side—with reason—attributes to the other ultimate desires and preferences incompatible with its own. Each side—again with cause—suspects that the other, given opportunity through a relative sufficiency of means, would bring its more remote desires and preferences into its pattern of efficient intentions. This reciprocal anxiety is nothing to puzzle about. Authentic spokesmen for the U.S.S.R. articulate goals in world affairs entirely at odds with conditions acceptable to a U.S. still able to exercise preferences in keeping with its order of values. Spokesmen on our side articulate world goals conceivably realizable only under conditions presupposing frustration of the U.S.S.R. amounting to historic defeat. That the articulated opposed goals lie beyond reach is beside the point. Each side makes plain enough what preferences it would establish as purposes of policy, only given capability to transcend the present standoff.

In analyzing interplay between inspection and the basic conflict of purposes, it is important to recognize that individuals may accept, draw upon, and apply orders of values prevalent within their culture even while ignoring or renouncing beliefs underlying them. One may act on monotheistic postulates while professing agnosticism or guide by dialectical modes of thought regarded with personal indifference. In this respect, hopes for détente founded on Khrushchev's indifference or even cynicism —often alleged but never demonstrated—regarding Marxist-Leninist tenets are in substance probably counterpart to a supposition that a Borgia pope, because inconstant on finer points of practice, might have been flexible on matters in controversy with Luther.

The mode of thought underlying the United States approach, whether or not recognized and acknowledged, rests on assumptions cognate with ideas of natural law. A unified creation, with a pattern of right reason inherent, is postulated. Good is identified with it. Principles are held as reflections of this good. What opposes good is ascribed to aberrant free will. Interests are seen as colored with such aberrant imperfections associated with misguided free will. Principles thus transcend interests. Social good inheres in upholding principles impartially. The concept of authority—which is to say, power to bind in conscience—is based on devotion to principles unswayed by interests and impartially applied. Facts are items of information developed impartially by authority and are an objective basis on which to apply principles. Such are justifying, if not always reigning, concepts in state life.

In the United States view, an inspectorate in connection with arms control comprises institutional arrangements for projecting onto the world scene, and especially onto the U.S.S.R., a fact-finding function based on the conception of authority described above. It must be above interests, impartial in endeavor—its

authority acknowledged, permitted scope, facilitated in operations, and submitted to without cavil or hindrance on occasions as it may require. Its existence and functions, thus
serving as both substantive and symbolic substitute for trust
between the great adversaries, would gradually evolve a basis
for confidence. It would serve to assemble and to verify facts to
bolster assurance or to confirm doubt. In extremity—that is, in
event of need to abrogate an agreement in face of unacceptable
violations of obligation by others—the system would provide
warrant and vindication. In sum, the U.S. plan for a disarming
or disarmed world is congenial to the U.S. view of legitimacy.

The U.S.S.R. view stands at odds. A basic aspect is totality of
claim on futurity asserted on a basis of dialectic concepts of
history. History is viewed as progressing by inherent momentum
toward a final perfection perceivable only in Communist doctrine. Concepts of legitimacy are derived from that postulated
law of history, conceived of as ordaining eventual, universal
triumph for Communist interests and purposes, which are accordingly averred to have exclusive access to legitimacy—to the
prejudice of all other interests and purposes, deemed deviant
and devoid of legitimacy. The ruling Communist party is considered sole interpreter and custodian of legitimacy. Rightfulness is thus cognate with the party and the outlook and interests
it epitomizes, and any other view is regressive. Bearers of party
authority are constrained not to concede legitimacy to any authority beyond their control.

No thread, I contend, has been more consistent in Communist conduct than this sensitivity to making any concessions to
external authority. It was manifested in the World War II period by obduracy against Western allies' scheduling of chain
bombing out of Russian airfields, stiffness over timing of return departures of lend-lease convoys, and impingements on
U.N.R.R.A. operations. Instances often cited as countervailing
turn out to be unconvincing under examination. Russia's acceptance of inspection in post-World War II occupation agreements, for example, pertained to domains not yet brought to
heel. Soviet agreement to inspection in Antarctica involved no

Communist area. Communist accession to inspection in North Korea under armistice terms has proved nugatory in real effect. According to a notion persistent within the so-called disarmament community, the U.S.S.R. did once offer concessions on inspection in preparatory discussions. Under scrutiny, the idea turns out to be equivalent to construing a martini recipe as an offer of a drink.

An index to the attitude is a U.S.S.R. practice linking inspection with the term *intrusion*. All too often, American discourse echoes the linkage, using *intrusive inspection* for inspection proper and *non-intrusive inspection* for monitoring. A standard definition of *intrusion* is "forcing of oneself into a place without right or welcome, the act of wrongfully entering onto property of another." *Inspection* is defined in lexicons as "the act of examining officially"—and *officially* means "with authority, with sanction." *Intrusive inspection* is a contradiction in terms and *non-intrusive inspection* a tautology—and both expressions should be banned from U.S. discourse. The heart of the matter involves questions whether entry is to be by leave or as a matter of right, whether the authority's scope of operation depends on its own choice or is set by the government of the area concerned, and whether the authority is merely empowered to confirm acknowledged deeds or is to have a warrant to search out things for itself. Soviet willingness to invite in an authenticating agency on occasion is quite conceivable but has no bearing on submitting to inspection. The U.S.S.R. persistently says this last is out—a stand consistent with the dogma. In face of this, it is difficult to explain lingering U.S. hopes that the U.S.S.R. really does not mean it and that obduracy can some day be overcome by adjusting details.

The United States may indeed exaggerate the efficacy of inspection. In this connection, notions of a potential in inspection for guiding the U.S.S.R. toward becoming an open society may be laid aside as inherently too marginal and speculative for serious consideration. The point of inquiry is whether inspection could do the job for which designed—let alone its potential for producing a windfall of history. I am not in position to state definitive views. I can only raise questions.

One question pertains to inspection as a way of ensuring compliance with any agreement. For the moment and for argument, formal acceptance of inspection terms by the U.S.S.R. and other Communist regimes may be assumed. Such a development would not necessarily support a conclusion regarding willingness to lend that degree of cooperation necessary to effective operation. The Korean armistice pattern might well be repeated —continuous frustration, postponement, avoidance, and administered ambiguity. Inspection would work only with dedicated good faith in making it work. It could be frustrated in myriad ways. In sum, establishing an international inspectorate would probably provide small, if any, assurance of compliance. The level and quality of information afforded might well be less than attainable through monitoring—that is, verification by means available to the United States irrespective of arrangements under an arms control and disarmament agreement.

A second question concerns qualities of an international inspectorate. To gain necessary respect and credit even under favorable conditions, such inspectorate would have to present a visage of high motivation and technical competence. Presumably it would have to draw heavily on people from uncommitted countries. Most of these countries are—and will remain for a long time—short on technicians. They will need to keep their best men at home.

Third, a question is in order concerning integrity—meaning soundness unaffected by extrinsic considerations—of findings by an international inspectorate. United States expectations are based on high valuation of the import and incontestability of what are called facts and on assumptions of universal comprehension of truth divorced from consequences. The approach envisages an international inspectorate disciplined and constrained to rigorous, exacting attitudes toward empirical data irrespective of preconceptions and preferences. While discounting such detachment from interests from Communists in an inspectorate, the approach counts essentially on such quality from neutral or neutralist participants—a matter for doubt.

The expectation overlooks a disposition, basic in the cultures of many of the neutralist countries, to view magisterial functions as intended not so much to forward triumph of good over its opposite in temporal affairs as to keep contention between them from getting out of hand—thus calling for temporizing, mitigating, hoping always to work out arrangements to save something all around but in a pinch favoring concessions to the more intransigent. F. S. C. Northrup's *Philosophical Anthropology and Practical Politics* reflects good insights into the attitude. I recall an illustrative instance. Representing the United States government at an International Red Cross Conference in 1952, I was forced to limits of patience in trying both to avoid a donnybrook and to preserve national prestige in face of outrageous attacks from Chinese Communist delegates. At intermission a delegate from a leading neutralist country, after praising me for reasonable forbearance, added, "These men are mad dogs. You should have let them have their way." It was *non sequitur* to me but obviously plausible to him.

To expect unequivocal findings by an international inspectorate which has neutrals in the swing position—especially with respect to crucial considerations likely to precipitate renewed competition on armament—is probably too much. Should the United States ever find itself constrained to abrogate a disarmament treaty, it would probably have to do so, and to face consequences, on its own sole sovereign discretion—without any international certificate. It could be—who can say for sure?—that inspection would not raise the level of technical surety over that achievable by monitoring. Some experts say this. Perhaps also the U.S. has not realistically appraised factors of feasibility in regard to plans for an inspectorate. These negative considerations, however valid, do not dispose of the matter. It is necessary also to take account of factors concerning political acceptability of an agreement within the United States—an aspect bearing on the juridic character of an agreement.

So systematic and far-reaching a venture as a formal agreement on arms control and disarmament should be an act of state of most solemn character—to be undertaken only on a basis of firm and demonstrated concurrence between the executive and the coordinate political branch. It should commit the nation beyond the term of an administration launching it, with a status above party contention. It should contract other parties to obligations equally durable and deep. A treaty seems appropriate, even indispensable, as an instrument for any such formal agreement.

In this perspective, limits, difficulties, and doubts regarding inspection recede to academic import. Questions of confidence and dependability are not merely technical. They never were. They might conceivably have become so if at some juncture relationships between the United States and the Communist imperium had turned onto a basically better course. Then armaments might conceivably have been susceptible of tethering without all the untested paraphernalia of inspection. The hypothesis is based on fantastic rather than realistic imagination. Whatever the theoretical possibilities under dreamt-up conditions, one now must take account of the autumn missile crisis. I have heard hopeful speculations regarding its effects as if fellowship might grow out of a shared crisis, as if wrestling a bear to the brink were a mutually endearing experience. I am skeptical. I see little in recent events to nourish the mystique of trust. An uninspected arms control compact seems out for the calculable future. The outlook is dour—indefinite impasse on formal terms, with abatement of the problems restricted to unilateral steps and to informal and tacit agreements, with or without more such crises as the one over Cuba.

THE CHINESE PUZZLE

The fifteenth General Assembly of the United Nations has settled down to quieter routines now, with the decline of the tumult and shouting and the departure of titans and kings. It has been a session unmatched for stately importance and un-stately surprises—and for sheer numbers as well. Two dozen chiefs of states or heads of governments have lent their presence. Seventeen neophyte states, mostly African, have expanded the membership to an unprecedented ninety-nine. The figure calls up a parable concerning a similar number once brought into a fold and a hundredth one that was absent and therefore the center of attention.

The conspicuous absentee is Communist China, third among nations in territorial scope, holding sway over a fourth of the world's people: by all odds the most numerous nation, with a population now estimated at 680,000,000 and increasing by annual increments about the size of the population of New York State.

The giant's absence surely leaves incomplete the image of a General Assembly designed to be a global town meeting. More than size lends importance, however. Red China's intentions and potential bear in all the topics laden with hope and fear touched upon in the Assembly's unprecedented spate of oratory. Red China is important to all and integral to most of the items on any list of grave issues—regulation and control of arma-ment, accommodation or protraction in the Cold War, relaxa-tion of international tensions, creation of a world order to succeed the vanishing imperial dispensation, economic develop-

From *The Commonweal*, November 11, 1960.

ment of backward areas, and encouragement of stable authority among the necessitous new lands. So Red China, conspicuously absent from the Assembly, is notably present in the calculations and appraisals of every world-conscious foreign office. What are the purposes and what are the assets and liabilities of Peking? The questions must be asked as searchingly in Moscow as in Washington.

It would be misleading to sort the answers into neat categories of means and ends or into a simple scheme of priorities. In policy, means and ends are inextricably connected, and assets and liabilities are ways of expressing the same realities. A nation's domestic needs and ambitions are intertwined with its world outlook and its historic goals. All this applies to the aims toward which Red China presses and the means it brings to bear. A nation may be said to consist of a territory, a people, and a pattern of authority. In China's case, all three relate to the potential and to the goals. Chineseness is intertwined with Marxism. The regime is at once dogmatically Communist and unequivocally racist.

One might start with the survival and the strengthening of the regime itself—the Communist regime which established its control eleven years ago upon the retreat of the precursor Nationalist regime to Formosa. Surely this qualifies as a pre-eminent goal. The regime's grip must be strengthened, its doctrine fastened upon the people, and its control riveted to all aspects of the national life, so that China shall respond with a unity and act with an effectiveness hitherto unknown in its long history.

An integral part of this is perseverance in a massive domestic economic revolution involving the subordination of production in all its aspects to central planning and control and designed to change the face of the land and to bring it by rigorous effort abreast of the industrialized countries of the West in the shortest possible time—the most massive savings program of history. This program leads in the broad purpose to propel China ahead as a great power in world affairs. As part of this Red China presses to reconstitute the Chinese family of nations—an historic expression representing a ring of protectorates ranging over Mongolia, Korea, Vietnam, Tibet, Bhutan, Burma, Malacca, Java, Luzon, and Ceylon. This purpose in turn intertwines with that of eliminating all Western influence from Eastern Asia—especially United States influence, for the United States, as leader among nations opposing the march of communism and as helper and ally to those disposed to stand independent of Red China, has been singled out as a supreme enemy to be humiliated, isolated, and brought to defeat.

The aim to dominate Eastern Asia connects with ambition to be the exemplar of Communist revolution for Asia. A like ambition extends to the necessitous emerging countries of other continents. This in turn relates to an ambition to establish Chinese pre-eminence in the Communist collaboration which, in the regime's view, is destined by a dictate of historic laws for a world-wide triumph. That culmination might with equal accuracy be described as pre-eminent, along with the strength and continuity of the regime. The rulership looks to its own position and interests as instruments of that postulated destiny. With regard to Communist dogma, its members are true believers. Their acts are subordinated to their view of an ineluctable struggle to achieve at last an historic plateau of world communism. In that course, war is taken as inevitable. Peaceful coexistence can only be an interlude to be accepted when the Communist cause is pushing to its destined triumph. Success in such junctures requires the proponents of communism to steel themselves against enemies, and this requires postulating, accepting, and acting upon the idea of inevitable war—to Peking an indispensable idea.

The regime is made up of true believers also in the sense of their assurance about the outcome. The policy of an adversary becomes, in their parlance, "a rotting bone in a graveyard." The decay of capitalism exemplified in the United States is postulated as a certain and current phenomenon. Adversary forces become "paper tigers." As the doctrinaire periodical *Red Flag* puts it, "None of the imperialist reactionaries who still seem outwardly strong can avoid the doom advanced by history."

Doomsday for the enemies will bring the true believers into their own as princes of a regenerated world.

What of the means for such a big order? Filling it must be largely a matter of tugging by bootstraps. Nature has not been bountiful to China in rainfall, soil, or subsoil wealth. The technological lag is woeful. For its ambitious endeavors China has two main basic resources—position and manpower. The thought must come to its rulers that Japan in its time cut a great swath with far less of both. Red China has little to spend beyond billions of man-years of effort to wring every possible bit of substance from the meager land. The mounting hundreds of millions of Chinese function both as the pre-eminent instrument for development and as the main charge against the assets produced—in a race to test whether denial and striving can enable production to make headway against requirements.

There is no place in this scheme for political deliberations and accommodations with the established powers of the West— and surely small incentive for cultivating diplomatic relations which would open China's domain to an influx of prying diplomats and inquisitive attachés from the adversary world. Rather, the image of being hemmed in by pressures from hostile forces must be intensified—so that every last ounce of effort may be exacted from a pressed and anxious populace for providing capital formation to undergird economic and strategic achievement.

Here the strength of the ruling apparatus is seen not only as an end but as a means. It is geared to manipulate people by hundreds of millions, stamping out every vestige of opposition, suppressing every impulse to individuality, eliminating every competing institution, obligation, and interest, and rendering a vast populace into an unquestioningly obedient mass. The dogma offers a goad as well as a goal. Its absolute promise of prevailing brings to the rulers the conviction to press their grandiose designs. It rules out doubt. It provides an enemy. It combines urgency for survival with the tonic sense of backing a sure thing. The ideological instrument links closely to the alliance with the Soviet Union, up to now an instrument of huge effectiveness. It has brought in material to redress deficiencies in military production. The intimidatory image of Soviet military power in the background has given Red China vicarious strength for risks and adventures beyond its own single capability.

Finally, an appreciation of Red China's role and scope requires understanding the relativeness of power, which means capacity to achieve intended results. Such capacity depends in part upon the strength of forces in opposition. The opportunities before Red China have arisen from the weaknesses in surrounding areas. In all too many of them tyranny and avarice have been the marks of rulership and apathy the curse of the ruled, bonds of identity and allegiance have been weak, and independence has brought only frustration. All this has raised the power quotient of Peking and has given the ring of plausibility to designs to revive the Chinese family of nations as a stepping stone to wider triumphs.

How can the thrust of Red China be controlled? That important question has produced an array of hopeful answers.

A current theory sees consolation in a prospect of irreconcilable cleavage within the Communist camp—with Soviet Russia presumably taking alarm over Peking's balky ambitions and resolving to bridle them with a replica of our containment policy. According to this theory, Khrushchev's recently demonstrated zeal to break down the United Nations barriers against Peking rose from an urgency to tame Red China by admitting the regime to responsibility and respectable fellowship.

One must put this theory into proportion. With completely unrelated cultures and languages, separate geographic positions, and contrasting internal requirements, the Soviet Union and China will tend to go on different courses, but they are likely to be more parallel than divergent. Whatever the frictions, they need each other. It is premature and beguiling to expect an unearned break for the West. Amid all the quarrels echoing from Communist realms, it is well to remember the tale of the missionary who, made captive in a jungle, was heartened by signs of a row among his captors—only to learn that the issue was over how to prepare the prospective stew. To place hopes in a supposedly moderate Khrushchev—as some are wont to do—would be simple folly. Khrushchev is not moderate. A position worse than having to depend on him to mediate our differences with a rampant China is hard to imagine.

A companion hope rises from a wish that the United States may wring some last benefit from its endeavor to bar Peking from the United Nations. This endeavor—which humors a fiction that the Nationalist regime located on Formosa still holds juridic authority over mainland China—has the look of an expiring policy. This gives rise to a notion of negotiating Red China into amenability as a condition precedent to the grant of membership coming increasingly into prospect. It is a wan hope. It is a fair question whether and how the regime might respond to opportunity for a role in the United Nations when and if the ban is lifted. It may see advantages in the facilities which membership would afford to its ambitions for pre-eminence in the Communist world, enhanced opportunity for contact with the fledgling states which it hopes to draw into its train by the power of its example in rigorous self-development, and a chance to make its persistent anti-American propaganda resound from a sanctuary within our own domain. If so, it may then accept membership, but it will do so arrogantly as a signification of triumph rather than obsequiously making amends and promises and showing gratitude for admission to respectable company long denied.

It is equally plausible that Red China might ignore, reject outright, or attach impossible conditions to the opportunity. No evidence—only conjectures, inferences, and Khrushchev's exhortations—supports an assumption that it wants in. It has not petitioned for a place. In dealing with other governments it has scarcely shown anxiety for acceptance. Its motivations bear rather toward humiliation of adversaries among the established powers than to participation in the normal usages of diplomacy. How better show disdain than by rejecting membership so long withheld when finally the opportunity is extended? Those who argue the advantage of having Red China represented in a world forum where it can be called to account for its actions should assume that the point, with values reversed, has not been lost on Peking.

The regime's long record of relationships with the United Nations has a bearing. The high point came in 1950, with the interposition of Red China's army, in the guise of volunteers, against the United Nations Command in Korea. Its spokesmen, invited before the General Assembly, came not as petitioners or defendants but as antagonists. After being tagged as aggressor for persisting in armed intervention, Red China fought on to a standstill—an immense source of prestige for it before its own people. In prolonged armistice negotiations its position was that of a bargainer on equal footing with the forces representing world authority. The position from which it bargained was one where its presence had been called aggressive, and the outcome left it in actual if not lawful control—a success of considerable moment for defiance. Indeed the Korean venture left the regime with enhanced prestige and a hugely stronger base at home. Red China has made a good thing out of defying the United Nations. If it should come in, it will scarcely be with hat in hand.

In seeking for solutions, one should keep in mind that Peking has tempered fanaticism in words with prudence in actions. Even the heady gamble in Korea—however risky when measured against the regime's newness, the tenuousness of its hold, and the meagerness of its resources—was undertaken only after long hesitation and was carefully kept from getting out of hand. China has pressed its territorial designs by pre-empting Tibet, an easy prize, and by indirect support of civil strife in other peripheral areas. Though it has deployed its arms into disputed areas even against India, it has generally kept a tight leash, preferring to position forces as a threat in being to neighbors, while exploiting weaknesses in environing areas by unconventional means such as infiltration, subversion and the like. For such efforts it has an auxiliary asset of considerable potential in Chinese populations living as minorities in Southern Asia—perhaps a foreboding precedent for the use it will seek to make of Chinese minorities in Africa and Latin America.

In conventional military strength Red China is powerful but not overpowering. However vociferous in manifesting hostile intent, it is likely to be tempted into military adventures only as want of external vigilance provides apparent riskless opportunity. In a short calculable future, Peking may have solved the problem of atomic energy and achieved symbolic weight as possessor of a few big bombs—a development more likely to increase truculence than to alter the preference for subversive means. Even when discounted to redress the excessive claims of propaganda, the Peking regime's achievements in development are formidable; they leave it closer to first than to third, but still second, in the Communist camp. For the calculable future, the main factor of concern to us must continue to be Soviet strength.

The prospect places a premium on the long tasks of shoring up the internal positions of potential victims of China's thrust. It requires of us a steady purpose to do what we can to overcome apathy in the environing countries and to guide backward regimes away from the temptation to tyranny. It means maintaining the symbols as well as the fact of United States strategic commitment to Southern and Eastern Asia. Doing so, we shall have to temporize with neutralists, but it is well to remember that some of the most vocal exponents of neutralism in the area are wont to be privately thankful that the United States retains a stake in their fate.

It is well to put in proportion the importance of what remains of Free China on Formosa, for its significance pertains not to its grandiose pretensions to a status long gone in fact—namely that of governing authority over China—but to its role as a source of restraint on China's rulers. It symbolizes from outside the possibility of alternative, the potential for popular revolt, and thus provides cautionary influence on the extent to which they feel free to make experimental exactions of their people.

As a recent report for the Senate Foreign Relations Committee puts it, "Communist China presents the most complicated and serious problem faced by the United States in Asia. It is also a problem more likely to grow than to diminish, and one for which there are no easy answers." By temperament and experience we are scarcely well geared for such problems. We prefer to sort situations into the hopeful and the hopeless and to try for quick answers. We can best get guidance not from our own past but from such historic processes as the long confrontation between Christendom and Islam.

Time may work its changes on Communist China. The present regime exemplifies the most enduring collaboration on the present world scene—thirty-five years in harness. This is a strong point, but also a weakness. Red China is evolving into a gerontocracy. Soon it must face a problem posed by the simultaneous superannuation of its top leadership and with it the test that overtakes every revolutionary regime—bridging from the first to the second generation. Then, virtually by default, power must devolve upon a second tier of leadership preponderantly now in the forty-five to sixty age group and military in outlook and background in consequence of past preoccupations and neglect of developing political successors. Below it, now in the thirty-five to forty-five age group, is a third tier of potential leadership brought into maturity since the establishment of the regime. Somewhere along the way there will be changes—perhaps for worse but maybe for better. We can best hope for the latter and be prepared to exploit whatever breaks may come our way—in the meantime taking care to keep our guard up, not expecting too much, but taking care never to do too little.

III.

RELATIONS WITH
NEW STATES

INTRODUCTION:

THE QUEST OF SOVEREIGNTY

A year after the firing of the shot that violated the laws of acoustics, our forebears came to a conclusion. Protection of their rights and improvement of their lot as wards of the Crown were no longer to be sufficient purposes. Instead of merely rebelling, the Americans would have a revolution—one designed not so much for turning domestic society topsy-turvy as for changing the status of the colonies in the juridic and political order in world affairs. The Americans would insist on standing among the subjects rather than the objects of policy—on being coordinate rather than subordinate elements in the scheme of importance. Vindicating their independent status required another seven years. The new nation then set about enhancing its place in the scheme of diplomacy. It was hard going. After a third of a century not even a dozen other governments had agreed to exchange envoys with the fledgling republic.

Aside from negotiation of commercial treaties with a few North African beyliks and sultanates in hope of preventing piratical raids on American vessels, the early overtures were all directed toward European sovereigns. A negus ruled then at Entotto, a shah at Ispahan, an emir at Qandahar, a mogul at Delhi, and a shogun at Kioto. Judged by the expanse of his sway, an emperor at Peking was probably the most puissant monarch of his time. All these and innumerable exotic princes, however, were then inconsequential in respect of world political affairs. The powers of the earth—the arbiters, the policymakers, the grantors of status—were located in Europe.

In our awareness, the American Revolution stands historically as the first move made outside Europe to challenge the legitimacy of the concentration in Europe of power in world affairs. As an Englishman once put it, the Declaration of Independence was, if not the death sentence of empire, at least its epitaph.[1] Whether or not it set the example, the new nation at least got in at the base point of a trend. The trend was slow to pick up momentum, however. How slow was borne in upon my consciousness recently by a chance reading of a manual for American diplomats issued in the closing weeks of Grover Cleveland's second presidency, roughly a century after the first American overtures in diplomacy and at a juncture within the lifespan of many still living.[2]

It would be diverting to dwell upon characteristics of a departed era of diplomacy as reflected in that manual: for example, an instruction to envoys on how to prepare their reports in longhand, a warning to mission chiefs against temptation to use cablegraph on pain of having to pay the tolls from their own pockets, forbiddance of concern in political situations within other countries, and so on. I must renounce such digression to get on to the point. The number of governments within the scope of United States diplomatic contacts had grown to forty-four—sixteen of them in Latin America, three in Africa, four in Asia, and one, namely the Kingdom of Hawaii, in the mid-Pacific. The rest were in Europe—still very much the center of importance. In the blunt discourse of that official document, the exterior world was sorted into civilized and uncivilized regions, and civilized countries classified as Christian and non-Christian. American nationals, partaking of the Frankish privileges of occidentals, were exempt from local jurisdiction in countries of that latter sort.

Such invidious distinctions of empire, once officially and candidly asserted by our own government, have gone by the board. The old structure of empire has all but disappeared. Certificates of statehood have been issued wholesale. It has become a com-

---

[1] W. T. Stead, *The Americanization of the World* (New York: Markley, 1901), p. 37.

[2] *Instructions to Diplomatic Officers of the United States* (Washington: Department of State, 1897).

monplace occurrence for yet another entity to go through formalities of assuming separate and equal station among the powers of the earth. Some approximations to indicate the scope of the phenomenon must serve. Roughly half of the world's states—containing roughly 40 per cent of the world's population and 30 per cent of its land surface—have come into independence since World War II. Poverty is a prevailing condition among them. These countries aggregate perhaps 5 per cent of the world's productive wealth. Their share of talents relevant to modernity is probably even smaller in proportion. Their potential wealth is problematic. By getting people off the land and starting afresh with an infusion of talent from abroad, some of these countries could theoretically leap into prosperity. The idea has no practical relevance, for no such opportunity is vouchsafed. These are the lands of the southern reaches—heavy in numbers, lacking in wealth, with populations generally inexperienced in what counts for making a success as a going concern under modern conditions. As political entities, as experiments in statehood, they are characteristically moved by ambitions hugely in excess of their power to fulfill. Sovereignty as an expression of juridic status is in hand, but sovereignty as the sum of attributes of a successful modern society seems beyond reach of many.

It comes easier to play the sovereign game in the former sense than in the latter. World affairs are a big thing for the fledgling states. Independence means instant importance. The nature of contemporary international organization provides opportunity to be courted and counted on issues far and wide. The United Nations is a place for debate even if debate is not allowed at home—a place for upholding rights to free elections for someone in a far land even while obstructing them in one's own. "The United Nations is, for a government like mine, what the stage is for an impoverished actor—a place to tread before bright lights, to utter noble lines, and to forget for the moment the unsatisfactoriness of the home situation," a knowing Asian politician once told me.

Independence comes as a right. What people do with it is

another matter. The universalistic fervor underlying our ancestors' bid for national autonomy—envisaging the United States
as exemplar for all peoples not only in establishing independence but also in showing what to do with it—has been buffeted
by events. We still tend to cheer and to abet every ambition
toward national independence. Yet our confidence in the American example with respect to political institutions has been
palled—especially, I think, by the failure of democratic regimes
to meet the test after being given their chance in Central and
Eastern Europe in the sequel of World War I. Lacking faith in
our example, some of us tend still to postulate faith in destiny.
Progress and goodness—so runs the faith—await every society
in independence as a matter virtually of right. Realization may
take time, but the outcome is almost certain. Every people has
native to itself—so goes the doctrine—some genius for success
in the venture. In Secretary of State Rusk's formulation, "History confirms that freedom must win because it is rooted in the
nature of man and in his relations with God." [3]

The matter is not all that simple, however. Not only freedom
but also the impulsions counter to it are rooted in human nature. No law of history guarantees a happy outcome. Peoples
have native to themselves only what they have been. In all
too many an instance this amounts to a society rendered static by
tradition, capable only of tribal conceptions of what is good,
and devoid of standards by which to make headway as a modern
polity. So in independence they must borrow—and yet must
feel constrained to disavow and to belabor the source of their
borrowing, often scorning what they would emulate.

As outsiders, exercising no control and even little influence,
we can feel compassionate about their predicaments without
feeling compelled to humor resultant fallacies. For one thing,
we can counter the proposition—comforting yet deceptive—
that, whatever their shortcomings, they are consequences of
having been in colonial status. We can remind them that success
in the venture of independence comes not as a matter of right,
not as a matter of claim upon others, but pre-eminently as a

[3] *Department of State Bulletin*, February 19, 1962, p. 276.

result of standards chosen and efforts put forth on their own. We can eschew that false charity that spares use of critical faculties.

The pieces selected for this final section pertain to problems posed by disparities between sovereignty as a status in world affairs and sovereignty as the sum of a state's attributes as a going concern.

THE GOLDEN AGE

IN PERSPECTIVE

In conversation a while back a lady of high civic zeal referred to her experiences in diplomacy as constituting the pleasantest way of spending a summer within her recollection. To my query for details, she told of a trip abroad. Along with her passport, she had been handed a brochure on proper conduct in foreign lands and had taken its hyperboles at face value and to heart. I have seen or heard the word *diplomacy* used and its cognates similarly invoked in relation to men of the fleet in a port of call, American lawyers in England for a professional conclave, touring glee clubs, Fulbright scholars, and foreign guides at a fair. A pianist recounts his experiences in concertizing abroad under the heading "Diplomacy by Keyboard."

With a rigor unfashionable in a time abundant with such notions as "people-to-people diplomacy," I prefer to use the term not to denote geniality among strangers but to refer to official representation and communication among governments, associated methods and conventions, the vocation devoted to them, and accumulated relevant lore. Such are the senses intended when someone represents diplomatic style as determining the character of relations among governments or cites relevant proprieties as a remedy, even *the* remedy, for the troubles of world politics. Usually the appeal couples diplomacy with a modifier denoting orthodoxy—some reference to standards presumably once upheld, then abandoned, and now requiring only to be embraced anew in order to move the world into safer, happier courses. The appeal to experience gives the idea an

From *Journal of International Affairs*, January, 1963.

advantage of plausibility. Characteristically, also, the proponents are men of scholarship and pertinent experience, not
lightly to be disputed.

With George F. Kennan, for example, the matters wished for
are "more effective use of the principles of professionalism" and
"diplomacy in the most old-fashioned sense of the term." Sir
Harold Nicolson, regarding a troubled world, has asserted belief
"that the principles of sound diplomacy, which are immutable,
will in the end prevail, and thus calm the chaos." Seeking a way
to "disentangle the skein," former Ambassador John Wiley has
urged a return to "conventional diplomatic framework." Senator Mike Mansfield pins hope on "the quiet art" of "traditional
diplomacy." Sir Ivone Kirkpatrick recommends "the classical
method of successful diplomacy." With Louis J. Halle—to
name another from a legion of examples—the prescription calls
for restoring "the practices associated with the Golden Age of
Diplomacy."

When, if ever, did such a Golden Age occur? Traditionalists
are wont to date the unfolding of a diplomatic Golden Age to
the second quarter of the seventeenth century, roughly two hun
dred years along from the origin of the modern state system.
Some identify it specifically with the tenure as France's chief
minister of Cardinal Richelieu, who, as Nicolson notes, "first
laid it down as a definite precept that diplomacy was not a mere
ad hoc operation but a continuous process . . . , surely . . .
an important concept to have originated." Others—Halle, for
example—place the time in 1648, when at last, in the Peace of
Westphalia, governments renounced trying to do each other in
for the glory of God.

Both versions are unconvincing. The Thirty Years' War went
on undeterred by Richelieu's innovations. The accommodation
at Westphalia brought two dozen years of peace. Then Louis
XIV began his onslaught against the state system. For forty-one
years institutions of diplomacy were in virtual abandonment.
Twenty-seven years without war on a grand scale followed before the launching of the three Silesian wars, the last of them
known as the Seven Years' War, persisting until 1763. The

three following decades were an interval of relative peace, with struggles marginal and formally unacknowledged. Then in 1792 gigantic hostility was resumed with the French Revolutionary Wars, which merged into the Napoleonic Wars ending with Waterloo. Only then did Europe's rulers, chastened by twenty-three years of conflict, begin giving persistent heed to keeping peace. Notions of Europe's having been, in an antecedent phase of the modern age, "a society of states, regularly constituted, in which each conformed its conduct to principles generally recognized by all," reach back, in Albert Sorel's phrase, to "one of the beautiful theories of philosophy in the eighteenth century."

The contrasting apparent stability of the ninety-nine years following Waterloo is reflected by the identicalness of the great powers involved in the deliberate construction of peace in 1815 with those participating in the precipitate dismantling of the structure in 1914—save only for one's change of name from Prussia to Germany. The near-century had been relatively peaceful. Most of its wars were fought away from centers of world politics. Issues at stake and destruction incurred in the brief, infrequent central wars were modest. Tranquility and continuity rested on general agreement among powers counting for much. Their regimes drew on a generally common fund of history. The frame of discourse among them was unified to a degree permitting any government participating significantly in world affairs to be confident of having its utterances understood by others in the sense intended. None was a revolutionary power. Ideologies were "a minor theme" through most of the period, and balance of power "seemed to be the political equivalent of the laws of economics, both self-operating," as A. J. P. Taylor puts it. The basis of general order was not at issue. A common notion of legitimacy prevailed. Looked back upon after an interval sufficient to soften details of enduring suspicions, recurring tensions, and occasional violence, the time, as no other, deserves celebrity as a Golden Age of Diplomacy.

Under precepts of the time, governments were normally to seek concord, finding ways of making purposes compatible through methods of discreet bargaining looking to contractual results. Participants in this distinctly rational way of conducting affairs did not delude themselves into regarding consent and coercion as disjoined. Some factor of constraint invariably underlies assent. Awareness of penalties of not agreeing is invariably a condition of agreement among governments. Recognizing these concepts, those handling policy had possibilities of resorting to force generally in back of their minds and sometimes in front. Though regularly involved in calculating relevant capabilities, they ordinarily refrained from flaunting the circumstance. " 'The rapine underneath was there,' " as Lord Vansittart has observed, "but relatively it was war in lace."

Bargaining and consent rested on a canon of equality, measured not so much in calculable strength, resources, size or technical achievement as in autonomous right to define one's interests and to make up one's own mind and of capacity to enter into contract. Participation in the pattern signified statehood. It denoted capacities to make and to effect decisions, to meet obligations, and to keep order within one's domain—capacities summed up as sovereignty, carrying title to be left alone by outsiders under a precept as stated by Kennan: " . . . once a state had been recognized as a sovereign entity, one did not attempt to extinguish it entirely, or to deny it the basic right to order its own internal affairs in accordance with its own tradition and ideas." What regimes needed to say to each other was supposed to be appropriate to, and confined to, channels provided by reciprocal presence of envoys. A deviation, such as an appeal by a government to another nation directed past a regime to its people, was regarded as an unstately trenching upon sovereignty.

As privacy was part of diplomatic usage, so circumspection, along with a stylized sort of courtesy, was a supposed quality of practitioners. It was considered fitting to appoint to diplomatic missions, and to use in foreign offices, men of aristocracy schooled to appropriate attitudes and well reputed. Professionalism thus developed in step with permanence of representation. A practitioner might meet his opposite number of the moment, and need his good will, at later stages in his career, and accordingly it was prudent to give heed even to an adversary colleague's interest in preserving standing with his principals and thus to avoid pushing too harsh a bargain. A practitioner owed obligations to his vocation as well as to his regime. Duality of obligation was supposed to enable a diplomat, dealing with his kind, both to advocate for his principal's interests and to mediate between them and rival interests. The extremes of policy were thus mitigated by negotiation, easing compromise much as in the manner of attorneys working out terms of agreement beyond reach of their principals in direct encounter. The profession was thus set apart—not only by a right of protection from local harassments and exemption from coercion by host regimes but also by attributes of "a certain freemasonry of diplomacy," in Francois de Callieres' phrase, transcending locality "like the knights of chivalry in the Middle Ages."

With eloquent emphasis, Kennan has embellished this view of the profession in an idealized interpretation of diplomatists as men rising above foibles otherwise affecting state business, spared of prejudice and ambition, guided only by reason, vouchsafed insights not accessible to other mortals concerned with public affairs, and standing superior and patronizing in relation to the sorry apparatus of the state much as physicians stand in relation to wayward patients or expert mechanics to outmoded and balky cars. In the tradition as celebrated for example, by Kennan, a government's will in external affairs and the processes of striking balance with external interests by negotiation tend to merge. The blending is as if the negotiators' role were, or should be, pre-eminent in setting policy and as if skill in parleying and reporting constituted the total requirement. The political character of foreign affairs, the element of conflicting purpose, fades into quiet professional interchange. The notion of rectifying a world through diplomacy amounts to having it regulated by diplomats.

If an accessible but overlooked set of techniques and a willing but slighted profession do indeed harbor workable but neglected solutions for otherwise obdurate and perilous international issues of our time, it is obviously urgent to make avail of them. The question entailed, whether the prescription of orthodox diplomacy is of practicable import or merely reflects a hankering for paradise lost, is easily disposed of.

Celebrators of a diplomatic Golden Age have, according to Robert W. Tucker, built the tradition into something "at times amounting almost to *mystique.*" It is worth a moment to examine the mystification. In its time of celebrity, professional diplomacy was a bureaucratic expression—elegant but still bureaucratic—of a political concord seemingly firm and universal but actually neither. "Every bureaucracy . . . , in accord with the peculiar emphasis of its own position," Karl Mannheim has observed, "tends to generalize its own experience and to overlook the fact that the realm of administration and of smoothly functioning order represents only a part of the total political reality."

Thus it is with the tradition surrounding diplomatic bureaucracy. Diplomacy, as Sorel made clear, "is the expression of political customs," not itself determinative of the character of political relations. The techniques of diplomacy did not create the Golden Age. Rather, the conditions of the time with Europe ascendant and superficially tranquil for the time being—provided opportunity for diplomacy and its practitioners to seem prodigious. The circumstances, while they lasted, were bound to be flattering to diplomats. Elements of success were in the environment, like a rainy spell for forest rangers or an abundance of duck for hunters.

The glow of diplomacy was but a reflection of assumptions prevailing within the societies mirrored in it—those of the West, especially Europe, in an auspicious time. Alfred North Whitehead recalled the latter decades of the period as one of "the happiest times I know of in the history of mankind," filled with "a sense of purpose and progress in the world." As Sir David Kelly reminds us, "Western man . . . regarded as obsolete the tendency to sheer wickedness. . . . Evil was associated with Nature, pestilence and earthquakes, and primitive man shared in the cruelty of Nature because he was still half-animal—but civilized man was envisaged as the innocent victim of evil and advancing rapidly to its conquest." The era, again in Sir David's phrase, was marked by "two obsessions—a dogmatic theory of linear progress and a belief that the local temporary conditions of Europe in the nineteenth century were final and stable."

Those conditions were indeed local and temporary. It is important to have clear in our minds the circumscription of the diplomatic order at the very high point of its contingent celebrity. Diplomacy and its equalitarian usages were strictly limited in application. Their time of eminence coincided with the heydey of empire—a general term summing up a variety of inequalitarian arrangements, accepted then as normal for handling relationships between governments within the Europe-centered state system and peoples of divergent cultures in remote areas.

The ranges both of diplomacy and of empire grew with the extension of European influence outward to other continents, beginning with what Sir Halford Mackinder called "the great adventure on the ocean that was to make the world European." The respective scopes altered from one juncture to another. Fastening of imperial arrangements onto one area might accompany a modification in the direction of diplomatic usages with respect to another. Sometimes—this happened especially as to parts of Africa—outlying areas and people might be brought tentatively and ambiguously within the diplomatic nexus only to be subjected later on to outright imperial domination. Again, forms of diplomacy might be applied but mitigated by inequality of privilege. The distinctions between equalitarian diplomacy and inequalitarian empire were not always of litmus-paper absoluteness. The point essential here concerns a misproportion involved in picturing a globe formerly ministered by diplomacy, while overlooking the complementary and no less significant role of imperial office—colonial ministers, viceroys, proconsuls, captains-general, and colonial governors—in holding together what there used to be of a world order in times now recalled as a Golden Age of Diplomacy. The oversight is of a bureaucratic sort, arising from tendencies to interpret realities in correspondence to departmental pigeonholes.

Indeed, diplomatic functions have suffered no reduction of scope or curtailment of numbers. Quite to the contrary, diplomacy has undergone sudden enormous extension—demonstrable by a visual count of automobiles illegally parked with legal impunity along Washington's curbs any day or by such a datum as a *Washington Post* news item placing at "more than 6,000" the number of persons enjoying diplomatic status in our national capital. Emissaries and their staffs abound and are kept busy far beyond past measure, and the work of burgeoning missions goes on at a volume and pace undreamt-of even a lifetime back. Surely not diplomacy but rather the imperial order has shrunk. The rate and sweep have been such as to make the change a major historic phenomenon.

With Americans, the characteristic relevant feeling is gratification, susceptible of being carried rather far in some cases. I recall once having read a woman journalist's account of being ordered at gunpoint to get off a sidewalk so as to make way for some passing minor functionaries in a newly independent Oriental land and of complying in thankfulness for opportunity thus to be demeaned in atonement for past imperial inequalities. I, for one, should find it difficult to summon up such large contrition for the circumstance that some governments, in whose acts neither I nor anyone of my acquaintance had a part, found it necessary, profitable, or convenient to interpose authority in other lands and over other peoples in times past. A more typical attitude toward proliferating new states would be a measure of misty pride in having other peoples in their fashion follow in our national footsteps.

Myriad factors, to be sure, must be added up as causes to balance against historic results of such scope as the wholesale movement into juridic independence in our time. A full accounting would encompass a complex of causes traceable over many centuries. Without the power of examples set at Concord, Philadelphia, and Yorktown, would the ideas carried far and wide by the thrust of empire—national identity, authority pervasive over a defined area, and a general will to make a place in history—have produced their now manifest consequences? No one can say for sure, but Americans are entitled to feel self-congratulatory for the nation's having got in on the start of a big trend—for having created, if not a model, then at least a precedent.

With ours, in Raymond Aron's phrase, "a world in which the grand principle of self-determination has somehow become an absolute," it is a prerogative of a multitude "to assume, among the powers of the earth, the separate and equal status" and to participate in diplomatic interchange. The novelty and anomaly of the resulting situation do not lie altogether in the multiplicity of participants, in the diminutiveness of a portion of them, or even in the meagerness of many of them as polities. One should have to turn back over less than a century to find a redundancy of states taking part in diplomacy, owing to the honeycombing of Central Europe and the Italian peninsula. Cyprus, Gabon, or Burundi has its numerical counterpart in Iceland or Honduras. The Balkans and Central America come to mind as examples of historic clusters of states with thin endowments for political life. What most of all distinguishes the present is a combination of unprecedented universality with unprecedented cleavages within the diplomatic framework—and therein lies a central part of the problem of order confronting diplomacy in a world "for the first time presented with a closed system," in Mackinder's phrase.

Whatever its contingency and injustices, the unequal imperial structure did serve a use in providing a frame of relationship among highly diverse entities.

> . . . How could communities . . .
> But by degree, stand in authentic place?
> Take but degree away, untune that string,
> And, hark, what discord follows!

Those lines from *Troilus and Cressida* are relevant. Filling in behind vanishing empire and for the first time being stretched to encompass a globe, the diplomatic nexus is called upon to join diversities hugely beyond what it enclosed in its eminent century. It has become surrogate to the imperial dispensation— under different and often inapposite rules. In comparison to its Golden Age, diplomacy is not so much neglected as baffled. It has no unified order matching its scope to stand upon, to minister, and to reflect.

The approach to realization of "a whole world consisting of peoples who have in the fullest sense entered history and become the concern, no longer of the colonial administrator or the anthropologist, but of the historian"—I quote Aron—implies universalization in a sense that every view of nationhood and history, whatever its quality, comes to count in the problem of order; but it does not mean universalization as an engrossing unity underlying order. Of the multiplicity of states in the increment, some are only nominally qualified—scarcely endowed with that unified view of will, action, and reality called a sense of history. "Man makes history," according to José Ortega y Gasset, "because, faced with a future which is not in his hands, he finds that the only thing he has, that he possesses, is his past . . . ; this is the small ship in which he sets sail toward the unquiet future . . ." Yet, as Robert L. Heilbroner has emphasized, "It can fairly be said that most of the underdeveloped world had no history," in the sense "of a shared political and social and economic self-consciousness which become part of the biographies of millions of human beings, helping to shape these biographies and to give them a common purpose." It is awesome for a people to be, in a phrase from Edmund Burke, "in so deep a play without any sort of knowledge of the game" —assuming nationhood and attempting a role in history without much of a grasp of either, trying to create a future with only a set of clichés for a past.

This proliferation of states without determined political character but with ambition to play a role in history occurs in a world already deeply riven over the meaning of history and, therefore, of the character of a legitimate order. I refer to the confrontation called the Cold War. The interplay between that division and the sudden vast extension of diplomacy—a unification without unity—is truly unprecedented. "Never before have states belonging to the same diplomatic system differed as they differ today," according to Aron. "Never before have people involved in a common enterprise been so disunited on fundamental issues."

ALLIANCES WITH

FLEDGLING STATES

If the laboratory method applied in foreign policy, it would be possible to appraise accurately and conclusively the effectiveness and import of specific undertakings. By running history over again under controlled changes of conditions we should be able to tell for sure how creative one policy or how misguided and delusory another actually was, and how much better or worse or how much of a nothing the putative alternatives were.

Did the Monroe Doctrine actually make much difference in the long run? Was Munich a default of good sense or an exercise of prudence by Chamberlain and Daladier, given the conditions? How differently and more favorably to our interests might other insights and a different approach have arranged matters at Yalta? Was the particular wording of Dean Acheson's speech at the Press Club actually construed as a come-on by the Communists in their designs on Korea, or was it actually a matter of no consequence at all? It would be interesting to have knowledge of such matters in place of the dogmatic assertion and the thin conjecture so often substituted for knowledge in this field.

Obviously, however, the professions of punditry and diplomatic history are in no danger of having their props knocked out from under them by the replacement of speculativeness with certainty in such matters. There is no way of telling for sure how different the actual would have been if it had been differ-

From *Alliance Policy in the Cold War*, Arnold Wolfers (ed.) (Baltimore: Johns Hopkins, 1959). Copyright © 1959 by The Johns Hopkins Press.

ent. Foreign policy, like all of history, gives no opportunity for the laboratory method. One may construct alternatives by hypothesis but not verify them by experiment.

In this light, it is impossible to say anything conclusive about recent United States undertakings in the contested areas of the Middle East and South Asia.

I understand, for example, the doubts raised about the Baghdad Pact, which the United States government has sponsored and encouraged though it has not actually joined. Perhaps it did serve mainly to push Egypt's Nasser into intractability and then to provide him a fulcrum by which to exercise leverage on Moscow. Perhaps without it in existence things would not have come to a head as they did in Baghdad itself, resulting in the destruction of the regime in the very city which gave the pact its name. I do not suppose it will ever be possible to affirm or to deny these suppositions for sure.

The effects of the Eisenhower Doctrine seem equally obscure. The only Middle Eastern government that put itself on the line for the doctrine wound up by having put itself on the spot instead. Maybe things would have come to such a bad pass for the Chamoun regime in any event—doctrine or no doctrine, endorsement or no endorsement. By the same token, it is hard to evaluate the intervention in Lebanon. Critics can point out its ambiguity—its stupendous-seeming start and its squeaky finish. Defenders of Secretary Dulles' policies may counter that matters in Lebanon and its environs might conceivably be much worse than they are and that the landing of United States forces saved the difference in a subtle way. Probably no one can be sure.

The same goes for SEATO. Apologists for it may point out that it was designed to stem Communist advances into Southeast Asia and that, since the whole place has not fallen yet, it obviously has achieved some success. Doubters may counter that the organization has served chiefly to divert working time and travel money away from more serious undertakings for meetings in which the participants orally exchange information that might better have been conveyed by paper. Moreover, a doubter may add, if any good is being done in the area, it is through the Colombo Plan, which has some sinew instead of just having meetings, agenda, and committees.

The inherent unsatisfactory character of politics is nowhere more apparent than among the fledgling states of Asia and Africa. The ambiguity of United States undertakings with respect to these areas results not so much from faults of policy as from the unsatisfactoriness of the political situations of the areas dealt with.

This suggests that the political character of the parties thereto has a bearing on the evaluation of alliances. It is well to understand an alliance as a political engagement between states. One must comprehend that one state may not be as highly developed as another in political capacity, that nominal states are not all alike in the level of their achievement of statehood, and that the contractive capacity of one may vary greatly from that of another.

One does not have to assume that these obvious considerations have been overlooked in recent United States foreign policy undertakings. The matter has been given explicit expression. An official high in the councils of the United States government in the field of foreign policy has laid down a doctrinal point: "There can be no first-class and second-class alliances. . . ." As if to clinch the point, he has said that this could no more be so than that the freedom of an individual in an Asian country, for example, could be considered to be worth less than that of an individual in a European country.[1]

As a moral proposition, as a judgment exercised from the standpoint of divine impartiality, the cited view about uniform concern for freedom is probably sound. An invasion of freedom in one political society should appeal to our compassion and concern just as much as the same thing in another. Yet politically one must take into account that the institutions of freedom are not really uniform from one country to another and that an impingement on freedom of individuals in one place may have

[1] Christian A. Herter as quoted in *Department of State Bulletin*, July 22, 1957, p. 138.

vastly more importance in what it forebodes for our policy than a similar impingement in another place. The fact that large numbers of persons are held in subjection approaching slavery on the African continent arouses our indignation as a violation of justice, but it would be sheer sentimentality to pretend that it moves us in a policy sense to the same degree as would a political development rendering an equal number of Englishmen to the same status. A sundering of a constitution and the imposition of military despotism in Pakistan concerns us, to be sure, but a like occurrence in Canada would concern us vastly more. This does not mean that we value Englishmen at a premium and Africans at a moral discount. Nor does it mean that Canadians are intrinsically more precious to us than subcontinentals. It means that the United States, world power though it may be, is not so powerful as to be uniformly involved in situations everywhere in the world.

It means also one state may be far ahead of another in political development, so that the toppling of a structure of government in one case may have far greater consequences for us than in another.

An ability to establish hierarchies of importance among external entities and situations is the most basic element of prudence in foreign policy. If, by proliferating alliances, we have suffered an impairment of this ability, then the consequences would be serious indeed. Moreover, if there could not be first class and second class alliances, then there obviously could only be second-class.

The point I am trying to make is, I trust, amply clear. Alliances are political arrangements for common objects and mutual benefit between allies. Allies are political entities aligned together and capable of doing each other some good. One alliance may be the equal of another as a liability—as a command on our sense of obligation, but surely they differ in their value as assets to us as the capacity of allies to do us good varies from one case to another.

Let us fasten our attention for the moment on the idea of the state as an association for doing good. Surely the ideal of self-determination rests on this notion. It assumes national freedom as an opportunity for a people to amount to something in the world. Surely also the idea of international cooperation assumes states as entities capable of being helpful to each other. The idea of the state as we accept it as a norm—a political entity geared up to play an historic role—grows out of a sixteenth-century Europe. One of its main characteristics is the existence of a population with the attributes of a populace—that is to say, a people conscious of political identity and of an historic role and identified with a defined territory by habit and history. Another characteristic of the state as we accept it as a norm is the existence of a government with faculties for making policy. It must be identified with the populace. It must be able to make and enforce public decisions requiring the allocation of resources to new patterns of effort. It is not enough to be able merely to provide peripheral security and to enforce custom and domestic order. These are the tasks of police strength and of administration. Government must be more than an arrangement for marshaling force and conducting an administration. It must be political.

Here, in the political quotient, seems to me to lie the distinguishing difference between colonial and national government. A colonial regime has military capacity. It may present administrative resources—often of a relatively high order. It lacks that rapport and identity that enable a regime and a people to relate themselves to each other with the pronoun "we" rather than "they." This lack is not necessarily redressed by the mere fact of juridic status as a state. This inherent colonial characteristic may endure in the unconscious habits of a people and a regime long after the achievement of nominal independence.

In my years of living in Pakistan, for example, I was struck repeatedly with this simple matter of pronouns. It emerged in the discourse not only of common citizens but also of high officials of the bureaucratic structure. In contexts where one might hope for the choice of pronoun to indicate identity between government and nation, regime and people, one would hear instead the pronoun of disjunction. This was a matter of no slight import. It revealed, in a way that no end of political orations would redress, the failure of the political process in the sequel to independence. It typified a default in those concepts whence derives the accountability of governments and the strength and stability of states.

These factors have an enormous bearing on the contractive capacity of governments. I mean not simply their capacity to sign on the dotted line of an international undertaking. I mean the political character that makes such a signature a real asset to the other party of the undertaking. This is the quality of a state as a going concern. Not all states have it in the same degree. I would no more say that there cannot be first-class and second-class alliances than I would say that all corporate contracts are of the same intrinsic relative value irrespective of the quality and deportment of the corporations making them.

We were surprised—at least some people were—when sudden events of July, 1958 wiped out what had been appraised as an asset to us—the whole relationship that the United States had enjoyed with the Iraqi regime, which had contracted into the Baghdad Pact. The initial response was to put this down as an intelligence failure, to cry out the words of Shakespeare's *King John:*

> O, where hath our intelligence been drunk?
> Where hath it slept?

Far more basic and important, however, was the policy surprise. Our appraisal of the regime's signature as an asset was based on an assumption of the regime's actual capability to contract. As things turned out, this proved a false assumption.

I happened not to have been surprised. This was owing to a deep impression that had been left upon me by a conversation with a Pakistani statesman, a man of deep discernment. He once related to me experiences in Baghdad during the immediate sequel to the Suez incursion in the fall of 1956. One day the people had demonstrated in the streets. Soon afterward the King and the Prime Minister, Nuri es-Said, had recounted this phenomenon to him. As he reported it, these two were "as wide-eyed as if a throng of lions or of men from Mars had suddenly materialized in the streets. The people had been out! Amazing! The place was full of Iraqis!" My friend pondered wisely the implications of the circumstance that those in seats of power could not relate themselves to a throng in the streets. He mused on the question of authority. He asked rhetorically: Could a regime really deliver in the face of such disjunction from its people?

Here surely was an instance of what Machiavelli had in mind in commenting on the folly of "alliances made with princes who . . . bring more reputation than substantial help to those who rely on them." [2] Nothing prevented our asking the same question of ourselves. That we did not ask it must have been a result of the fallacy of thinking every alliance is of the first class. There is surely no patent on the item of wisdom that lack of a political base is a grievous weakness in a government.

Surely the deficiency in statehood of a great many of the entities having nominal status as states is one of the deep and serious political characteristics of our time. The American disposition is an equalitarian one. We incline to accept the equality of states not only as the juridic principle, which it properly and solely is, but also as a guideline to world politics. We tend to overlook the special advantages that enabled this country to develop so rapidly from colonial status into a prototype of the states of Europe from which we had derived the example of statehood. The American habit has been to assume parallels between the facts of our own case and the potentials of others and thus to regard every political entity in colonial subordination as a frustrated state and independence as the removal of impediments to development toward a mature and reasonably effective entity according to inherent teleological elements.

In the light of such assumptions we have gone on, in our policies, to postulate economic aid as bound to help the evolutionary process along in the states receiving it, military assistance as necessarily helpful in strengthening the executive au-

---

[2] *Discourses on the First Ten Books of Titus Livius*, Bk. II, chap. xi.

thority and thereby conducive to stability, and alliances, where feasible, as bound to be beneficial in demonstrating and thereby helping to enhance the contractive character of the fledgling states making compact with us.

We need to make careful appraisal of the fledgling states in regard to their characteristics, which bear, I think, basically on their capacity for contractual relations. One characteristic is lack of a pattern of interest groups having political focus. This relates to a characteristic disjunction between political discussion and actual policy and to the emotive and generalized character of political ideas, which show a negative tendency to be against some exterior or interior adversary but not for much of anything. The tendency is to make ideology rather than a line of policy the basis of consensus. Clique control, with an accompanying tendency of the clique enjoying power to consign all rival cliques to the status of enemies of the state, prevails in place of political competition between groups presenting alternative lines of policy. All of this makes for a deficiency in contractive character—that is, in the corporateness that enables a regime to commit its people and its successors.

Every state is *sui generis*, and this is true of the fledgling states as it is of the states well established. The characteristics named above apply to them in varying degrees, but the generalization is sound enough for the purposes at hand. The problems of world politics for us are not only how to fend against the threat of Communist penetration; they include also the development of the fledgling states into states in the full sense of the term. They must become politically as well as economically and militarily viable. Indeed, it is important to understand the degree in which viability in the last two senses is contingent upon viability in the first sense. It is important also for us to understand the ways in which the effort to help along with economic and political viability, especially military viability, may militate against the political goals we should have in mind.

Machiavelli suggested that any state paying over money to others—"though they may be more feeble than herself"—gives sure signs of great weakness and places itself in position of being a tributary.[3] This has more truth in it than we sometimes like to see in our bighearted way with the world. Once we make another state the beneficiary of our aid, we tend in some degree to invest prestige in it. If the receiving state has marked political weaknesses, our giving of aid tends to plight us to the correction of its weaknesses. If this purpose fails, not only the recipient but also the donor feels the consequences.

These aspects take on special relevance when the government with which we enter into contractual relations is not one in the sense of our usual understanding but rather a clique, an in-group. In such instances inevitably the tendency is to commit the prestige of the United States—and by prestige we mean not simply a superficial matter of pride but that standing by which a state is able to command respect, that promise of efficacy that makes for efficacy—to the fortunes and tenure of such an in-group. The recipient group will probably be fully aware of this, even if our own government does not adequately take heed of it at the moment of making commitment. The recipient regime may be able to make use of these factors so as to make its own necessitousness a source of advantage in the relationship.[4] Moreover, commitment to an in-group in the guise of a government in the usual sense tends to foreclose the United States from interchange with rival potential in-groups, which the clique in power will be disposed to regard not simply as rivals but as enemies of the state. The resulting embarrassment to relationships when, as sometimes happens, the in-group loses its grip is obvious. A companion tendency is to subordinate intelligence and reporting functions to the view of the in-group dealt with, so that United States appreciations become derivatives of what the in-group wishes to have accepted.

Through such steps the donor of aid tends to become in some degree the client. It gets a vested interest in the position of the

---

[3] *Ibid.*, chap. xxx.

[4] Something akin to this has happened with respect to the problem of the Formosa Strait, where, by the accounts given out by our own leaders of policy, the subjective requirements of a necessitous regime have become paramount considerations overriding even the factors of military good sense in determining our obligations and commitments.

counterpart group and in shoring up its weaknesses against the perils of a political process.[5] This has a bearing on the simple faith we tend to give repeatedly to the strong-man figure as he rises from time to time in the politically underdeveloped countries. It has become a cliché of our reportage on such areas to observe their prematurity for political processes and as a substitute uncritically to accept every self-vaunted strongman at face value as the solution for the problems of stability and security—overlooking the point, I think easily demonstrable by experience, that strongman rule has been as brittle and perishable as any other kind in the areas concerned.

This brings me to a basic paradox of our world position. As a people disinclined to militarism, at least inclined to regard ourselves as so disinclined, and as a people who above all assert a position against economic determinism and should certainly stand for the primacy of politics in the life and health of the state, we seem to have projected a reverse image of ourselves to the underdeveloped areas. As a people historically and sentimentally disposed against colonialism, we have worked ourselves altogether too much into the position of appearing to stake our interests on the prolongation of colonial conditions of politics in such areas.

Of course, we have not intended to do so. Our actions in this regard have been unwitting rather than purposive. Yet the effect described is inherent in our permitting ourselves to become identified with economic and military solutions, primarily and to the exclusion of others, in the fledgling states. The purposes for which we advocate become limited to strong administration, which we deem necessary to efficacy in economic programs, and to military policy.

Lucian Pye has written on the excessiveness of our expectations first of military policy and second of economic aid. He refers to "our habit of greatly oversimplifying the relationship between public policy and social behavior." In a context refer-

---

[5] Machiavelli was surely inadequate in seeing only the dangers of alliance with a stronger power. (*The Prince*, chap. xxi.) Alliances with weakness have perils of even more subtle character.

ring to Asia but equally applicable to other areas, he notes our addiction to "the notion that political loyalties are largely determined by people's discriminating reaction to alternative policy proposals." Pye continues:

> . . . in societies where the central problem is that of building an effective national community, we often forget that it is the dynamic process of politics and not the degree of rationality in public policies or the particular values expressed by such policies that gives coherence to a people. . . .

He does not dismiss public policy and administrative programs as unimportant. He says simply that they are not enough "to bring order and direction to the transitional societies. . . ." He draws a contrast between communism, "still on the rise in Asia" because "it has focused its energies on political relationships and the possibilities of introducing Western principles into the political sphere," and the non-Communist effort to modernize Asia, the latter concentrating "on administrative and bureaucratic measures," with a result that the West, "as in the past under colonialism, . . . is now seen in Asia largely in the role of the administrator rather than in that of the politician." Mr. Pye concludes:

> . . . the politician in Asia, as elsewhere, is generally held to be shrewder, more subtle and flexible, less rational, less respectable and, above all, more understanding of the complexities of human motivation and behavior than the administrator. Much of the success of the Communists in Asia in filling the role of politician has been due to lack of competition, for competent non-Communists have largely ignored this role in favor of that of the administrator, or the soldier, or the leader who stands above politics.[6]

Mr. Pye adequately describes what happens when we over-concentrate on stability and on administrative and military ave-

[6] "Communist Strategies and Asian Societies," *World Politics,* October, 1958, pp. 118, 127

nues thereto. This, I think, is a large weakness of our attempts at alliances among the politically underdeveloped states. We seem to think the whole thing can be done through firepower and an increment of productive efficiency, whereas the states concerned need above all to progress as political societies; they need to fulfill their nominal status as states.

UNCONVENTIONAL WARFARE

AS A CONCERN OF

AMERICAN FOREIGN POLICY

Sir Keith Hancock has described the plight of a soldier pitted against a sullen and estranged people: "He was living all the time inside enemy lines without ever knowing who his enemy was or where he was. A group of men playing pitch and toss by the roadside was such a common sight . . . that an enemy patrol could easily camouflage itself in this way. Men apparently engaged in work on the land could quickly form an ambush along the hedges whenever a scout or a small boy brought news of approaching troops." [1]

The words are about Ireland in 1921. In essence they might apply to a number of countries at present. The situation depicted is that of unconventional war—a phrase much in vogue, because the phenomena are widely present and the problems posed to our foreign policy are thorny and exasperating. The phrase tends in one respect to be misleading. In suggesting departure from usage, it implies aberration and rarity. Quite the contrary, what one calls unconventional warfare, now active or latent over large parts of the world, is nothing really extraordinary in experience—including our national experience.

From the *Annals of the American Academy of Political and Social Science*, May, 1962. Copyright 1962 by the American Academy of Political and Social Science.

Also from *Nation's Business*, October, 1962, and from an address delivered before a session of the Council for Asian Studies, Philadelphia, Pa., March 26, 1963.

[1] W. K. Hancock, *Four Studies of War and Peace in This Century* (Cambridge, England: Cambridge University Press, 1961), p. 15.

The art in a widely displayed beer advertisement serves as reminder of one famous incident of unconventional war in the American past. It depicts the annihilation in 1876 of a United States cavalry battalion—the word *squadron* was then not yet in style—in a scrape with a heterogeneous collection of aborigines. What overtook Custer and his men at the hands of Chief Gall's Uncapapas, Crazy Horse's Ogalallas, and Two Moons' Cheyennes was not the first or the last instance of the doing-in of disciplined troops in full panoply by primitive foemen. The campaign climaxed by the Custer Massacre was one of many waged by United States troops against red Indians—not to mention a large number of similar efforts carried on by our colonial antecedents. American experiences relevant to unconventional warfare have not been confined to military ventures against primitive foes. In some phases of the war of the American Revolution the Americans were the ones in a primitive role, pitted against British forces which preserved stately forms of combat. All of our conventional wars have had unconventional aspects—especially the Civil War of a century ago, when both sides got involved in bushwhacking.

So irregular war is an old story for the United States, but the present problems require more light than the long past can give. Proceeding from some basic and simple abstractions, I hope to add clarity to the relevant problems confronting United States policy. The topic suggests such abstract treatment as an alternative to handling it by reciting empirical characteristics of a number of local situations in a way likely to be overtaken by events as soon as published if not before.

My own qualifications leave no choice, for, though I share the bias for the actual over the abstract owned to by Mark Twain when he said he liked to hear war talk by men who had been to war better than moon talk by poets who had not been to the moon, the fact remains that I have not engaged in, witnessed, or even planned any unconventional warfare and so am confined to what I have read or heard or can surmise. The subject bears on the attributes of authority and the nature of conflict and civil order in relation to the sort of human association called the state. My generalizations focus on these concepts.

A distinction—however obvious—between coercion and consent is basic to them. These two terms concern methods of adjustment among intentions. An intention encompasses a desire extracted from the realm of wishing and made into a purpose, the action envisaged for realizing it, and the means pertinent to such action. Where individuals are not solitary—that is, in any social situation—intentions tend to intersect, and paths of action to cross, and entities must cooperate or compete with others for control of means and accept the purposes of others, oppose them, or get their own purposes accepted instead. All collaboration within society involves adjustment among intentions. The basic ways to such adjustment involve action on the purpose or on the means aspect of intentions. To get another's compliance on a basis of recognized common or compatible purposes is to proceed by consent. To get it by action or threat or intimation of action to deprive him of choice of acting adversely to one's own intentions—that is, to constrain him by actual or potential force brought to bear on his means—is to coerce him. *Coerce* and its cognate, *coercion*, are sometimes used more loosely to include irresistible suasion. The sense as used here is a restrictive one integrally involving physical compulsion.

Compliance to some pattern of intentions, whether through consent or coercion or a mixture of both, is basic to all human associations. A characteristic of a state as a human association, though this does not exhaust its attributes, is the intention to establish and to maintain a monopoly of the right to use or to license coercion pervasively over a particular area—a point requiring restatement from time to time even though presumably well known virtually to everybody.

Probably no association bearing title to statehood maintains a monopoly of coercion as an unexceptionable operative fact. The authority of even the firmest state is chronically challenged by coercion lawlessly undertaken. Less solidly established states —the present world abounds with them, old and new—may be confronted by tribal or other forms of particular coercion left over from the past and still suffered to persist or still defiantly asserted against state prerogative. The test of statehood in this respect is one of tendencies rather than of perfection. When that monopoly is effectively asserted only in a few alcoves of authority but ignored widely across the countryside, the state concerned represents unfulfilled ambition. When such a monopoly, formerly however effective, begins to feel a challenge of competition beyond its power to cope, the essence of the state concerned is ebbing.

Rounding out and shoring up its asserted monopoly of coercion are ever unfinished business for any state—in societies entitled to be called free as well as those unfree, in pluralistic systems as well as totalitarian. The point of distinction between such types is not whether coercion is centralized or divided around but whether those in charge of the apparatus of coercion —that is, those governing—are effectively bridled in respect of power to choose purposes for which and modes by which to apply coercion through being made dependent on institutional concurrences not themselves subject to coercion.

Still another proportion on the matter is the tendency of consent and coercion to merge. They are not necessarily opposed to each other. It is wrong to think of them as antithetic in such a way that the more there is of one, the less there can be of the other. Successful statecraft uses each to enhance the other. A firm grasp on power to coerce, however essential, is not enough alone to ensure strength in a state. The range of purposes achievable through sheer compulsion by a governing apparatus is small. A regime with no means beyond those of force and fear for ensuring compliance would be able to do little beyond maintaining a fragile order among a sullen populace—an exhaustive, expensive, and dubious process when carried out through coercion alone. Consent is highly perishable unless sustained by power to protect—a power dependent on ability to bring force to bear, which ability in turn is determined in some degree by a regime's being able to count on willing support among a people.

Such rudimentary observations concerning the nature of state and authority must suffice for the time being so as to permit a shift of attention to the character of war as a phenomenon of states. The term *war*—though often loosely applied to any rigorous conflict, especially one involving violence—more accurately refers to a contest of purpose carried on between or among organized groups having or aspiring to have the attribute of statehood represented in title to a monopoly of coercion over a given area. Each side in war seeks, to its own conclusive advantage, a redress of relative capabilities for coercion between itself and the adversary—this as a condition necessary to enable its own purposes to prevail. The contending sides may go about this in many ways—mobilizing their resources, instilling support for their respective causes, and trying to impair support, confidence, and will within the adversary establishment. Whatever else they may do, the contending sides must, as an essential element, bring force to bear upon each other. Indeed, the term *war,* strictly used, is reserved to circumstances involving use of force in the direct, unequivocal sense of discharging energy with destructive intent. The component of violence and the requirement of the contenders' having or coveting a monopoly of coercion deserve stress as characteristics: without the one, there is only tension; without the other, there may be only violence for particular advantage in defiance of state authority but without a purpose to assume a part of state authority.

The characteristics of war stated above relate to war as a phenomenon whether between or within states—war across or within state boundaries, war as an international or as a civil phenomenon. The distinctions between those two sorts are less materially relevant here than distinctions between war as an acknowledged enterprise overtly prosecuted and war as a clandestine activity. It would be convenient to be able to state simple correlations between war as an international strife and war as an acknowledged activity and between civil war and clandestine war. Such links come easily—too easily—to mind; international wars have characteristically been acknowledged wars, and civil wars have often been clandestine. Analysis permits no such litmus-paper precision, however. Acknowledged wars usually have clandestine aspects. International wars often entail civil conflict. Rare is a civil conflict without some stimulus and abetment from outside. Civil wars may rise to the acknowledged status of international wars.

Acknowledged wars are those taking on the character described by John Locke as sedate hostility. Among states, each existing on a basis of a putative monopoly of coercion within its area, a certain community of culture inheres. Different and disparate as they may be, certain elements of symmetry apply between them. At some demarcation or frontier zone, the span of state jurisdiction leaves off. Each has a licit and known organization to keep internal order and formally identified forces for defending its bounds and moving against external enemies. Each is disposed to make constantly manifest its control over its domain. Each has official forms for making its purposes known and channels, direct or through intermediaries, for communicating them to an adversary state. These and other such circumstances form a basis for a pattern of conventions—a term itself implicit of culture in common—affecting warfare. They enable one to tell with fair accuracy where, when, and whence a boundary was transgressed, to mark a commencement of hostilities, and to identify the parties. Issues of war and conditions of peace become ascertainable. It may be feasible—to name a few aspects of mutual management of hostilities—to arrange between antagonists dependable understandings about exchange of prisoners, exemption of stipulated areas from military use and reprisal, and the interruption and cessation of hostilities. In the degree of the approach to symmetry between the side attempting to firm up or to hold on to title to the monopoly of coercion and the side seeking to withhold it or to wrest some or all of it away, civil war also tends to become conditioned by such conventions.

Unconventional war, multifarious in its patterns, is war relatively or entirely unconditioned by elements of the common culture relevant to hostilities. In a particular situation this characteristic may be due to one or more of a number of circumstances: an unbridgeable inherent difference of culture between antagonists, as in myriad instances of aboriginal resistance to state authority—for example, in the desultory wars once fought by Indians against the establishment of state dominion in this continent; an inherent impossibility of any concession of legitimacy between the contending sides, as in the account in the Book of Judges of the onslaught by Gideon's band on behalf of Jehovah against the prevailing worship of Baal; a pronounced disparity in numbers or weapons such as to foreclose one side from venturing openly into the field and to force it to avoid identification of its forces; or the vicarious involvement of outside parties constrained by expediency to keep their role concealed or at least deniable.

Whatever the determining circumstances, unconventional war is amorphous war, generally characterized by asymmetry in juridical status and military resources at hand as between antagonists. One side is overtly in dominion and holds the structure of government, public channels of communication, centers of administration, and military posts. The other side's forces must operate in the interstices, hiding their identity, not wearing military uniforms whether for lack of them or for expediency, taking protective coloration from the milieu, and being furtive about support from outside, using tactics of harassment—disrupting revenue, impeding communications. The protagonist's aim at this stage is to disintegrate rather than to overwhelm the ruling establishment. The direction of attack is vague. It is difficult to mark the onset of hostilities, to gauge the state of battle, and to appraise the relative situations of the two sides, and often, virtually impossible to manage hostilities along to a formal and precise conclusion.

In a typical situation falling within the range of concern here —that is, an instance of internal aggression—the protagonist's side is intent upon impairing the effectiveness of the regime's writ, undermining its reputation for effectiveness in punishing its enemies and protecting its adherents, in sum trying to undercut the competence and capacity of the rulership to command allegiance. The aim, however, is not merely to destroy the manifest effectiveness of the regime but ultimately to take over as successor to the regime. The asymmetrical relation between the two sides and the concomitant unconventionality of hostilities are a temporary necessity. The aim is not to protract unconventional war as an end in itself but, rather, to redress the asymmetry of the relationship as rapidly as feasible and prudent, to get popular support or acquiescence, to take overt control of a stretch of land, to stake out a claim on legitimacy, to assume a governing role, to affect the conventions of belligerency, to claim a right to receive assistance from abroad, to move into a position enabling the protagonist side to reverse the factors of asymmetry to the disadvantage of the present ruling apparatus so that it becomes the side forced into the interstices while the challengers take over the structure of government and effect their claim to the monopoly of coercion. This—the basis and title of rulership—is the central prize of the conflict.

While it lasts, unconventional war thus represents frustration both to the protagonist group and to the governing establishment. It does so to the former because its aim is to get out of the marginal situation, to raise the level of combat to that of conventional hostilities, and then to prevail and to succeed in establishing its own monopoly of coercion. Protracted unconventional war represents frustration to the governing group because its ambition must be to round out or to redeem its control, to suppress competition in coercion, and to eliminate all challenge to its ascendancy.

The asymmetry of the situation attending unconventional war represents an inherent advantage to the ruling group. So long as the asymmetrical character obtains, the opposition is kept from prevailing. The ruling group must strive to keep the struggle unconventional—confining combat to the back areas, forcing its enemy to remain furtive, denying him sufficient control of territory to justify a title to govern and a right to receive outside assistance. Beyond that, the ruling group must strive to find, to fix, to fight, and to finish the irregular forces. All the while, it must maintain its hold on the structure of government, on main lines of communication, the centers of administration, and the centers of its military system.

This last point deserves stress. It is counter to a tendency to regard the military requirements of a government beset by a guerrilla threat as confined to meeting the challenge solely on its own grounds and terms—to suppose the prudent course to be that of putting aside other military concerns, adopting a guerrilla-like guise for its own forces, and deploying them into the bush to shoot it out with the foe. It is, indeed, necessary to carry the initiative against the enemy, meeting him on his own terms—likely to be at best a tedious, exacting process. Beyond that, it is necessary also to hold onto a monopoly of formal military posture as a symbolic and essential aspect of state authority. The final business of stamping out the guerrilla force, moreover, is likely to be a job for conventional forces.

Battle is only one aspect of the competition between government and challenger. The contest covers other factors of fitness to govern—involving capacity to elicit consent as well as capacity to apply coercion and, especially, the talent for using each to enhance the other. Each side, according to its lights, presents the best practicable combination of intimidation and justice. Finding a favorable milieu among the people of a countryside, internal aggression prospers. Deprived of their support, the cause withers—and the inherent military advantage resting with the regime takes its effect. The affection or disaffection of the local society thus is a decisive factor in the outcome of the armed aspects of the struggle. For either side, winning consent is inseparable from capability to exact retribution of its enemies and to protect its adherents—that is, coercive power. The relation is reciprocal.

The easy answer is to suggest the undertaking of internal reform to satisfy a people's requirements and to win their affection as a way to fend off or to roll back a threat of internal aggression. This is too easy an answer, for it tends to beg the crucial questions. Internal aggression is a malady of politically weak societies. No politically viable society is an easy mark for it. Giving effect to internal reform itself demands a large degree of political strength. A regime with thin margins of support is likely to be in poor position for prodigies of creativeness and initiative in policy. Yet the answer is inherently the right and necessary one. Curing a susceptibility to internal aggression requires correction of the constitutional deficiencies inviting it— using constitutional in a broad sense.

Again, it is not easy. Creativeness in government has always been a matter of lifting by bootstraps. Maintaining a viable order has normally been a touch-and-go business in political history. A basic, broad circumstance of the contemporary scene is an extraordinary incidence of weakness among regimes. This may be attributed to a number of causes. One is surely the rise of self-determination as virtually a political absolute of our time —so that many peoples are in position of essaying national independence while scarcely grasping the rudiments of nationhood. An attendant circumstance is the progressive decline and disappearance of the imperial-colonial order—this concomitant with the emergence into independence of increasing numbers of political entities with unformed political character. An aggravating circumstance—attributable to the efficacy of modern communications—is a heightening of awareness of economic, social, and political disparities among peoples, with the effect of intensifying demands for improvement among those disadvantaged and often arousing expectations beyond the power of available talents and resources to fulfill.

These are the marks of societies thrust toward modernity without the habits and institutions required for coping with it. The basic factors of deficiency are variant from one situation to another. They stem from tribal backgrounds, from communal divisions, and from varieties of traditional inhibitions. Typically they are aggravated by discontinuities in economic change, by cultural dislocations, by accompanying personal and group anxieties, by power of modern communications to elicit mass responses, and often by dynamics of population growth.

In some instances a relevant deficiency may be a lack of identity among a population—identity related to a sense of history and a realistic set of expectations held in common. Again, the attribute lacking may be linkage between the populace and a defined territory held in its consciousness as the scene of its history and its expectations. A relevant deficiency may also be the lack of a regime sharing identity with the people and endowed with true policy-making attributes and administrative capacity—in other words, capability to make and to give effect to decisions marking new directions in public effort and new allocations of resources. Still another characteristic deficiency is a lack of such sense of proportion and assurance in political affairs as to enable a regime to tolerate political opposition and not to harry it into hostility and as to enable individuals and groups to temper their criticism of those in authority with some regard for the limits of the feasible and to impose a regime's policies without venturing into sedition. These are rare and fragile attributes. It is easy enough to list them. It may be infinitely difficult to remedy a lack of them; yet of such are the deficiencies rendering a society vulnerable to internal aggression.

A second major condition underlying the importance of indirect aggression and unconventional war in the current world situation is the combination of position, power, and purpose represented in the world Communist movement. This aspect needs to be put in proportion. Communism and indirect aggression go hand in hand in our consciousness. In an oversimple corollary, without communism there would be no woes of weakness, internal disorder, and subversion, and every state would enjoy a serene, assured existence. Such woes have in fact been rife in large parts of the world over considerable recurrent spans of time without any stimulus from communism. Imaginably, some of the mischief in the form of internal aggression which Communist regimes have sponsored and abetted against other governments might have occurred under quite different auspices. For example, a still czarist Russia might conceivably have supported guerrilla warfare in Greece, and China consolidated under any persuasion might have pursued its ambitions by vicarious assault on other governments in Southeast Asia. Hypotheses of this character, frequently propounded by analysts disposed to discount the significance of communism as a force per se in international affairs, are not susceptible of refutation. One might just as well accept them. It scarcely disposes of a problem to allege the possibility of its existence in another form under different circumstances.

What is important to take into account is the universality of the claim on the future asserted on behalf of communism. Its exponents profess to regard their own system as designated under a law of history to exercise receivership over every society after the inevitable failure of alternate methods of governing. They presume a natural prerogative with respect to every society's future. All outlooks, interests, and purposes other than their own are deviant and inherently lacking in legitimacy, but Communists are capable of discriminating among them in accordance with the degree in which they are assumed to conduce to the furtherance of Communist purposes and opportunities. Violence in furtherance of Communist aims is inherently justifiable. Disorder is rationalized as an agent of order when it serves to further Communist advantage. War is regarded as illegitimate only if it opposes the asserted momentum of history toward Communist ascendancy and is condoned and extolled when it conduces toward expansion of the Communist position.

Propositions of this tenor, standard elements of Communist discourse and policy, were rounded out and proclaimed in the declaration of Communist leaders of eighty-one countries convening in Moscow in November of 1960 and reiterated in the program of the Communist party of the Soviet Union adopted at the Twenty-second Congress in October of 1961. They implicitly endorse indirect aggression aimed at any non-Communist regime—save, of course, such as may be fomented by interests working in opposition to Communist purposes.

One should not construe from such propositions a conclusion that the Communist powers have contracted themselves into underwriting every outbreak of war, conventional or unconventional, prosecuted against another regime and likely to promote Communist aims. What is asserted is a right to interpose with support whenever the Communist powers find it opportune. The two polar capitals of communism, Moscow and Peking, may diverge on their estimates of opportunity, but they are agreed on the basic assertion of the rightfulness of helping history along whenever it is opportune. The Communist view specifically abjures the idea of an analogous right of other governments to interpose in support of any effort to overthrow a regime identified with or regarded as favorable to or veering toward communism. Under the Communist assumption about the movement of history, each Communist interposition is regarded as innocent assistance solely of a domestic character, but such anti-Communist interposition is illicit and properly raises international issues.

Obviously, the developing rivalry and enmity between the Soviet Union and China make a difference with respect to the character and strength of the threat posed by Communist purposes to the internal security of other societies, but it is not a determining difference. The problems are altered but not disposed of. The combination of systematic animosity and a great base of operations still presses upon other societies in the degree that they are made vulnerable by propinquity and by factors of internal weakness.

By the Communist premise, any faltering regime is an eligible target for Communist purposes. In one sort of typical case, doubt over its own popular standing may cause a regime to seek survival in an oppressive order, leaving effective political communication to clandestine adversaries and propelling opposition into surreptitious armed activity against the regime. In another instance, political forces representing revolutionary impulses may take over on a basis of rallying mass emotion behind aspirations all too likely to be beyond capacity to fulfill. Instances of the one sort present a danger of permitting Communists to pre-empt the evocative aspects of political life within a country and to become the agents of an internal aggression enjoying, if not active, at least passive support from oppositionist elements and the disenchanted with no place else to go. Instances of the other sort present a danger of making the Communists the receivers for bankrupt revolution. Either course presents the

Communist movement opportunity for reinforcing its claim to the mantle of revolution and for a rising momentum of Communist success without resort to acknowledged war—an eventuality too weighted with uncontrollable destructiveness to be a practicable instrument of policy for the great powers under present circumstances.

It would be presumptuous to regard any society, including our own, as so perfected, so assured in the habits of order and accommodation, and so unified in spirit, as to be beyond any possible danger of internal division and exempt from internal aggression. Let authority falter, let large numbers lose confidence in the system of justice, and let communication break down among large blocs of the populace, and such danger may become clear and present in any land. The areas where the threat, active or abeyant, is significantly high are along the Asian littoral, in much of the Middle East, and through Africa and much of Latin America. The threat is compounded among necessitous countries in proximity to sources of Communist material support and in chronic latent danger of invasion by massed Communist forces.

With respect to such countries, whether subject to a single threat of internal aggression or to a compounded threat of both internal attack and external pressure, the United States policy is to render what assistance it can in improving the capability of states to make their way as going concerns in face of the challenges of modernity and, where required and opportune, to assist them with respect to the military factors of the problem of security.

Expressed in broad abstraction, United States foreign policy is directed toward the ultimate goal of an order representing collaboration among juridically free and equal states viable in independence—this in succession to the now largely eroded imperial-colonial dispensation. In application, this aspiration is greatly affected by precepts out of the American past. These honor, besides public order and responsibility, the ideas of popular government and national independence. In the American outlook, any people anywhere is to be regarded as an inherent community with an inherent potential for succeeding as a civil polity. If something appears radically amiss in the general conditions of another land, then the American presumption attributes fault to the rulership. Government of the people, by the people, and for the people is taken to be the universal formula for proper and secure government. Any regime imposed from outside is by definition violative of that requirement.

Accordingly, the American attitude likes to encourage order in another land but also tends to sympathize with those who rise against authority on domestic considerations voiced as demands for a better break in life. It regards as wholly unconscionable the projection of forcible interference across a boundary to stimulate such trouble or to suppress it. With all these attitudes in mind, United States policy does its best to work out a consistent mode of operation.

Obviously, the United States' policy has in it a notable amount of self-projection. I do not call this reprehensible. It is inevitable. Any nation can advocate only for the values it accepts. In striving to help any other society become as we think it should be, inevitably we think along lines of encouraging it to be like ourselves. Yet the thought abashes us, and our spokesmen feel constrained to proclaim preservation and enhancement of diversity as our aims in dealing with necessitous societies.

Communist policy—being predicated on an ultimate destiny of all other peoples, after successive failures of every other attempted course, to be compelled into the pattern of Marxism-Leninism—presents an instance of self-projection counterpart to ours. Indeed, the conceptual parallels between the Communist approach and our own are striking. Those with a wont to express all foreign policy issues in analytic models are likely to find so much likeness as to conclude that no worthwhile difference obtains. No labored answer is necessary. It was William James, I believe, who once quoted a philosophic farmer as observing that after all there was not much difference between the best and the worst fellow in town but that such difference as there was was all important.

The focus here is not on justification but on the practical

prospects. One often hears the issues of the contemporary world expounded as a contest between versions of world order, one of which is bound to prevail to the exclusion of the other. No one knows. The great globe may well prove too vast and obdurate to be fitted into any scheme of order. The final score in world affairs is not necessarily to be determined by a toting up of advantages and disadvantages in competition for affecting the future of feeble and vulnerable states.

With this disclaimer, I see few reasons for assurance that the United States will be able to deal successfully with the problems of shoring up societies subject to the dangers in question. This dour appraisal is ventured despite two successful efforts to suppress internal aggression enjoying external Communist support —in Greece and in the Philippines. Both were special cases. Every instance of the phenomena is a special case in the sense that relevant lessons transferable from one case to another are hard to find.

In the Greek instance, success turned primarily on closure of Communist access from the outside—a development made possible by Yugoslavia's decision to resist domination by the Soviet Union. Also, despite age-old natural obstacles to unity in Greece, an ancient historic tradition deep in general consciousness was latent and could be invoked against divisive forces at work.

In the instance of the Philippines—perhaps the most significant success involving the United States in helping to allay danger from internal, unconventional war—the distinguishing characteristics are more varied. The instance still bemuses us. I have often heard participants in that effort extol it as a model for all ventures to cope with such danger. The formula goes like this: the way to shore up a country against the guerrilla menace is to have it be a preponderantly Catholic country, with four centuries of close rule by a European state in its background, these 400 years followed by a half century or so of tutelage by the United States, with the United States having formed and trained its constabulary and its army and having had a hand in its educational institutions and in building its roads, and so on; add to all that a charismatic leader of great reliability, energy, imagination, and sense of how to govern; and the situation is well on the road to solution.

Our cause would be well favored if conditions affecting the outcome in the Greek and Philippine instances could be duplicated elsewhere—I have in mind Southeast Asia, especially South Vietnam and Laos—but they are not likely to be. Moreover, in general, the material aspects both of economic development and of military security—exacting as they are—are yet for us the simplest parts of the broad problem. The more obdurate parts of the problem are those falling within the jurisdiction of the societies concerned—largely beyond reach of benign assistance from abroad. These aspects relate to the views of human possibilities within their cultures, to the attitudes toward each other taken by regimes and peoples, to the intangibles of allegiance and authority.

Making up for such deficiencies—if they could be redressed at all—would require in extreme cases interposition of a most deep and pervasive sort. Many circumstances of the contemporary world militate against such action. For one thing, the great states are subject to judgment by whatever standards they proclaim. Equitably or not—those proclaiming lofty principles are held to account more rigorously for that very fact. As exponents of nonintervention, we are obliged to abide by what we assert. An analytic precisionist might insist on terming our actions interventions in any case. I should not dispute the point. The interventions available to a power prepossessed by the concept of nonintervention are constricted by the requirement of keeping a measure of consistency. Ours is probably the first instance of a people and a government essaying at once to adhere to the gospel of nonintervention and to play the role of a great power with responsibilities and commitments of truly imperial scope. In consequence, we may not be entirely inhibited against intervening, but such ventures, constrained to be ambiguous, are likely to be awkward and ineffectual.

A second inhibiting circumstance is American fastidiousness about warfare. However much of it there may have been in the past, including the national past, the present attitude takes war as an aberrant phenomenon—a disgraceful departure from the norm. The American fastidiousness about warfare may be summed up in a general's famous abjuration, at the time of the Korean War, against getting involved in the wrong war in the wrong place at the wrong time. The point has a self-evident cogency. Unfortunately, any unconventional war in which the nation may find itself involved is all too likely to prove to be precisely such a triply unfavorable sort of war. Such conflict is likely to be indeterminate. Industrial proficiency and high military technology—points of excellence in the American method in war—are at a discount. The measure of gain is elusive. The idea of winning seems intangible. These aspects tax the patience of a people disposed to expect, to compute, and to report rapid progress in all endeavors.

A regime beset by internal aggression, moreover, is not likely to fill the bill completely as an appealing ally. Societies with great public spirit and regimes full of civic virtue are unlikely targets for such conflict. Any regime needing our help in such extremity would likely present characteristics troublesome to liberal sensibilities. That counsel of perfection disposed to urge the withholding of effort except on behalf of unequivocally meritorious causes would have an array of moral arguments for remaining aloof. Those with an exclusive preponderance for backing sure winners would be in position to cite expediential reasons for remaining unentangled.

The threat posed by unconventional war, however, does not humor such preconceptions. The choices afforded are characteristically miserable. If unable or unwilling to respond to the demands posed by this type of conflict, the United States must eventually choose between relinquishing the field and assuming military initiatives on its own terms.

The advantages accruing to the Communist purpose in this competition are obvious, for the Communist cause epitomizes, on a world scale and in a historic span, essential characteristics of unconventional warfare—an onslaught both within and outside the framework of states, impairing as it can what it cannot control in hope of eventually taking it over, an amorphous but relentless aggression flowing toward every point of opportunity, taking care to avoid identifying itself until time to claim the reward of power, and ever remaining beyond reach of settled understanding.

The greatest advantage accruing to the adversary—perhaps I should say adversaries—is retention of uncontested initiative for internal aggression. Along the Asian littoral, for example, Communist resources sustain unacknowledged war against beset non-Communist regimes. Against these onslaughts there is defense—supported by our assistance—but no riposte in the form of unconventional warfare waged with our assistance within Communist-ruled areas. This unequal relationship is explicable on the basis of enormous obstacles to such action within a realm subject to unabashed totalitarian controls.[2] It reflects also the disposition, on this side of the confrontation, ever to hope for settlement along some line of equilibrium and a reluctance to risk heightening the wider dangers of the world situation by disturbing the balances to the adversary's disadvantage. Here, as in other respects, our policy is limited to the thankless defensive.

Our policy is meliorative. The adversary's is revolutionary. Our policy, as leaders occasionally remind us, is premised on the United Nations Charter and indulges hopes in a tendency toward accommodation—an unfolding toward a happy time when all nations, including those within the adversary's span, will at last bring their purposes into harmony with each other in keeping with the Charter's principles. The adversary asserts an expectation to win a world, and an intention to push this expectation toward fulfillment. He has, in effect, made a unilateral amendment of the Charter. This difference underlies the asymmetry of the situation. It is scarcely conceivable—even if we were to will it—that the asymmetry of attitudes toward unconventional war could be redressed on the basis of adherence to present policy. It is inconceivable simply because unconventional war can scarcely be raised for the ends of amelioration, accommodation, or the easing of tensions.

[2] Franklin A. Lindsay, "Unconventional Warfare," *Foreign Affairs*, Vol. 40, No. 2 (January, 1962), p. 272.

ON UNDERSTANDING

THE UNALIGNED

Any American having lived, as I have, for a considerable time in a distant but relatively accessible non-Western country is likely to have recollections of at least one homeland friend who stopped off on tour, saw the museums and landmarks, shopped in the bazaars, conversed with some cabinet ministers at tea, met a few bureaucrats and professors of the locality, chatted with students, and, after a week, went on his way aglow and atwitter with a sense of new understanding of the land and its people—leaving his host to muse upon the contrast between his guest's quick, confident conclusions and his own wariness about claiming to understand the environment. Apparent points of identity induced a sympathetic response in the guest, and this made him sure of having gained insights, whereas the more skeptical host would ponder on the subtleties of cultural diversity, the elusiveness of real insight, the ephemeral and misleading nature of sympathy without insight as a base, and the ambiguity of understanding.

That last word is one likely to recur frequently in discourse on foreign policy, whether at sentimental levels of discussion or in exacting forums of decision. Hardly a speaker nowadays omits urging international understanding. Rare is the report or resolution that fails to invoke it. Obviously, the quality and the function represented by this word deserve reason's endorsement. It is difficult to imagine anyone openly advocating its

From *Neutralism and Nonalignment*, Laurence W. Martin (ed.) (New York: Praeger, 1962). Copyright 1962 by The Washington Center of Foreign Policy Research.

opposite, *misunderstanding*. The synonymity of the word for *stranger* and that for *enemy* in most primitive languages suggests at least a tendency of comprehension to abate hostility and promote friendship in human affairs. The idea of creating understanding underlies a great many current undertakings in international relations. Its truth and utility, however, should be seen as relative rather than absolute. Either must be weighed against warnings of dangers in intimacy uttered by such wise men as Aesop, Publilius Syrus, and Shakespeare.[1] Professor John Stoessinger has aptly pointed out limits to the idea of a necessary linkage between better understanding and closer mutuality.[2] A recent book by Stuart Cloete reflects the possibilities of increasing one's awareness of estrangement through greater knowledge of exotic cultures.[3] My own advocacy of understanding in world affairs—now recorded to fulfill the formalities —is conditioned only by a caveat against assumptions equating it invariably with affinity.

Here, however, the purpose is not so much to take a stand in favor of understanding as to examine what it entails, especially in the sectors of policy comprising the precepts and endeavors by which a government undertakes to relate itself to the portions of the world lying beyond the span of its jurisdiction.

Two of the several meanings of the ambiguous term "understanding" are relevant. It seems like a good idea to distinguish between them and then to relate them to each other. They are almost alike but not quite, and the difference is important. First is understanding in a sense of gaining a full mental grasp of the nature, significance, or explanation of something. Second is understanding in a sense including all such comprehension and, besides all that, developing a sympathetic attitude regarding the object of comprehension. Objective appreciation is common to both meanings, but the second has in addition a quality of favorable subjective response. The first involves taking measure

---

[1] According to each of the three, familiarity breeds contempt.

[2] John G. Stoessinger, *The Might of Nations* (New York: Random House, 1961), p. 25.

[3] Stuart Cloete, *West with the Sun* (New York: Doubleday, 1962).

of something, while the second involves that plus accord. The first embraces comprehension of qualities, but the second includes also some degree of community of qualities. Even adversaries may understand each other in the first sense of the term—and indeed, as Professor Stoessinger has made amply clear, it is highly important for them to seek to do so.[4] Allies and friends understand each other in the second sense—at least to the extent of their understanding in this sense, nations may be described as being in accord.

The first sense of the term applies to consideration of phenomena in a detached, scientific fashion unencumbered by preferences and invoking no frame of values. The approach is akin to that ascribed to an anthropologist by Ruth Benedict:

> To the anthropologist, our customs and those of a New Guinea tribe are two possible social schemes for dealing with a common problem, and in so far as he remains an anthropologist he is bound to avoid any weighting of one in favor of the other. He is interested in human behavior, not as it is shaped by one tradition, our own, but as it has been shaped by any tradition whatsoever.[5]

Though intent to comprehend the values of any social group, one taking this approach does not himself invoke any scheme of values. He wants to enhance understanding solely as comprehension—not as a concept entailing sympathy, accord, or identity. He notes likeness and diversity as qualities of relationship between or among entities from which he stands intellectually aloof, but not as qualities of relationship between himself and others.

Far from being, like an anthropologist, concerned merely with comprehending other societies while remaining indifferent to points of community or diversity between his own society and any other, a policy-maker is enormously concerned about them. Points in common, in so far as they obtain or can be devel-

---

[4] Stoessinger, *The Might of Nations*, pp. 406–20.
[5] Ruth Benedict, *Patterns of Culture* (Boston: Houghton Mifflin, 1961), p. 1.

oped, are essential to the dialogue of policy and diplomacy. To find none whatever—to be in a world devoid of points of response—would amount to being alienated and isolated in the world of policy. The proponents of policy must seek points of community between the home base and the world environment. Recurring allusions in our discourse to the preservation and nourishment of diversity as an aim of our foreign policy tend to obscure this idea. The elements of diversity in the world are likely to suffice without being given attentive care. Policy must seek to bridge diversity—not merely to recognize it or to preserve it. This is not an absolute statement. Only a foreign policy dogmatic and totalitarian to the utmost degree conceivable would aim to wipe out all diversity or even to maintain animus against all diversity. Nevertheless, the concept of a need to bridge diversity is essential to the understanding of understanding in foreign policy.

Moreover, policy is concerned not only with understanding circumstances but also with affecting them. Policy involves the exercise of preferences; choice is its very essence. The grasp of the world and the view of history underlying any version of foreign policy are not simply passive intellectual appreciations of the external environment and of the nature of human affairs. They constitute major premises, articulated or unarticulated, by which to exercise choice, to make decisions, and to bring will to bear. Political decisions—like all decisions—involve opting for one course and renouncing alternatives, favoring one possibility to the disadvantage of another, committing influence and resources to a particular course in preference to something else. The business of states and governments, in so far as it is political, involves choosing sides and thus entails weighing values, not with uninvolved objectivity, but with an aim to invoking them as guides to action.

It would misstate the case to imply mutual exclusion between the two kinds of understanding, associating one solely with political endeavor and the other with scientific approaches. The two are neither inextricably linked nor altogether separate. The description given for an anthropologist's outlook surely serves in the field of policy. It applies to the approach of a political scientist as distinct from a policy-maker. Yet, walks of life other than political, even the most coldly detached and scientific, have aspects requiring understanding in the sense entailing accord or sympathy. For example, however objective and indifferent to questions of community of values in surveying the workings of society as an object of scientific interest, an anthropologist is involved, in a different sense, and must operate with a different kind of understanding in dealing with, say, colleagues and superiors. For then society is the element he swims in, rather than that which he scans and measures as it flows past. The point of distinction is which kind of understanding is instrumental and which is purposive. In the field of anthropology—to labor the example—a scientist may employ the second kind of understanding of the working of society to ensure an opportunity to pursue the first kind of understanding. In the field of policy, understanding in the first sense is instrumental to understanding in the second. Thus, while the anthropologist seeks to keep his preferences walled off from the phenomena he studies, the proponent of policy must surely find understanding in the sense of objective knowledge of use only as he brings it to bear in clarifying, refining, and helping to realize a set of preferences.

The policy-maker works at understanding the world from a base consisting of the essences of his own society's character, possibilities, and requirements, as he understands them. From this base, he sorts out what is relevant or irrelevant, important or unimportant, favorable or unfavorable, alarming or reassuring, and feasible or unfeasible in the environment. In doing so, he focuses on the frames of understanding, so far as he can understand them, dominant in other governments and other societies. He embraces in this quest an understanding of their understanding of his own government's understanding of them, and assumes that the process is reciprocated. He looks for points of response and assumes that potential respondents are doing likewise in return, in a complex and continuous interaction. The basic concepts from which the process of understanding begins can be subtly affected by the process—and here, again, the effects are assumed to be reciprocal. The continuously interacting essays in understanding elude measurement and definition. Approximations and generalizations must do. To gain even an approximate understanding of the understanding thus operative within another government's frame of policy is to understand it in the first sense of the term used here. To be able to concur substantially in another government's frame of understanding as thus understood and to sense a reciprocal concurrence is to approach understanding in the second sense of the term.

Anyone in a foreign government undertaking to understand the American understanding of the world would surely be well advised to take into account the body of premises and conclusions engrossed in the Declaration of Independence. The document was, in its time, primarily an undertaking in propaganda and psychological warfare. It was designed to explain the sundering of a bond of authority; it was not intended and could not have served as an instrument for governing. Its assumptions were in some degree subsequently modified and superseded by the Constitution. Notwithstanding these considerations—and despite the far greater numbers, scope, and ethnic diversity that now distinguish the nation from what it was at its advent in independence—the Declaration remains basic in the American appreciation of history and of the rights and reasons of nationhood. Its propositions—even though not memorized by all or even a great many Americans or invoked by them each time they appraise an event or an issue on the world horizon—nevertheless enter deeply into American assumptions and perspectives.

The doctrine in the Declaration is that of a people "born free"—an effective phrase used, in Professor Louis Hartz's *The Liberal Tradition in America,*[6] as an echo of Alexis de Tocqueville, who in turn echoed it from the Apostle Paul. In Hartz's context, it describes the condition of being unencumbered by an overlay of relationships and restrictions left over from feudal

[6] Louis Hartz, *The Liberal Tradition in America* (New York: Harcourt, Brace, 1956), p. 309.

order or a tribal system, the condition of being able to make a conscious collective choice about the character and limits of governing authority, to act as a society in ordaining an apparatus of government and bridling it, and to make such basic decisions as a society antecedent to the governing authority rather than being in essential respects a creature of it. Such are the conditions assumed in John Locke's theories of the state. The Americans fulfilled them on coming into independence. They regarded themselves as vindicating rights assumed inherited from ancestors who, in Thomas Jefferson's words, "before their emigration to America, were the free inhabitants of the British dominions of Europe and possessed a right, which nature has given to all men, of departing from the country in which chance, not choice, has placed them, of going in quest of new habitations, and of there establishing new societies, under such laws and regulations as to them shall seem most likely to promote public happiness." [7] These ancestors had been colonial in a classic sense of bearing elements of a metropolitan culture to distant lands and there applying them as the basis of new communities pervasive of the new locations. The situation was distinguishable from that of being colonial in the sense applicable to a people and a land subject to a superimposed alien authority. The American venture into independence arose from differences of constitutional interpretation and preference between political groups, however estranged by time and distance, still sharing common ancestry and language and drawing largely upon a common fund of history—namely, those groups dominant in the life of the British colonies in America, on the one hand, and those dominant in the political life of the homeland, on the other. Autonomy and self-government were asserted not as goals to be pursued but as realities to be preserved. Separation from a kindred people in an erstwhile homeland was proclaimed on the premise of its necessity to the preservation of conditions of government to which the Americans asserting in-

[7] As quoted in Edward Dumbauld, *The Declaration of Independence and What It Means Today* (Norman: University of Oklahoma Press, 1950), p. 51.

dependence not only felt entitled, but also were accustomed.

These points, however obvious, are often overlooked in facile attempts to overdraw the parallels between the American experience in venturing into juridic independence and the quest of independence among colonial peoples of the contemporary world. Those in colonial status today are characteristically peoples whose ancestors were once placed in colonial status through conquest by forces intruding from abroad. No simple formula for this can be presented. The presence of descendants of the Dutch in South Africa and of Portuguese-descended persons in the Portuguese enclaves of Africa, for example, is inveighed against as imperialistic even though, presumably, their ancestors got there ahead of the now subordinated Negro populations. Moreover, the equities, case by case, may become enormously complex. Often the rights asserted against imperial rule are those of peoples whose own ancestors, in their own time, arrived as conquerors.[8] The contemporary case against imperial rule seems largely to be based on impugning the last conquest and overlooking what conquests preceded it. In the main, the ones last coming from afar, or descendants of theirs, are the ones from whom, rather than by whom, independence is asserted. The American thrust for independence and the contemporary instances do have in common a repugnance for being ruled from afar, and the parallel between the American case and the present typical case would be more apt if the American quest of independence had been the work of Mohawks, Shawnees, Cherokees, and the like, rather than being, as it was, an effort raised by groups preponderantly of British antecedents on behalf of reasons appealing to them in part from British backgrounds inherited from British ancestry.

[8] An item in the *Washington Post* for February 1, 1962, relates charges of Arab dominance in the Sudan made by refugee Negro political leaders in Brazzaville. The gist is that Arab groups ruling since the withdrawal of British control are descendants of conquerors from the outside, with no more right to be in the country than the British had. Presumably, investigation might show even the complainers in this instance to be descendants of tribesmen who, in a distant past, captured land from earlier occupants. The notion of retroactively correcting the results of every conquest obviously soon reaches absurdity.

In asserting independence, the Americans might conceivably have stated their case solely on pragmatic grounds having particular application to their situation. They might thus have asserted that rule from abroad was not the sort of thing they were accustomed to and that they were simply not going to put up with it. This attitude, they could have added, made such rule unworkable, since it was scarcely feasible for the Crown to generate support enough to make it effective, and force sufficient to make up for the lack of support was proving excessively difficult and expensive to maintain. They could have pointed out that authority so far removed from the scene of its effects could not make practicable decisions and was bound to blunder. They could have asserted their own superior comprehension of their own problems. They could have concluded by saying that was the way they wanted things to be—and that King and Parliament had better take a practical view, recognize their reluctance for what it was, and yield to realities.

Besides marshaling particular reasons for a particular desired effect, the Americans had also, and more importantly, to use other and more abstract grounds. In that age, the dominant intellectual forces were strongly inclined toward universal concepts. The Americans had to find grounds convincing to themselves as partakers in the intellectual style of the times, and to those abroad whose support they needed, including sympathizers within the onetime mother country. They placed high store on the efficacy, as a factor swaying the policy of governments, of the group opinion of private men as distinguished from regimes—"a decent respect to the opinions of mankind." Arguments merely of practicability and self-interest would not have sufficed. Accordingly, the exponents of independence raised universal postulates, invoked principles declared to have validity everywhere, premised certain attributes as inherent in all men, argued for corollary restraining principles as incumbent upon all governments, asserted the obligation of obedience to be contingent upon fulfillment of these principles by governments, cited divine authority, invoked natural law as a premise for their case, and asserted that governments fit to command allegiance must be lawful in that sense of law, and that in order to fulfill this requirement they must be based on the consent of the governed.

This argument was set down lucidly and dramatically. It was an argument designed for history, expressed with the apparent intention of producing a deep impression over a wide scope. The argument thus fashioned along a high line may be found circular if carried to a certain length. That is beside the point, for circular logic inheres in perhaps all deeply held political creeds. At some point, any proponent of such is likely to find himself having to rely on the fact of belief as his justification for believing. The aspect in focus here is a different one, of a sort latent in any instance of asserting eternal, universal reasons on behalf of a particular purpose. The question is whether the proponents were citing such huge reasons for restricted results or really hoped to see their purposes reverberate through a scope as wide as their argument. Were the Americans announcing independence concerned only with explaining themselves to the world and explaining the world to themselves, or did they intend to shape the world as well?

An answer at one extreme is the notion of a chosen people— to use Professor Hartz's apt way of characterizing it.[9] It involves in no degree the weakening of the assertion of universal principles. Rather, it combines it with a claim of their peculiar applicability. It argues that the application of the inherently valid principles must be deserved by those who would invoke them. The qualifications are a special grace and set of insights, accessible only to the elect. From this viewpoint, the precepts underlying American independence are regarded as giving the nation a special role in history, one setting the nation apart from others, rather than serving to relate it to others. The attributes making up the national character are therefore to be guarded rather than shared. Being rightly governed derives from talents in the people. Whether others in due course see the same light and thus are led to qualify is their concern, not that of the assertedly elect, and the validity of the insights by which the

[9] Hartz, *The Liberal Tradition in America*, p. 35.

elect guide their affairs is not to be verified or discounted by the degree of their appeal and success among the rest of mankind.

At a contrasting extreme is the concept of a people with a universalizing mission—not the role of a chosen people, but one in accord with the injunction, "Go ye therefore, and teach all nations. . . ." [10] In keeping with it, the principles redeeming the political life of a nation are not to be hoarded, but rather exemplified, advocated, and promoted wherever feasible. This may come naturally enough to men who, besides believing themselves possessors of a great truth regarding the best of all possible ways to govern, hold some notion of a community or brotherhood of all. The precepts of governing, according to this view, rightly cannot be fulfilled if a nation is governed without its consent. Government by popular consent is obviously incompatible with government imposed from afar; therefore, it follows that every nation should have opportunity to determine its own government as a condition precedent to being governed rightly. It is, then, seen as a national mission to promote political self-determination everywhere and, beyond that, to coax, to educate, to abet, and to press other nations to use independence rightly to develop political constitutions and practices consistent with the right way of governing.

As abstractions, either of those approaches can be made to appear either plausible or unsound. A nation disposed to regard itself as a chosen people leading a life in history all its own can be thought of as either modest or self-centered. The elitist idea implicit may be judged unbecoming in an age inclined to emphasize community and equality, but the busybody implication of the contrasting extreme may be equally subject to criticism. It is not reprehensible for a nation to do the best it can with its own opportunities without engaging in the dangerous folly of trying to determine history for everyone else as well. The notion of a universal political mission is likely to entangle a nation endlessly and vainly in other people's problems through the assumption of a general warrant to intervene. On the other hand, there are the clichés about no nation's being an island

[10] Matthew 28:19.

sufficient to itself. It is pretentious for an informed people to pose as uninterested in what may happen beyond its domain. It is fallacious to suppose that good may be the result of sparing other nations from critical judgment of their acts and standards. If the judgment of outsiders is to count, why should not our own be included? To assign ourselves no role beyond that of approving or remaining indifferent to whatever others may do is to make of us a nation with nothing to communicate, no standard to advocate in history.

How plausible either side of the argument may be made to sound was impressed upon me by an incident in Buenos Aires still recalled vividly from 1948. At an American Club luncheon, a visiting United States Senator, guest of honor of the occasion, spoke. Juan Peron was then in sway, and the United States' relations with the Peron regime was the speaker's theme. The drift of his argument was: Out in the world at large, Americans must see in proportion the principles which they value in their own institutions. Americans are for representative government, accountable authority, and free elections, and they are against dictatorship and totalitarianism. These abstractions are good, but it is pointless and mischievous to intrude on other nations with them. Whatever government suits the Argentines deserves American approval and cooperation. They owe that much to their neighbors. The important thing is to do business and to put aside any concern over the inconsequential question of how another nation is governed. A good rule is to run your own affairs and let other people run theirs.

The Senator spoke well and conclusively—or at least so it seemed for a moment, until someone offered a spontaneous rebuttal from the floor. The challenger introduced himself as an American in business in Argentina. This is what he said, as I caught it in notes at the time: "On arriving here a few years ago, calling myself a hardheaded, realistic business operator, I would have agreed with what the Senator has just said. I know better now. Tyranny is not an abstraction. The fears and indignities of life under an oppressive, vengeful, self-centered, unaccountable rule are realities. The notions of a free order and constitutional government are practical, sensible proportions. If how men govern is not important, then what is? The founders of our nation thought it so. Nothing has disproved them. We cannot impose their ideas on Argentina, but that is not the issue. The question is whether we still stand for them. Nothing compels us to yield our sense of truth. That we cannot order the situation to our liking is no reason for saying we like it. If we cannot give effect to our standards, we can at least avoid the futile relativism of declaring that whatever is, is good. I cannot think of business as separate from the human condition. We owe something to those Argentines aware and ashamed of the regime's true character. We owe them a recognition of their ordeal and a sign that we too hope for something better for their land."

The dialogue between these two propositions started at the beginning of the American experience in independence, as Professor Hartz has pointed out,[11] and continues into our own time. Its effect on the set of understandings composing United States policy toward the exterior world has been determined not solely, or perhaps even primarily, by intrinsic merits of the argument, but more importantly by the external situation and the prevailing estimates of opportunity and the factors of national power in relation to it.

It is relevant to recall the broad circumstances of the early decades of independence as background to the approach reflected in United States policy in those times. The state system, far from being universal, was centered in Europe and largely confined there. The metropolitan societies participating in it shared, at least as states, large elements of common culture. Diplomacy, as a set of equalitarian usages for relating different political societies to each other, operated within the limits of the state system. Relationships among entities of highly diverse cultures far removed from each other were carried on, if at all, through inequalitarian practices of an imperial-colonial order, distinct from the usages of diplomacy. In winning a place in independence, the Americans, in effect, succeeded in transferring their relationships with other areas from the nexus of the

[11] Hartz, *The Liberal Tradition in America*, pp. 36–37.

imperial-colonial order to the system of diplomacy. It was a highly contingent success. In Professor Thomas A. Bailey's phrase, the United States was then the "world's ugly duckling." For the time being, the newcomers to independence were having an extremely difficult time putting into practice the independence and self-government they had asserted. "Most Europeans," Professor Bailey recounts, "did not bother their heads about the new infant in the family of nations; or, if they did, their opinions were obscured by ignorance." Their indifference, however, he adds, "was not shared by the monarchs of Europe. . . . The ruling classes of the Old World were anxious, therefore, that the American experiment should fail. This attitude continued to be a basic factor in the relations between the United States and Europe far into the nineteenth century." [12]

In these circumstances, merely to hold onto national existence was enough as an exemplification of the precept of independence to the world. Of necessity, the role of a chosen people prevailed in policy, whatever was the temptation to indulge the notion of a universalizing mission in sentiment and rhetoric. The prevailing concept provided a dignified rationalization for a people still engrossed in realizing its asserted nationhood, preoccupied with filling out its land position, still striving to establish itself. The attendant habit of mind—in an oversimplifying correlation—underlay the United States' historic isolation and the accompanying attitude called isolationism, and its marks still linger and are important.[13] Conversely, the idea of a peo-

[12] Thomas A. Bailey, *A Diplomatic History of the American People* (New York: Appleton-Century-Crofts, 1947), p. 37.

[13] My colleague Ralph McCabe points out that in internal undertakings the Americans who got the nation under way in independence adhered to the concept that self-government was not something to be bestowed without restraint, but rather an attribute to be earned through rigorous qualification. Self-government, he points out, was not spontaneously extended to territories of the United States. To the contrary, participation in the nexus of self-government through admission to statehood was made contingent upon qualifying for it through meeting standards laid down by the Congress to require appropriate willingness and capacity on the part of the population. This practice has continued into our own time. In this respect, internal practice implicitly has been consistent with the concept of a chosen people.

ple with a universalizing mission tended to become reflected in United States policy in connection with an increasing role in world affairs—a development corresponding with what, for want of a better term, may be called the enhancement of United States power. This, in turn, has related closely to successive changes in the dominant position of the imperial-colonial system centered in Europe.

The first relevant change was an erosion of that system with the assertion of independence by a cluster of Latin-American countries during a temporary breakdown of the European state system marking the Napoleonic period. Whether or not the North American colonies' earlier success in cutting transatlantic strings was a necessary condition for the emergence of Latin Americans into independence, the development gave Americans opportunity to claim authorship of a historic precedent, and the hope of having established an archetype for new nations. Henry Clay's prediction that "they will establish free governments" typified this hope. He saw the United States as "their great example." "They adopt our principles, copy our institutions . . . and employ the very language and sentiments of our revolutionary papers," Clay said. In answer to those doubtful of the Latin Americans' capacity to follow the American example, he assailed "the doctrine of thrones that man is too ignorant to govern himself" and asserted self-government to be "the natural government of man." [14] Doubt was typified by John Quincy Adams: "I have seen and yet see no prospect that they will establish free or liberal institutions of government," he said of the same claimants to nationhood. "They have not the first element of good government. Arbitrary power, military and ecclesiastical, is stamped upon their education, upon their habits and upon all their institutions. Nor is there any appearance of a disposition to take any political lessons from us." [15]

The differences in estimate did not produce differences in policy. Both views united on propositions of sponsoring the

[14] As quoted in Dexter Perkins, *The United States and Latin America* (Baton Rouge: Louisiana State University Press, 1961), p. 48.
[15] *Ibid.,* p. 50.

independence of the emerging states by early diplomatic recognition, and of asserting the exemption of the American continents from extension or renewal of European dominion. Both actions were consistent with the attitude of isolationism in respect to Europe but tended also toward assumption of ranging responsibilities pertaining to the Western hemisphere. Yet, for more than half of the intervening experience of roughly 140 years, the relationship was mainly one of mutual indifference. In the next phase, which lasted about thirty years, the United States set a high mark for activity but an indifferent record for success in the role of exemplar and mentor of the forms and standards of the political life of its neighbors. For roughly the last three decades, effort has been guided toward combined enterprise in ensuring the political standards of the hemisphere.[16]

Much of this broad range of experience has borne out the dour predictions of Adams. Yet the notion of governments republican in form with accountable institutions and free elections, and with authority the reward for excelling in a free competition for political support, has come to prevail as a norm, if not as a pervasive fact, in the American hemisphere. Failures to fulfill the pattern have customarily and conveniently been accounted for as tutelary phases and aberrations. That some of the participants have met the standards only intermittently, and others scarcely at all, has not disposed of the tradition. The notion of all American republics as destined some day to succeed in prosperity and democratic institutions is still honored in discourse, along with the idea of "this hemisphere" as having a life apart—a new world "insulated from the follies and wickedness of the old." [17] The vaunted archetype has not been fulfilled; it has been challenged, but it has not been discarded. The goal remains easier to eulogize than to realize.

In considering the interplay in American attitudes and policy between the concept of a chosen people, withdrawn and living its history alone, and that of a people with a universalizing mission, one is tempted to dwell upon the Wilsonian period,

[16] *Ibid.*, pp. 51–86.
[17] *Ibid.*, p. 57.

concomitant with the making of war and peace in the second great breakdown of the European state system. With respect not only to Latin America in particular, but also to a larger frame, American discourse in Woodrow Wilson's time set a high point in projection of the assumed American archetype and the concept of self-determination. Here it would be easy to confuse the implicit universality of rhetoric of policy with actualities. In Professor Rupert Emerson's description, however,

> The ringing phrases . . . had all the sound of universality, but for practical purposes . . . were regarded as matters for application in Europe. The rest of the world barely entered in. . . . It is symbolic of the times that the man who set out to make the world safe for democracy went no further than to suggest that the interests—not the national desires—of the colonial peoples should be lifted to an equality with the claims of their alien rulers.[18]

All the great discourse on self-determination, self-government, and rights of representation undoubtedly entered into the world's general store of ideas and thus may have served as a factor in producing long-term results, unintended at the moment of utterance, in the great movements for independence and the proliferation of new states that developed a quarter-century later out of circumstances following the third great breakdown of the European state system in World War II.

If so, it could have been only a minor and marginal factor in phenomena whose causes and consequences reach into multifarious aspects of recent history and contemporary events. These phenomena are, of course, first, the wide and rapid progressive decline and disappearance of imperial-colonial relationships, inequalitarian in character, formerly serving as a basis for order between peoples of highly diverse cultures and levels of economic development living in widely separated places; and second, the concomitant emergence into juridic independence of

---

[18] Rupert Emerson, *From Empire to Nation* (Cambridge, Mass.: Harvard University Press, 1960), p. 25.

increasing numbers of political entities with unformed political character.

Characteristically, though the degree of difficulty varies widely from one instance to another, these newcomers are having a hard time finding their place in the conditions of the middle of the twentieth century, striking a practical balance between ambition and capability and finding adequate standards for public life in independence. These trials are not unique to them, for even long-established political societies have to strive in order to cope with the demands of the times. Obviously some states are distinctly better off than others for having developed a sense of their place in history, a pattern of identity and allegiance, and institutions adequate to the requirement of making and carrying out decisions. Not all states of long standing have achieved these attributes in a satisfactory degree. Not all of the states newly arrived in independence are beset by a critical lack of them. Yet, broadly speaking, necessitousness in this respect does characterize the new states—along with what President de Gaulle of France has aptly described as "a passion for self-determination, for the right to make their own decisions" and "a growing desire to see their own living standards rise." [19] Characteristically, they are conscious of having a long way to cover before becoming going concerns, and they are not sure of how to close the gap.

Among these newcomers to independence, one finds prevalent the tendency called neutralism and nonalignment—an attitude showing some appeal among Latin-Americans as well. Each of the abstractions requires a referent. Neutralist and nonaligned in what respect? To name three illustrative examples, Indonesia is certainly aligned with respect to West New Guinea, as India is with respect to Kashmir, or Afghanistan with respect to a dream of access to the Arabian Sea, and all of them have in common the emotions of self-determination. Actually, a considerable tangle of alignments on one issue or another obtains among them. A disposition to describe them as neutralist and nonaligned reflects a recognition that what counts in their ap-

[19] *New York Times*, November 11, 1959.

praisals is not merely different but, indeed, notably different from what prevails in our own policy. There are gaps in understanding between them and ourselves—gaps important enough not to be obscured by customary sentiments regarding international understanding.

Neutralism—meaning merely a tendency toward vehement profession of expediential nonalignment—appeals to some of them as a way of bridging a gap between neediness and ambition for significance. It reflects at once a desire to avoid commitment—an understandable attitude for any people of meager resources—and a wish to be among those who count in world affairs. It is a way not of withdrawing but of playing a role in global politics, of getting into the game but staying out of the scrimmages. The character of contemporary international organization puts a premium on this approach. Being among those who are counted almost necessarily entails being among those who count. A state truly desirous of avoiding some role in world affairs would virtually have to exclude itself from the state system and avoid the United Nations membership, which now seems to follow almost *ipso facto* on the attainment of juridic independence, and, as the Western Samoans have done, renounce "the status symbols of world politics." [20] This is a course likely to appeal only in marginal instances. The motives guiding some underdeveloped new states to wish to frequent the machine shop and, at the same time, keep out of the machinery should present no puzzle to us. Even in the form of trying especially hard to placate the presumably less placable of the great antagonists in the contemporary world, the motives are readily understandable, in the first sense of understanding given above, however perplexing it may be to our own view of the realities and, therefore, less understandable to us in the second sense of the term.

A far deeper and more enduring significance implicit in the phenomenon of neutralism is a disjunction of ideas between ourselves and a great part of the emerging world. This gap in

[20] "Samoa's Coming of Age," *The New Republic*, February 12, 1962, p. 12.

communication is due not to failure to say enough back and forth, not to a failure as yet to hit upon a right combination of words, not simply to a lack of common knowledge and terms, and not to an insufficiency of exchanges of visitors and students. It is, however, ascribable to some basic disagreements as to what counts, what is feasible, what the nature of authority is, and what the nature of history is in which nations have their being. If the lack were simply quantitative—a failure of parties to meet each other halfway—it could be readily met by doing more, giving more time, spending more on the effort to communicate. In fact, however, unprecedented volumes of words go into international communication, cultural exchange operates at a high level, and official good-will visits and the like have become commonplace. The problem seems to be not quantitative but qualitative; the question is not whether to meet each other halfway, but how to approach each other on intersecting tangents.

Professor Saul Padover, an astute observer, has stressed the point that, "although a measure of misunderstanding among nations is unavoidable, that which exists between the United States and a large part of the world is monumental and unprecedented. . . . Unless corrected, at least to the extent that it is possible to do so under the circumstances, the gap . . . may become unbridgeable. . . ." [21]

"Can a people 'born free' ever understand peoples elsewhere that have to become so?" The question is raised at the conclusion of *The Liberal Tradition*.[22] The phrase "born free" has been dwelt upon. The word "understand," in this context, presumably embraces both senses of the term discussed above, and especially, in relation to policy, the sense of mutually recognized common views. The "peoples elsewhere that have to become so" are a significant portion of the world exterior to the United States. The phrase "have to become" is indicative, moreover, of something unfulfilled, but not of historic necessity.

[21] Saul K. Padover, "Asia Puts Some Sharp Questions to Us," *New York Times Magazine*, March 4, 1962, pp. 14, 88.
[22] Hartz, *The Liberal Tradition in America*, p. 309.

No law of being compels peoples to achieve the state of being free. The process of becoming so is by no means necessarily to be equated with the achievement of juridicial independence. If it were, in actuality, equivalent, then the progressive disappearance of the imperial-colonial order could be taken to signal the universalization of freedom in the domestic character of the societies concerned, as well as the riddance of rule from afar— an unwarrantedly optimistic conclusion.

Professor Hartz leaves his question unanswered, but the implication of his text is scarcely more affirmative than Professor Padover's account of "a measure of misunderstanding . . . which . . . is monumental and unprecedented." That question of understanding was obviated as a consideration of policy so long as the United States, in a marginal and highly insecure position in the early sequel to gaining independence, adhered in practice to the concept of being a chosen people. In later times, with widened scope, Americans have had to think of themselves as a people with a mission, although without a clear formula for performing it. Simple projection of the American image, as it appealed to Clay and Wilson, for example, seems scarcely adequate to cope with exigencies in the present. To a people whose independence was based on generalizations as wide as ours and whose founders declared "a new order of the ages," this is disconcerting. It is a concern not only of sentiment and pride, for it has a central bearing on the character of what new order, if any, will replace the disintegrated imperial-colonial system.

It is perhaps relevant to refer to some of the common expedients offered for getting around the difficulties. One of these is to cleave to old assurances of a world destined to follow the American example into independence and, thereafter, the American pattern of national success and affluence with freedom. This is coupled with assertions of American authorship and inspiration for recent and current surges into independence, and interprets the emerging world in the pattern of an American prototype. One notes, for example, an address by one of the State Department's hierarchs postulating the relevance and utility of the United States' early history as the key to understanding the future of the nascent states of Africa. He likened one-party authoritarian rulerships currently prevailing among them to the overwhelming American consensus behind George Washington as the first President, discerning therefore a prospect among them of early polarization of politics along lines of a two-party competitive system as here. This, he said, equated their disposition for neutralism to the tenor of Washington's Farewell Address.[23] In a similar vein, an official of the United States Information Agency has asserted that the inspiration of African independence is American—citing as proof his having met some rioters knowledgeable of Jefferson.[24]

Another expedient is to view independence itself as a final good, ignoring all consideration of what to do with it. This attitude maintains that whatever practice may be indigenous is suitable, and whatever is suitable, is good. It judges the quality of government solely on the basis of the territorial location of authority, and is relativistic with respect to other qualities. It is reflected in an often-heard proposition that the all-important challenge for the emerging peoples is to find institutional patterns of their own suitable to native genius. That states only a fraction of the requirement. Government must be not only native but also effective; and if the society concerned proposes to act as and to be regarded as a going concern in a modern, respectable sense, the effectiveness must be judged by the relevant standards. An analogue to Edmund Burke's warning of the folly of regarding freedom as a final good, irrespective of what was to be done with it, must surely apply to independence.[25]

A third approach is to pin hope on economic development as

---

[23] *Washington Post and Times-Herald,* January 21, 1962.

[24] *Ibid.,* February 11, 1962.

[25] "Is it because liberty in the abstract may be classed amongst the blessings of mankind, that I am seriously to felicitate a madman, who has escaped from the protecting restraint and wholesome darkness of his cell, on his restoration to the enjoyment of light and liberty? Am I to congratulate a highwayman and murderer, who has broke prison, upon the recovery of his natural rights?" Edmund Burke, *Reflections on the Revolution in France* (London and New York: Oxford University Press, 1950), p. 8.

the key to the character of states and nations—a premise often encountered among the more enthusiastic rationalizations of foreign aid. The line of reasoning is simple and, within its limits, plausible enough: to be free and successful, societies must be able to make choices; to make choices, they must have alternatives; having alternatives requires margins; margins require increments of productivity; this will materialize in ratio to outside assistance supplied. Mr. Robert L. Garner, former Vice President of the International Bank for Reconstruction and Development, has cogently pointed out the questions begged by these propositions. Good use of foreign aid requires antecedent characteristics in a society and its government. It is Mr. Garner's "conclusion that economic development or lack of it is primarily due to difference in people and in their attitudes, customs, traditions and the consequent differences in their political, social and religious institutions." He declares it "no service to truth and realism to avoid the fact that much effort and sacrifice of the accustomed ways are the inevitable price of advancement." [26]

A fourth escape defines a solution in a negative term: anticommunism. It attempts to describe a course by indicating a pitfall, to define a goal in terms of what it should not be. To a query of how to set up a going concern, it gives an answer of how not to do it. It supposes that things will end well if the emerging societies avoid the Communist formula, and that no guidance beyond that is required. This is far short of what is needed by a society in the predicament of being partly in modernity and partly still in the grip of a traditional past.

Much of the bias against the forces and ideas summed up in the term *the West* are consequences of a sense of that predicament, one suspects. Generally, the societies concerned were brought into such a predicament through contact with the West. What they label as imperialism are the experiences and influences that put before them concepts they feel able neither to achieve nor to renounce. So they tend to associate their frustra-

[26] *New York Times*, September 22, 1961.

tions with Western societies and cultures, with a consequent bias that sometimes affects their views on great issues.[27]

Our end of the dialogue with them is perhaps excessively affected by our sensitivity to this bias. Our interest can be served better by comprehending the bias for what it is and understanding how it arises than by humoring it with uncalled-for sympathy. There is indeed a morbidity—not too strong a word, I think—in the preoccupation with the West and its values and precepts and in the related dissents and grievances found among the peoples of the emergent countries.

On a recent occasion, I heard a minister of education from one of the more underdeveloped and militant of the new African countries expound plans to eliminate Western influences and to restore indigenous values in the educational undertakings of his government. It was an eloquent exposition on inculcation of national morale, enrichment of public life, and development of a sense of a place in history. At the luncheon afterward, a wise Nigerian observed: "He said those basic ideas in French, and he could not possibly have said them in the tongue of his tribe. Such is the dilemma. To express his aspiration he must embrace that which he would scorn." This reminded me of thoughts I had once addressed to an Asian and African group, and I repeat them now in closing:

> At Bandung . . . a recurring theme was the necessity for the new states of Asia and Africa to develop political institutions and traditions distinguishable from those of the West. Those bespeaking this theme did so almost invariably in English—and not merely as a matter of convenience in communication, for in the general case it would not have been possible to express in the native tongue the political abstractions being spoken of. I have heard the same idea

[27] This sense of frustration related to the West and imperialism can indeed be carried to inordinate lengths. For example, a scholar from India recently told me: "Our grievance is not only because of what was taken from us but also for what we were prevented from doing. Electricity, atomic energy, the internal combustion engine—all those would have been within our capabilities. We should have had them first if it had not been for the burden and blight of imperialism."

over and over again from Asians and sometimes also from Africans, and one can understand the impulses behind it without being persuaded of the merits. It is folly to take a position for abandoning ideas merely because they and the West have had something to do with each other, and one should not abandon a source before making sure that he has an alternative at least as good. It is folly—understandable folly, perhaps, but still folly—to speak of finding one's political traditions in the background of one's own country when that country manifestly has no traditions adequate for the problems of a political going concern under the conditions of the mid-twentieth century.

There is nothing wrong, moreover, with such ideas as accountability of ministers, with the right to be judged under law on the basis of evidence and with opportunity to put up a defense, or with the notion that bureaucrats should make their decisions on the basis of some pattern of public policy arrived at by discussion and established by processes free of coercion. These are hard things to achieve. They are not practiced perfectly anywhere. To maintain them is an onerous, Sisyphean task. The West, in its best sense, represents the achievement of such ideas and in its worst sense the failure of them; but for better or worse, they are identified with the West in some degree. To feel free to cut loose from them merely because they are in some way of the West is a course of egregious folly. The important thing is not that they are Western but that they represent the better impulses of men in the life of the state. The struggle between the better and the worse impulses as they affect political life is a general struggle. It knows no point of the compass. Anyway, the abandonment of something of value in the politics of any part of the world hurts all of it.[28]

[28] Charles Burton Marshall, "Political Relations with the New States," *United Asia* (Bombay), November, 1959, pp. 403, 406–7.

INDEX

THE EXERCISE OF SOVEREIGNTY
Papers on Foreign Policy
BY CHARLES BURTON MARSHALL

designer	:	Athena Blackorby
typesetter	:	Vail-Ballou Press, Inc.
typefaces	:	Times Roman, Perpetua
printer	:	Vail-Ballou Press, Inc.
paper	:	Warren's 1854 Medium
binder	:	Vail-Ballou Press, Inc.
cover material	:	Bancroft Linen Finish